DRUG TREATMENT AND CRIMINAL JUSTICE

SAGE CRIMINAL JUSTICE SYSTEM ANNUALS

Volumes in the **Sage Criminal Justice System Annuals** focus on and develop topics and themes that are important to the study of criminal justice. Each edited volume combines multiple perspectives to provide an interdisciplinary approach that is useful to students, researchers, and policymakers.

Recent Books in This Series:

Volume 27. **Sage** Criminal Justice System Annuals

DRUG TREATMENT AND CRIMINAL JUSTICE

James A. Inciardi
Editor

SAGE Publications
International Educational and Professional Publisher
Newbury Park London New Delhi

For information address:

SAGE Publications, Inc.
2455 Teller Road
Newbury Park, California 91320

SAGE Publications Ltd.
6 Bonhill Street
London EC2A 4PU
United Kingdom

SAGE Publications India Pvt. Ltd.
M-32 Market
Greater Kailash I
New Delhi 110 048 India

Printed in the United States of America

Library of Congress Cataloging-in-Publication Data

Main entry under title:

Drug treatment and criminal justice / edited by James A. Inciardi.
     p.   cm. — (Sage criminal justice system annuals ; v. 27)
    Includes bibliographical references and index.
    ISBN 0-8039-4909-X — ISBN 0-8039-4910-3 (pbk.)
    1. Prisoners—United States—Drug use. 2. Drug abuse—Treatment—United States. 3. Drug abuse counseling—United States. 4. Drug abuse and crime—United States. 5. Criminal justice, Administration of—United States. I. Inciardi, James A. II. Series.
HV8836.5.D79   1993
365'.6—dc20   93-15517

93 94 95 96 10 9 8 7 6 5 4 3 2 1

Sage Production Editor: Astrid Virding

CONTENTS

Chapter 1

INTRODUCTION
A Response to the War on Drugs

JAMES A. INCIARDI

During the closing years of the 1970s, just prior to the beginning of the presidency of Ronald Reagan, a new epidemic of drug use was noticed in the United States. Rather than heroin, which had defined the parameters of "the drug problem" for more than two decades, the difficulty this time was a derivative on the rather innocuous Peruvian shrub *Erythroxylon coca* Lam.—cocaine (see Inciardi, 1992). Cocaine was nothing new to the United States, having first appeared a century earlier. However, by the late 1970s the drug was being smuggled into the country from South America in record quantities. Moreover, the use of cocaine appeared to be escalating, particularly in the inner cities. And a concomitant of the increased presence of cocaine on the streets of America was a rising rate of crime—particularly violent crime.

The 1980s also witnessed the rediscovery of *crack*-cocaine. The American crack experience is fairly well known, having been reported, and perhaps overreported, in the media since early 1986. There are the "highs," binges, and "crashes" that induce addicts to sell their belongings and their bodies in pursuit of more crack; the high addiction liability of the drug that instigates users to commit any manner and variety of crimes to support their habits; the rivalries in crack distribution networks that have turned some inner-city communities into urban "dead zones" where homicide rates are so high that police have written them off as anarchic badlands; the involvement of many ghetto youths in the crack business, including the "peewees" and "wannabees" (want-to-be's), those street gang acolytes in grade school and junior high who patrol the streets with walkie-talkies in the vicinity of crack houses serving in networks of lookouts, spotters, and steerers, and who aspire to be "rollers" (short for "high-rollers") in the drug distribution business; the child abuse, child neglect, and child abandonment by crack-addicted mothers; and finally, the growing cohort of "crack babies" who appear troubled not only physically but emotionally and behaviorally as well (Inciardi, 1992; Inciardi, Lockwood, & Pottieger, 1993).

As both drug use and crime escalated, the federal government responded, as did legislators and criminal justice systems at all jurisdictional levels. From federal policymakers there were dramatic increases in the funding of a war on drugs, with much of the new monies earmarked for law enforcement activities. In addition, there were the RICO (Racketeer-Influenced and Corrupt Organizations) and CCE (Continuing Criminal Enterprise) statutes. As asset forfeiture provisions, RICO and CCE mandate forfeiture of the fruits of criminal activities. Their intent is to eliminate the rights of traffickers to their personal assets, whether these be cash, bank accounts, real estate, automobiles, jewelry and art, equity in businesses, directorships in companies, or any kind of goods or entitlement that are obtained in or used for a criminal enterprise (Dombrink & Meeker, 1986).

Another component in the federal drug war armamentarium was "zero tolerance," a 1988 White House antidrug policy that expanded the war on drugs from suppliers and dealers to users as well—especially casual users—and provided that planes, vessels, and vehicles could be confiscated for carrying even the smallest amount of a controlled substance (U.S. Department of Transportation, 1988). At state and local levels, zero tolerance gave birth to the many "user accountability" statutes. User accountability was based on the notion that if there were no drug users there would be no drug problems and that casual users of drugs, like addicts, were responsible for creating the demand that made trafficking in drugs a lucrative criminal enterprise. As such, the new laws called for mandatory penalties for those found in possession of small quantities of drugs. User accountability, however, played only a small part in the local initiatives against drugs. More significant, drug enforcement measures in municipal and state police departments were expanded, new laws were enacted to create mandatory penalties for certain drug crimes, and special courts were established to process the increased number of drug cases.

When George Bush was sworn in as the 41st president of the United States in 1989, the complexities involved in waging the drug war were well known to him. Not only had he served as vice president during Reagan's drug war, but also in the early part of the 1980s he had directed the South Florida Task Force, a special federal antidrug initiative designed to reduce the flow of cocaine through the Port of Miami. As president, Bush expanded Reagan's antidrug effort with increased funding. And finally, Bush's drug war policies were developed and coordinated through the newly established Office of National Drug Control Policy (ONDCP), a White House-level office that had been created by the National Narcotics Leadership Act of 1988, a piece of legislation drafted by Senator Joseph R. Biden of Delaware.

Amid this period of rising crime rates, the escalating war on drugs engendered a criminal justice process that appeared to be "drug driven" in almost every respect. In the legislative sector, new laws were created to deter drug involvement and to increase penalties for drug-related crime. In the police sector, funding served to expand street-level drug enforcement initiatives, which, in turn, increased the number of drug-crime arrests. In the judicial sector, the increased flow of drug cases resulted in overcrowded dockets and courtrooms as well as the creation of new drug courts, special dispositional alternatives for drug offenders, and higher conviction and incarceration rates. In the correctional sector, the results included the further crowding of already overpopulated jails and penitentiaries and the establishment of liberal release policies.

On the more positive side of this equation, the packed courtrooms and dockets and the overcrowded jails and prisons engendered by the war on drugs initiated a number of humane changes in criminal justice processing. In the courts, diversion to drug treatment as an alternative to incarceration became more widespread; drug treatment programs were established in jail and prison; and, for those in the post-incarceration phase of corrections, treatment alternatives became available as supplements to parole and work-release supervision. Although treatment within the context of criminal justice is decades old, it became far more widespread during the second half of the 1980s and the early 1990s. The papers in this volume document a number of the more innovative projects, programs, and advances during this recent time.

REFERENCES

Dombrink, J., & Meeker, J. W. (1986). Beyond "buy and bust": Nontraditional sanctions in federal drug law enforcement. *Contemporary Drug Problems, 13*, 711-740.

Inciardi, J. A. (1992). *The war on drugs II: The continuing epic of heroin, cocaine, crack, crime, AIDS, and public policy.* Mountain View, CA: Mayfield.

Inciardi, J. A., Lockwood, D., & Pottieger, A. E. (1993). *Women and crack-cocaine.* New York: Macmillan.

U.S. Department of Transportation, Office of Public Affairs. (1988, June 6). Zero tolerance policy on illegal drugs. *Transportation Facts.*

Chapter 2

TREATMENT STRATEGIES FOR DRUG-ABUSING WOMEN OFFENDERS

JEAN WELLISCH

M. DOUGLAS ANGLIN

MICHAEL L. PRENDERGAST

INTRODUCTION

Convictions for drug offenses are a major contributor to the increasing offender population, and women constitute the fastest growing segment of convictions at all levels: local, state, and federal. Most women who are arrested test positive for one or more drugs, and much of the crime perpetrated by women is for drug offenses or is associated with drug use. To decrease the level of crime committed by women and to mitigate the subsequent impact on society and the criminal justice system, effective strategies must be devised to prevent, control, and treat women's drug use.

The preponderance of empirical evidence indicates that treatment for drug-abusing women is effective and that its effectiveness is not diminished when women offenders are coerced into treatment by the criminal justice system prior to sentencing or as a condition of postconviction probation or parole. Despite its effectiveness, however, only a very small

AUTHORS' NOTE: This chapter was prepared in part with support from California Department of Alcohol and Drug Programs contracts D-0004-9 and PE-001-C and from National Institute of Justice grant 91-IJ-CX-K009. M. Douglas Anglin is also supported by NIDA Research Scientist Development Award DA00146. Thanks are due to Renee Pitts and Rowan Roberts for word processing.

Jean Wellisch, Research Associate, M. Douglas Anglin, Director, and Michael L. Prendergast, Assistant Research Historian, are affiliated with the Drug Abuse Research Center of the University of California, Los Angeles.

percentage of drug-abusing women offenders are being treated within the nation's jails and prisons, and only a small percentage of those who could benefit from treatment are being diverted into treatment prior to sentencing in lieu of incarceration or as a condition of probation or parole.

Not all treatment programs are equally effective, however. Results obtained from the few available program evaluations, based mainly on programs for non-incarcerated offenders, indicate that outcomes can vary widely, depending to a large extent on how the programs are implemented. Thus, a critical question arises as to how programs directed toward women offenders should be structured to achieve the greatest benefit. This issue of effective treatment strategies for adult women offenders is the concern of this chapter.

Women in the criminal justice system who are identified as drug abusers may, in some jurisdictions, be able to enter drug abuse treatment through several avenues, depending on state and local administrative and adjudication policies. These alternatives include: diversion from trial, which may occur through formal legal procedure or through operational practices without the formality of specific law; referral into treatment and sentencing alternatives, pre- or post-trial, that are provided through specific diversionary programs such as Treatment Alternatives to Street Crime (TASC) or through TASC-like programs; civil commitment, a legal process that allows for the involuntary commitment of certain persons into drug treatment; or admittance to treatment, usually on a voluntary basis, for offenders in custody.

A relatively small percentage of drug-abusing women offenders, perhaps as few as 10%, are provided treatment within jail or prison.[1] Both because most convicted offenders are on probation or parole and because of the limited treatment availability in in-custody settings, most women offenders who enter treatment do so in the community. Women offenders who enter community-based treatment may be referred before sentencing by the court, district attorney, public defender, pre-trial services, or social services in lieu of custody, or as a condition of probation, early release from custody, or parole. Some community-based treatment programs serve only clients from the criminal justice system (CJS) and, in effect, are an extension of the criminal justice system. Other community-based treatment programs serve a variety of clients—self-referred or referred by social agencies, hospitals, or other programs—as well as clients referred by the CJS.

Community-based programs provide four principal treatment modalities: medical detoxification, outpatient methadone maintenance for narcotic addicts, residential or therapeutic communities, and outpatient drug-free programs—which together account for over 90% of clients in the public treatment system (Butynski & Canova, 1989).

Historically (and even at present), most community-based treatment programs were developed for the treatment of men. Not surprisingly, given the lack of adequate funding for innovation and the few models of specialized treatment for women, comprehensive in-custody programs for women offenders have been largely modeled on the treatment generally provided in community-based residential programs. There is some justification for this approach since long-term, heavy drug abusers found in community-based residential treatment are similar to drug abusers in prison. In fact, many residents have been in prison at some time in their adult lives, and most have engaged in criminal activity to support their drug use. Despite this similarity in population characteristics, such programs are usually no more appropriate for women inmates than they are for non-incarcerated women. In recognition of this fact, federal grant initiatives have recently been implemented for the development of programs specifically designed for women.

Until very recently, nearly all evaluation of drug abuse treatment was of community-based treatment programs. Most of these programs are publicly financed, and clients often include persons who have been referred into treatment by CJS. Studies of community-based programs that provide services for both men and women offenders have found that legal referral is not a strong predictor of posttreatment outcome (DeLeon, 1988); that is, offenders who are legally coerced into treatment do as well as voluntary clients (who themselves may have been coerced into treatment by various forces such as family pressures, ultimatum from employer, fear of physical deterioration, dissatisfaction with the addict life style, or other factors).

Although legal coercion is not a determinant of treatment success, time-in-treatment is a strong predictor of treatment outcome, and those who are legally referred tend to remain in treatment significantly longer than do voluntary admissions. Overriding the issue as to motivation for treatment entry, however, is the overwhelming evidence that treatment (coerced or voluntary) leads to reduced drug use, reduced crime, and more prosocial behavior (Anglin & Hser, 1990).

The remainder of this chapter is divided into four main topics. In the following section, we discuss current directions in CJS drug abuse treatment for women, and include brief descriptions of several programs that have been specifically designed for women offenders. Next we present a section summarizing findings on outcomes of several in-custody programs and another section on the attributes of successful programs. Finally, we conclude with remarks on the future of drug abuse treatment for women offenders.

DIRECTIONS IN CJS TREATMENT
FOR WOMEN OFFENDERS

There is a considerable body of descriptive and outcome literature on community-based treatment in general but relatively little that is focused on women and even less on women offenders who are in community-based treatment (see Austin, Bloom, & Donahue, 1992, and Wellisch, Anglin, & Prendergast, 1991, for recent reviews). However, over the last few years, in part through seed money provided by federal grants, a number of community-based programs are being developed specifically for women. This same movement toward recognition of women's needs is also evident in several comprehensive treatment programs that have only recently been implemented in prisons and jails.

Theoretical and Practical Considerations
Underlying Program Development for Women Offenders

The current trend in the development of substance abuse treatment programs for women in the CJS appears to have two main thrusts, one philosophical and one practical. The former is to empower women so that they perceive themselves as actors, rather than victims, able to direct their own lives. The latter, which is complementary, is to provide these women with the coping skills that will permit them to implement desired changes in their lives. In addition, many of the newer programs incorporate a number of service components and strategies aimed at responding to women's identified needs, mainly related to their status as single parents: parenting, health and nutrition education, family planning, assertiveness training, and vocational training. Some programs attempt to operate on a biopsychosocial model of treatment, providing diverse components that deal with a wide range of problems and needs. For example, one recently implemented drug abuse treatment program aims to remedy the drug dependent women's major deficits, which are defined as a "combination of inadequate and maladaptive social-behavioral and cognitive skills" (Mental Health Systems, 1990, p. 4).

Also, given the chronic relapsing nature of drug dependence, there seems to be acute awareness among both program designers and operations personnel of the critical importance of continued supervision and support after women are released, either from in-custody programs or community-based intensive programs. Largely depending on the funds available for in-custody treatment and for the parole support and supervision following release and depending on the treatment resources available in the community, transition and aftercare in the newer programs are provided with varying levels of intensity and duration.

The least structured and intensive of such linkages to community support is through the Anonymous Fellowships, primarily AA, NA, and CA. It appears that, with few exceptions, both in-custody drug treatment and outpatient treatment for women in the CJS include the requirement or recommendation for attendance at a specified number of Anonymous Fellowship meetings each week. Beyond the belief shared by many in the treatment field that such meetings are important in promoting abstinence, there are two main reasons for this emphasis. First, for many years AA, and more recently NA and CA, have provided volunteer in-custody meetings for inmates in many correctional facilities. In the majority of jails and prisons, such meetings were the only form of drug abuse treatment available. Even today, along with some courses in drug abuse education, the Anonymous Fellowship meetings are still the only form of substance abuse treatment available to most alcohol- and other substance-abusing women in custody. Therefore, such meetings become a familiar and expected component of CJS-associated drug treatment. Second, the Anonymous Fellowship meetings are available and accessible to women in almost every community, so that this linkage to community support can be assured, and transition from in-custody meetings to community meetings can be accomplished easily. Such transition is sometimes inaugurated in the near-release period.

More structured and intense transitional aftercare includes gradations in supervision from living in a community-based residential community for several months, to halfway houses, to cooperative living arrangements with one or more recovering women, and to intensive supervision, usually provided through probation or parole officers. In addition to intensive supervision, some parole agencies are employing systems of graduated sanctions where each subsequent infraction merits an increased number of days in jail. Random urine-testing is almost always a requirement of supervised aftercare, whether directly administered by CJS personnel or as a component of treatment.

Although graduated support and monitoring are considered critical in reintegrating (or, in many cases, integrating) the woman offender into the community, the resources needed to implement long-term continuous supervision and support are rarely available. Logistically, transition programs that provide continuity of treatment care and supervision are most easily managed as an extension of jail programs, since most of the women in the jail program reside in the same local community. Currently, many local communities are implementing jail/transition programs directed toward the treatment of drug-abusing women offenders, for example, Cook County, Illinois; Multnomah County, Oregon; and Contra Costa County, California. By contrast, in prison, it is much more difficult, and expensive, to provide uniform and systematic continuity of care for inmates who participate in treatment programs because, on release, the women may be widely dispersed—each prison tends to service a broad geographic area that may incorporate several towns, cities, and counties. In an effort to deal with this geographic dispersion of released offenders and the problems of multiple jurisdictions, some area networks that incorporate parole and social agencies of several counties have recently been formed, for example, in Oregon and the Bay Area in California.

There are indications (conditional on the availability of funding) that we may see significant breakthroughs over the next few years in treatment for women coming out of the demonstration and pilot programs and studies of programs funded by the Department of Justice, the Center for Substance Abuse Treatment, the National Institute of Corrections, the Federal Bureau of Prisons, and various state governments.

Today, many counties and local communities have new prison and jail programs and transition programs that have been specifically designed for women—drawing from what seems to work for women, or at least what seems to meet women's identified needs. Although still grossly insufficient to meet the need, the programs are too numerous to describe in full, but a few examples are provided to highlight both the similarities and the unique characteristics of programs developed specifically for women offenders.

Examples of Programs Designed for Women Offenders

We start with in-custody programs—a federal program, several state programs, and one local jail program. These are followed by outpatient programs serving women offenders.

Federal Bureau of Prisons

The Federal Corrections Institute in Lexington, Atwood Hall Drug Abuse Program[2] is a traditional 12-step program in which drug abuse is viewed as a disease that leads to physical deterioration, emotional instability, and spiritual bankruptcy. The program emphasizes large-group therapy in which the women prisoners, working with the 12-step philosophy, deal with issues of denial, recovery, and relapse prevention and, in the process, strengthen cognitive coping skills. There are also small-group general psychotherapy groups, and women receive individual counseling for a minimum of 1 hour a week. Academic/vocational training is provided, and peer counseling is used for advanced students.

The program is housed in a separate correctional facility that contains single- and multiple-occupancy cells, laundry facilities, recreational areas, day rooms, meeting rooms, and staff offices. Women are in the program area 10½ hours a day. Meals and some recreational activities take place with the other inmates, and educational and vocational programs are conducted outside of the program area. Urinalysis monitoring is continuous throughout the duration of the program.

Program duration is 12 months, with 6 months supervised aftercare. There are 150 slots in the program, and 12 full-time staff. Criteria for admission to the program are these: meets clinical criteria determined by the score on the Inventory of Substance Use Problems; 20-25 months until release; no outstanding legal matters that would conflict with stay in a halfway house after release; no serious medical, psychiatric, or psychological problems; and no violent institutional infractions within the last 12 months. Women who meet the criteria are randomly selected from a list of volunteers.

State Prison Programs

Passages.[3] The Wisconsin Department of Corrections has a range of drug and alcohol treatment programs designed to provide a continuum of services from drug education to programs modeled on the therapeutic community lasting 6 months or longer. Offenders are diagnosed based on the Alcohol Use Inventory and the Inmate Drug Use History; they are assigned to the program by combining needs assessment from these two instruments with profiles from the MMPI in the case management classification system.

The Passages program for women offenders was created in mid-1988 as a demonstration of nontraditional treatment methods for drug-using women offenders. Originally funded by the U.S. Department of Justice, the program is currently funded through federal block grants to the Wisconsin Department of Corrections. The program is a joint venture of the Kettle Moraine Hospital and the Inter-city Council on Alcoholism under contract to the Wisconsin Department of Corrections. General oversight of the program is provided by the Director of the Office of Drug Programs in the Division of Program Services; ongoing daily supervision is the responsibility of the Superintendent of the Women's Correctional Center (WCC).

Prior to Passages, a program with a specific female perspective primarily served drug-using women in the Taycheedah Correctional Institution. It was a half-time, 12-week program supported by five day-care slots in the De Paul Hospital, used for crisis intervention. These treatment offerings were found to be insufficient to meet the department's needs. In addition, use of traditional treatment for drug abuse based on the medical model did not appear to promote positive change in women inmates, and the department found that women failed to complete programs offered by a therapeutic community. Therefore, Passages was developed as a demonstration of a program designed to respond to women's specific problems and needs. The program is geared to handle 60 women a year; 15 are programmed at a time; when one women graduates, another enters.

Passages is designed on an empowerment model.[4] Women inmates are seen as victims—used and abused—who do not believe that they can change the direction of their lives and who do not possess the coping skills for self-actualization (see Bandura, 1982, and literature cited therein).

The Passages program is 8 hours a day, 5 days a week, for 12 weeks. Services are provided in a facility separate from the Women's Correctional Center (WCC). Women who are diagnosed as having chemical dependency problems and who are classified as minimum security risks, regardless of offense, are eligible for admission to Passages. Women who are admitted into the program live at WCC and are transported by van to the office building in which the Passages program is offered. Staffing for the program consists of one supervisor and three counselors, all of whom are recovering substance abusers.

The program has three phases. Phase I is based on the 12-step program, including assessment of chemical use and criminal activity, responsibility for decisions and behavior, relapse, and values clarification. In Phase II, emphasis shifts from discovery to the development of skills for personal growth and for relating to others. In this phase, it had been anticipated that community resources (e.g., Family Services, Planned Parenthood, YMCA/ YWCA, Health Department) would be available to expand program offerings, but except for the involvement of Anonymous Fellowship groups, this support was not forthcoming. In Phase III, clients continue working on their skills and pursue individual treatment issues. In some groups, clients are expected to assume leadership roles; in others, they role play, learning assertiveness, conflict resolution, communication, and other skills.

In each phase, attendance is required at a minimum of two AA/NA/CA meetings per week, and clients are subjected to ongoing random urinalysis. Program planners had wanted to include a fourth phase of aftercare and alumni support lasting 4 weeks or more, but according to a recent report on the program (Falkin, Wayson, Wexler, & Lipton, 1991), it appears that this phase was dropped from the formal program structure. Instead, women who complete the 12-week program spend their days at WCC preparing for reentry or participating in work/study release.

California Institute for Women (CIW).[5] The CIW program is a demonstration project just getting under way. It is managed by the California Department of Corrections (CDC), which will also conduct an evaluation of the program. Approximately 340 inmates (3 cohorts of about 120 each) will be treated over a 17-month period. All participants are volunteers; if more women volunteer than can be accommodated, eligible volunteers are selected randomly. To be eligible for selection, women must have a substance abuse problem, must have no recent history of violence or commitment for a predatory crime, and must be close to the end of confinement but have sufficient time left for the 4-month program.

Mental Health Systems is the contractor responsible for administering the treatment program. They describe the program as consisting of six components: a model of relapse prevention (Gorski & Miller, 1986), aggression replacement training (Goldstein & Glick, 1987), a 12-step program, small-group activities, individual counseling, and case management.

During the first month, for 1 hour each, training is provided in relapse prevention and pre-treatment stabilization; drug education; 12-step; and small-group. During the following three months, aggression replacement training (ART) replaces drug education. As required, women may replace a session of 12-step or small-group with individual counseling. The relapse prevention component is based on Gorski and Miller (1986) and treats addiction as a biopsychosocial dependence.

As described in the abstract to Mental Health Systems' (1990) proposal:

> Relapse Prevention is a cognitive behavioral program of drug education, recovery planning and counseling. It is designed to deal with the psychological effects of early trauma. ART is a highly structured behavioral, emotional and cognitive re-structuring program. It addresses elementary and complex social skills; develops alternatives to aggression; and addresses arrested moral development. Twelve-step programs are widely recognized as the single most effective component of a recovery program and will serve in this program not only as ongoing support but as an important means of release transition. Small-group experiences will address specific subjects such as parenting. Equally important, they will provide a milieu in which skills learned in other program components can be used. Individual counseling will be an important component of the program involving treatment planning, assessment of progress, and individual treatment. Case Management performed by the individual counselor will become increasingly intense as women progress in the program. Ultimately, Case Management will provide a release transition plan, the implementation of which will begin while women are still in the program. Personal contacts will be made with community providers to ensure support during the difficult transition period from prison to parole.

The treatment program is scheduled for 4 hours per day for 4 months. The California Department of Corrections had planned for a 6-month in-custody program followed by 4 months of aftercare in the community. However, given the short duration of most inmates' stay in CIW (much of their sentences are spent in the county system), a 6-month in-custody program was unfeasible; instead, the design was altered to provide 4 months of in-custody treatment and 6 months of aftercare in the community. Inmates who are paroled to Los Angeles, Orange, Riverside, or San Bernardino counties will be offered a continuation of residential substance abuse treatment services. Intensive supervision will be provided by parole staff in each of the four counties. It is expected that about 70 women will participate in community services offered in the demonstration counties— women from nondemonstration counties will be encouraged to seek services on their own.

Stay'n Out. The Stay'n Out program for 40 women is housed in a correctional building in New York City and is similar to residential programs found in the community (Wexler, Falkin, & Lipton, 1990). Clients are housed in facilities separate from the general population, although the

Stay'n Out inmates eat in the common prison dining areas and attend morning activities with the other prison inmates. The program begins with highly structured activities and then gives participants greater freedom for decision and choice and greater responsibility as they prove themselves ready. It appears that the staff is mainly composed of ex-inmates, recovered addicts, and a support network of formally trained professionals. Therapeutic groups are a mainstay of the treatment program, and encounter groups meet twice weekly. Treatment duration in Stay'n Out, typically, is 6 to 9 months.

In-Custody Jail Programs

Project DEUCE.[6] Project DEUCE—which stands for Deciding, Educating, Understanding, Counseling, and Evaluation—is a joint effort of the Contra Costa (California) County Office of Education and the Contra Costa County Sheriff's Department. The project is under the supervision of the Adult Education Program Administrator, the Facility Commander, and the Inmate Services Director. Instructors in the program are under the supervision of the County Office of Education Adult Education Program Administrator.

The DEUCE Marsh Creek program for women has an 80-bed capacity and is housed in a self-contained dormitory. It is a voluntary three-phased residential program designed for a stay of 3 months; however, inmates with a minimum of 30 days left to serve may be admitted and those with longer than 90 days left may remain in the program until release. DEUCE is described as a two-track program—one track geared toward drug abuse intervention and prevention and the other toward increasing inmates' employability.

Attendance at the structured day program is mandatory for those in the program; in addition, inmates are strongly encouraged to avail themselves of the elective classes offered during Phases I and II. Phase I lasts 4 weeks and provides intensive alcohol- and substance abuse education and guidance. Phase II, also 4 weeks, continues to focus on addiction but, in addition, begins to examine inmates' relationships. During this stage, inmates also obtain family counseling and may enroll in various courses such as computer literacy, ABE, high school completion, art, creative writing, and employability. Beginning in Phase III, inmates are given passes for preplanned activities (e.g., Anonymous Fellowship meetings, recreational activities, church attendance) and visits with family. In Phase IV, also 4 weeks, inmates develop individual action plans that focus on relapse prevention, employability, and transition into the community. There is a voluntary Post-Phase "Out-Mate" support group. Probation department staff work with inmates in designing an aftercare plan.

Outpatient Jail Programs

The Santa Clara County (California) Criminal Justice Treatment Division provides a number of outpatient programs for persons who are charged or sentenced for a drug violation and are referred by a criminal justice system provider.[7] The three programs that provide drug abuse treatment services for women are Women's Treatment Alternatives (WTA), which will accept both pre-sentenced and sentenced women; Treatment Alternatives Program (TAP), which is for adult men and women who have been sentenced by the court for one or more drug offenses; and Women's Relapse Prevention Program, a treatment continuation program that was developed jointly by the Criminal Justice Treatment Division of Santa Clara County and the Combined Addicts and Professional Services, Inc. (CAPS) of San Jose, California. These three programs are briefly described here.

Women admitted to WTA may be voluntary or court-ordered but the referral must come from a criminal justice system provider. They may be pre-sentence or sentenced. Most women admitted to TAP have been sentenced and are remanded to treatment. In both programs the women must agree to attend classes, submit to random urine testing, and participate in the program, which consists of one individual and one group counseling session per week, two recovery classes per week, and attendance at a minimum of three group support (12-step or other self-help) meetings per week. Both WTA and Tap are 90-day programs; women who are admitted to TAP in lieu of incarceration in jail are expected to participate a minimum of 140 hours.

After completion of WTA or TAP, women are encouraged or required, depending on their legal status, to attend the Women's Relapse Prevention Program. This 120-day program provides intake assessment, individual treatment planning, referral, and participation with outside agencies as required. The relapse prevention program is divided into two phases. In Phase I, clients attend two individual and two group counseling sessions and two 12-step meetings and submit to two urine tests per week. In Phase II, they have one individual and one group counseling session and participate in three 12-step meetings. The program provides continuing treatment oriented toward helping the drug-dependent woman change her attitudes, behavior, and life-style. Both voluntary and court-ordered clients are accepted, but clients must be involved with the criminal justice system and must have completed at least 90 days of primary treatment.

Commonalities in Program Characteristics

Many of the newly developed or modified programs serving women offenders, a few of which have been described here, tend to be similarly structured, include the same or similar components, and employ the same range of strategies.

1. In-custody program activities, particularly in prison programs, tend to be conducted in separate settings. Participants' living arrangements may also be separate, but meals, work assignments, and recreation may be with the general prison population.

2. Programs for inmates usually operate on a volunteer basis, and in the main, women are not promised extrinsic rewards such as better food or accommodations, shortened sentences, or early parole consideration because of participation. However, in those states where treatment is required before the inmate is eligible for parole (e.g., Wisconsin), women can meet their parole requirement by participating.

3. Inmate volunteers are screened before admission to programs. Typical criteria for program admission include history of heavy drug use, no major psychiatric disorders, no history of violence, near release, and no outstanding legal difficulties that would make it impossible to complete the program or be paroled shortly after completion but with enough time left to complete the program. In addition, programs with a cognitive component may require some level of literacy or indication of normal aptitude.

4. Drug use is monitored with random urinalysis; standards of behavior are set and consistently enforced. Penalties are exacted for infractions and include discharge back to the general jail or prison population for major infractions.

5. Programs tend to be structured in phases, the first primarily concerned with drug education and self, the second with relationships and the beginnings of skill acquisition, and the third with development of coping skills and preparation for community reentry. Relapse prevention tends to be a major emphasis throughout.

6. Participation in a specified number of Anonymous Fellowship group meetings is usually mandatory.

7. A wide range of strategies is employed, including individual and group counseling, lectures, films, therapeutic groups, writing assignments, and work assignments.

The distinctive characteristic of these programs—that which differentiates them from the traditional programs used in the treatment of women offenders in the community and in custody—is that they have been specifically developed or extensively modified for treating women and they attempt to provide for the specific needs of drug-abusing women offenders. Although rigorous evaluation data on such programs for women offenders are sparse, in part because of the newness of some of the programs, some findings of interest are reported in the following section.

FINDINGS FROM IN-CUSTODY TREATMENT PROGRAMS

In the past, few states, local government agencies, or treatment projects formally evaluated their drug abuse treatment programs. Few even maintained adequate records on participants' recidivism. However, all of the newer programs for women offenders mentioned above have plans for evaluating program effectiveness. Older programs (e.g., Passages and Stay'n Out) have been studied and appear to produce successful outcomes.

In regard to Passages, the Wisconsin state prison program for women, the consensus of the corrections staff, treatment staff, and prison administration (as reported by Falkin, Wayson, Wexler, & Lipton, 1991) was that the program showed a number of benefits, including the following:

- Breaking down communication barriers between inmates and prison staff
- Improving clients' self-esteem
- Saving administration's time in preparing for aftercare because Passages arranges halfway houses, AA groups, and other services
- Reducing staff stress at the prison, reinforcing actions of the prison management, and providing greater confidentiality (by separating treatment from custody)
- Keeping the women in treatment occupied in meaningful activities, and benefitting other inmates because Passages clients speak with them about women's dependency issues
- Helping its clients deal with important women's issues (assertiveness, sexual assaults) as well as with drug dependency

- Increasing the likelihood of parole because state goals for inmates to receive alcohol and drug treatment are being met

Although the Stay'n Out program appears to be more similar to the traditional community-based therapeutic community than it is to more recent trends in custody programs for women, it is of particular interest because it has been studied and evaluated over a period of several years. Wexler and Williams (1986), based on an evaluation that used a quasi-experimental design, report a reduction in recidivism rates and lower rates for parole revocations for those who were positively discharged from the program than for those who dropped out prior to 6 months. Recently, in further examination of the influence of time-in-treatment, Wexler, Falkin, and Lipton (1990) report that they found consistent improvement in postrelease behavior as time-in-treatment increased from 9 to 12 months but an unanticipated decline as time-in-treatment exceeded 12 months.

Simon Fraser University conducts a highly innovative Canadian in-custody program for men and women that provides inmates with a liberal arts education. It had the lowest recidivism rates of four programs described by Chaiken (1989), all of which had lower recidivism rates for program participants than for inmates who were not in treatment.

As an indication of the effectiveness of the in-custody jail program DEUCE, the California Legislature in Assembly Bill No. 3649 recommended replicating Project DEUCE, which is referred to as a "self-esteem based" program (AB 3649, March 1, 1990, *Legislative Analyst Digest,* p. 2). The bill states that inmates participating in the DEUCE 90-day education program were half as likely to be rearrested within the 12 months following release as a control group. Because the program appears to be working, several correctional agencies within the state, in addition to the March Creek Detention Facility in Contra Costa County, have implemented Project DEUCE.

A number of programs in Multnomah County, Oregon, report greater numbers who remain drug-free and lower recidivism rates for women offenders engaged in treatment (Beebe, 1991; Eisen, 1991; Griffiths, 1991; McFarland, 1991). Oregon's experience offers confirmation that "while there is some indication that close monitoring, methodical sanctioning systems, and substance abuse treatment all contribute to positive outcomes, the most demonstrable outcomes occur when these three are combined" (Field, McGuire, & Nelke, 1991, p. 1; Petersilia & Turner, 1990).

ATTRIBUTES OF SUCCESSFUL PROGRAMS

Almost all researchers who have published in the area of compulsory treatment for drug-abusing offenders, prison treatment programs, and drug abuse treatment for women have explicitly or inferentially indicated what they consider to be the sine qua non of effective treatment (for example, see Anglin & Hser, 1990; Ball & Corty, 1988; Beschner & Thompson, 1981; Chaiken, 1989; DeLeon, 1984, 1985, 1987; Joseph, 1988; Leukefeld & Tims, 1988; Maddux, 1988; Reed, Beschner, & Mondanaro, 1982; and Wexler, Blackmore, & Lipton, 1991). Some researchers have also identified barriers or impediments to the implementation of effective treatment programs in prisons. Unfortunately, few researchers have developed prescriptions specifically directed toward effective programs for women offenders, especially programs for women who are incarcerated. To remedy this omission, we focus here on in-custody treatment—first, the institutional and structural attributes of successful programs, which presumably apply to women's programs as well as to programs for the general inmate population, and second, the special requirements of programs for women.

Institutional and Structural Attributes

Many of the institutional and structural attributes of successful programs have broad acceptance—they occur in guidelines established by the National Institute of Corrections (1991) and in the recommendations of many of the researchers cited above as well as of practitioners (see, for example, Anglin & Maugh, 1992, and Chaiken, 1989). Our recommendations are briefly stated below as directives for program development.

1. *Develop support within the correctional system to implement the program.* This may involve overcoming entrenched negative attitudes and educating personnel at all levels within CJS to the benefits of corrections-based interventions and community treatment in conjunction with legal supervision. According to Wexler, Lipton, and Johnson (1988), most prison-based treatment programs operate under so many bureaucratic and political constraints that they are programmed to fail from their inception.

2. *Set up formal communications channels* (useful informal ones will develop naturally in a cooperative environment) with legislators, state administrators, administrators and supervisors within the corrections institution, and security personnel and parole officers to keep people

informed, as appropriate to their needs, on the plans, implementation, and progress of the program.

3. *Set up the treatment program to be independent (within security strictures) of the prison administration.* The program should constitute an autonomous unit within the prison with its own funding. This may best be achieved if programs are conducted by independent organizations on a contract basis, with incentives linked to reductions in recidivism and increases in prosocial behavior (Wexler, Lipton, & Johnson, 1988). Program participants should be separated, to the extent feasible, from other inmates, although in most cases it is most cost-efficient for basic services— meals, housing, security, and medical and dental care—to be provided by the correctional institution.

4. *Enroll prisoners in treatment programs when their remaining period of incarceration is only as long or slightly longer than the length of the in-custody part of the treatment program.* Most authorities agree that too early enrollment may erode the gains made in treatment because the prisoners will remain in an environment—the prison—that is conducive to relapse (Wexler, Lipton, & Foster, 1985).

5. *Select a high-quality professional staff, composed mainly of women who have professional skills and can function as role models.* To the extent possible, the staff should reflect the ethnic mix of the program participants. The importance of high-quality staff cannot be overemphasized. Joe, Simpson, and Sells (in press), for example, found that positive treatment outcomes were associated with higher quality of professional specialty of the staff involved in diagnosing clients at admission and designing treatment plans. Chaiken (1989) found that across the four successful in-custody programs that she studied, staff were drawn from outside of the field of corrections or were considered atypical corrections personnel.

6. *Clearly define and separate the kinds of infractions that are dealt with by prison authorities and the kinds that program personnel are empowered to deal with.* Intermittent drug use that does not seriously disrupt the individual's program plan, as other program infractions, should be dealt with on an individual basis in the context of the program participant's overall adjustment. Drug abuse treatment requires individuation and a degree of flexibility that is not consonant with most prison operations.

7. *Implement strategies that give participants a stake in the success of the program as a whole and in their own rehabilitation.* Chaiken (1989) found that the successful programs she studied had inmate organizations

to deal with management of activities—assigning, operating, and monitoring. Wexler, Lipton, and Johnson (1988) recommend adopting an incentive system to tie socially desirable behavior to rewards for inmates.

8. *Make continuing care during transition and return to the community, and a lengthy period of supervision in the community, integral parts of the treatment program.* Because dependence on drugs is a chronically relapsing condition, in most cases several cycles of treatment, aftercare, and relapse will occur. The typical successful intervention achieves longer periods in which the dependence is controlled and there are shorter periods of relapse. Most studies have shown that the longer an individual is retained in a treatment program, the more likely it is that drug use and associated criminal activities will be reduced (DeLeon & Schwartz, 1984; McGlothlin, Anglin, & Wilson, 1977; Simpson, 1979, 1981; Wexler, Lipton, & Foster, 1985).

9. *Early in program development, plan for transitioning inmates into the community.* Such plans can include having dedicated parole officers who get to know inmates during treatment; where indicated, arranging for transition of inmates into residential treatment programs; and setting up contacts and liaison with appropriate agencies within the community for services that inmates may require on reentry (e.g., medical, legal, housing).

10. *Separate surveillance and treatment functions of field supervision officers to maintain confidentiality and trust among those supervised.* Ideally, surveillance and treatment should be handled by staffs who work separately but cooperatively to avoid role confusion for both officer and offender (Wexler, Lipton, & Johnson, 1988). The treatment team should also rotate between working in prison and in the community to maintain continuity between the rehabilitation efforts in both environments.

11. *Build into the treatment program data collection and methodology for process and outcome evaluation.* All intervention programs should be regularly evaluated to determine overall effectiveness and effectiveness of particular treatment components. Feedback loops should be built into the program, and programs should be flexible enough to implement changes in response to changing needs and characteristics of program participants and to advances in drug addiction treatment.

Attributes to Meet Special Requirements for Women

In most, if not all, jails and prisons, services needed to satisfy the special requirements of drug-dependent women inmates (as well as all women inmates) will be the responsibility and function of the correctional institution and not of the drug abuse treatment program. However, it must be recognized that the services identified below are integral to the well-being of the women and to the success of the drug abuse treatment program.[8]

1. *Provide the means for women to maintain or reestablish contact with their children.* Many women prisoners are sent to correctional institutions that may be distant from their homes and that are often almost inaccessible by public transportation. Even when homes are nearby, if children are made wards of the state when their mothers are incarcerated, the mothers may lose track of the whereabouts of the children and find their efforts to maintain contact difficult or impossible. Often the women do not understand the child welfare system and do not even know the name of the social worker or judge who oversees their case. Also, there may be shame on the part of the mother, and anger, resentment, and shame on the part of the children—feelings that make maintaining contact difficult. Some prisons, such as the Georgia Women's Correctional Institution at Hardwick, have created bright, toy-filled visiting rooms, but more typically facilities are grim and frightening for the children. In some prisons, visiting children are separated from their mother by glass.

2. *Provide vocational training and career opportunities in higher-paying fields for women,* rather than in traditional low-paying jobs such as launderer or beautician. Most women offenders with children are the sole providers for their children; rarely do they receive any help from the fathers of their children, and yet many leave prison less equipped to earn an adequate living than do men who have been incarcerated. According to Paul Bestolarides, who directs a program at the Northern California Women's Facility that provides courses in landscaping and electrical work, women inmates are more motivated in terms of career than men. Most women are unemployed at the time of their offense or conviction, but opportunities for further education and vocational training are extremely limited and what training is offered tends to be in traditional low-paying jobs for women. A recent survey by the American Correctional Association (1990) shows that of the nearly 50% of women who attended vocational school, 36% received training in the business and secretarial area; 19% in medical and dental technology; and 13% in cosmetology. Only about 4% were trained in the male-dominated construction trades which offer higher pay.

3. *Ensure that women offenders receive adequate health care.* Most prisoners suffer a lack of adequate health care, but it is more serious for

women because of their need for gynecological care and precautionary
testing such as Pap smears and mammary examination. One source (not
named) reports that 25% of the women in prison are pregnant or have
recently given birth (Women in Jail, 1990).[9] In addition, women who are
dependent on drugs or alcohol, are HIV positive, or have other sexually
transmitted diseases need special attention. Moreover, since a large percentage of incarcerated women have been subjected to physical and sexual
abuse, they require counseling and psychological support in addition to
general health care.

THE FUTURE OF DRUG ABUSE TREATMENT
FOR WOMEN OFFENDERS

Although the evaluative information on treatment process and outcome
needed for the design of effective programs is still scarce, a few states
have already been monitoring their programs and do make their data
accessible. For example, the Washington State Department of Corrections
(1988) has been evaluating its drug treatment programs for women since
1984 and has reported some interesting findings. Although the evaluation
found no significant reduction in the frequency of substance abuse infractions, it did find significant reductions in the frequency of other types of
infractions; in addition, a significantly smaller percentage of those who
had treatment returned to prison within 2 years after release as compared
to those with substance abuse problems who did not have treatment. Over
the next few years, we can expect to see more states begin to develop,
improve, and assess their programs, given the impetus of Project RECOV-
ERY, a program initially supported by the Bureau of Justice Assistance of
the U.S. Department of Justice and now supported as Project REFORM
by the Center for Substance Abuse Treatment. Project REFORM/
RECOVERY (Wexler, Blackmore, & Lipton, 1991) provides expert technical assistance to selected states to help them reduce drug abuse and
recidivism through the development of effective drug abuse treatment
programs. Currently, ten states are participating.

In addition, the Center for Substance Abuse Treatment (CSAT) is also
supporting a number of drug abuse treatment demonstration projects,
mainly based on the therapeutic community model, that will impact adult
offenders (men and women) who are in custody. These demonstrations
include state prison projects in Alabama, Connecticut, New York, and
Hawaii, and comprehensive care models for jail populations in King County,

Washington; Cook County, Illinois; and Montgomery County, Maryland. In addition to in-custody projects, CSAT is supporting demonstration projects for non-incarcerated populations that include women offenders. These include diversionary projects in Tucson and Birmingham, and special treatment for high-risk probation/parole clients in Washington, DC, Oregon, South Carolina, and California.

Given that drug abuse intervention prior to sentencing, in jail or prison, and during periods of probation or parole can be effective, and that in both the short and the long run treatment is cost-effective, it is incumbent on policymakers to increase treatment availability and, to the extent that current knowledge permits, optimize the effectiveness of treatment programs. With increased general awareness of the association between drug abuse and crime and of the efficacy of drug abuse treatment in reducing crime, and given the impetus of federal and state support for the development of innovative programs, we can expect to see more funding for innovative women's treatment programs in prisons and jails and in the community.

NOTES

1. No doubt a considerably larger percentage of women are impacted if we include those who participate in treatment that consists only of Anonymous Fellowship meetings or drug education programs. However, since research has not demonstrated that such programs by themselves are effective with heavy drug users, we are restricting the discussion of "treatment programs" to those that are relatively comprehensive.

2. This description of the Atwood Hall Drug Abuse Program is based on information provided by Dr. Mark Simpson, Drug Abuse Program Coordinator, and material contained in the orientation handbook for the program.

3. This discussion of Passages is based on information provided by the Wisconsin Department of Corrections (1988, 1989), and Falkin, Wayson, Wexler, and Lipton (1991). Because Passages is a program that was specifically designed to be responsive to women's problems and needs, has been in operation since mid-1988 and likely influenced the design of many subsequent women's programs, and has recently been studied by Narcotic and Drug Research, Inc. (Falkin, Wayson, Wexler, & Lipton, 1991), it is described here in somewhat more detail than other programs.

4. The idea of empowerment comes out of the self-efficacy concept, which is the idea that persons' perceptions of their self-efficacy (knowledge and ability to take appropriate action to accomplish some goal) greatly influence their performance. Findings from research on self-efficacy indicate that the higher a person's perceived self-efficacy, the higher is their performance and the lower their emotionally induced physiological stress. As stated by Bandura (1982), "Perceived self-efficacy helps to account for such diverse phenomena as changes in coping behavior produced by different modes of influence, level of physiological stress reactions, self-regulation of refractory behavior, resignation, and despondency to

failure experiences, self-debilitating effects of proxy control and illusory inefficaciousness, achievement strivings, growth of intrinsic interest, and career pursuits" (p. 122).

5. The following description of the drug treatment program at CIW is based on the plan proposed by Mental Health Systems, Inc. (1990), the company responsible for designing and administering the program, and the plan for evaluating the program, prepared by Lois Lowe (1990), of the Office of Substance Abuse Programs, California Department of Corrections.

6. The description of this program is based on the student handbook for Project DEUCE; the Legislative Counsel's Digest of AB No. 3649; and a summary of the training and observation schedule and groups currently using DEUCE, all of which were kindly provided by the program administrator, Mary Lou Browning.

7. Information on these programs was provided by Carla Noto, MA, LMFCC. At this writing, the programs are about 2 years old. Currently, 75 clients are being served, and 40 are women. A tracking system is being implemented that will provide follow-up information at three points—90 days, 6 months, and 1 year. Currently, the programs operate at no cost to the clients, but they are expected to pay fees starting in fiscal 1992. The fees will be based on a sliding scale, and Medi-Cal payment will be accepted.

8. Discussion of special requirements concerning visits by children and medical and vocational needs is based largely on Barry (1987) and recent reports from *Newsweek* (Women in Jail, 1990) and *Time* (View from Behind Bars, 1990).

9. Ellen Barry, director of legal services for prisoners with children, reports (personal communication) on a woman addicted to heroin who was 6 months pregnant when sentenced to serve 6 months in a county jail in California. She was forced to go through withdrawal without benefit of medication and suffered shakes, chills, nausea, and vomiting; slept on an inch-thick mattress on the floor, which gave her severe back pain; and saw an obstetrician only once, although she was experiencing a high-risk pregnancy. Such extreme cases are, no doubt, unusual, but a report by the American Correctional Association (1990) indicates that it is not unusual for gynecological and obstetrical services to be inadequate to meet the needs of jailed women.

REFERENCES

American Correctional Association. (1990). *The female offender: What does the future hold?* Washington, DC: St. Mary's Press.

Anglin, M. D., & Hser, Y. I. (1990). Treatment of drug abuse. In M. Tonry & J. Q. Wilson (Eds.), *Drugs and crime* (pp. 393-460). Chicago, IL: University of Chicago Press.

Anglin, M. D., & Maugh, T. H. (1992). Ensuring success in interventions with drug-using offenders. *Annals of the American Academy of Political and Social Science, 521*, 66-90.

Austin, J., Bloom, B., & Donahue, T. (1992). *Women offenders in the community: An analysis of innovative strategies and programs.* Washington, DC: National Institute of Corrections.

Ball, J. C., & Corty, E. (1988). Basic issues pertaining to the effectiveness of methadone maintenance treatment. In C. G. Leukefeld & F. M. Tims (Eds.), *Compulsory treatment of drug abuse: Research and clinical practical* (NIDA Research Monograph 86, pp. 236-251). Rockville, MD: National Institute on Drug Abuse.

Bandura, S. (1982). Self-efficacy mechanisms in human agency. *American Psychologist, 37*(2), 122-147.

Barry, E. M. (1987). Imprisoned mothers face extra hardships. *Journal of the National Prison Project, 14*, 1-4.

Beebe, K. (1991). *Community sanctions and alternatives fund quarterly report.* Salem, OR: Burnside Projects.

Beschner, G. M., & Thompson, P. (1981). *Women and drug abuse treatment: Needs and services.* (DHHS Pub. No. [ADM]81-1057). Rockville, MD: National Institute on Drug Abuse.

Butynski, W., & Canova, D. M. (1989). *State resources and services related to alcohol and drug abuse services, fiscal year 1988: An analysis of the state alcohol and drug abuse profile data.* Washington, DC: National Association of State Alcohol and Drug Abuse Directors.

Chaiken, M. R. (1989). *In-prison programs for drug-involved offenders.* Washington, DC: U.S. Department of Justice, National Institute of Justice, Office of Communication and Research Utilization.

DeLeon, G. (1984). Program-based evaluation research in therapeutic communities. In F. M. Tims, & J. Ludford (Eds.), *Drug abuse treatment evaluation: Strategies, progress, and prospects* (NIDA Research Monograph 51, pp. 69-87). Rockville, MD: National Institute on Drug Abuse.

DeLeon, G. (1985). The therapeutic community: Status and evolution. *International Journal of the Addictions, 20,* 823-844.

DeLeon, G. (1987). Alcohol use among drug abusers: Treatment outcomes in a therapeutic community. *Alcoholism: Clinical and Experimental Research, 11*(5), 430-436.

DeLeon, G. (1988). Legal pressure in therapeutic communities. In C. G. Leukefeld & F. M. Tims (Eds.), *Compulsory treatment of drug abuse: Research and clinical practice* (NIDA Research Monograph 86, pp. 160-177). Rockville, MD: National Institute on Drug Abuse.

DeLeon, G., & Schwartz, S. (1984). The therapeutic community: What are the retention rates? *American Journal of Drug and Alcohol Abuse, 10,* 267-284.

Eisen, D. (1991). *Community sanctions and alternatives fund quarterly report.* Salem, OR: Portland Addictions Acupuncture Clinic.

Falkin, G. P., Wayson, B. L., Wexler, H. K., & Lipton, D. S. (1991). *Treating prisoners for drug abuse: An implementation study of six prison programs.* New York, NY: Narcotic and Drug Research, Inc.

Field, G., McGuire, B., & Nelke, V. (1991). *Effective Oregon programs: Outcome studies of community treatment and control efforts with substance-abusing offenders in Oregon.* Salem, OR: Department of Corrections.

Goldstein, A., & Glick, B. (1987). *Aggression replacement training.* Champaign, IL: Research Press.

Gorski, T. T., & Miller, M. (1986). *Staying sober: A guide for relapse prevention.* Independence, MO: Independence Press.

Griffiths, B. (1991). *Community sanctions and alternatives fund quarterly report.* Salem, OR: Linn County Community Corrections.

Joe, G. W., Simpson, D. D., & Sells, S. B. (in press). Treatment process and relapse to opioid use during methadone maintenance. *American Journal of Drug and Alcohol Abuse.*

Joseph, H. (1988). The criminal justice system and opiate addiction: A historical perspective. In C. G. Leukefeld & F. M. Tims (Eds.), *Compulsory treatment of drug abuse: Research and clinical practice* (NIDA Research Monograph 86, pp. 106-125). Rockville, MD: National Institute on Drug Abuse.

Leukefeld, C. G., & Tims, F. M. (1988). Compulsory treatment: A review of findings. In C. G. Leukefeld & F. M. Tims (Eds.), *Compulsory treatment of drug abuse: Research and clinical practice* (NIDA Research Monograph 86, pp. 236-251). Rockville, MD: National Institute on Drug Abuse.

Lowe, L. (1990). *An evaluation of the California Department of Corrections Female Offender Substance Abuse Project: Evaluation research protocol.* Sacramento, CA: Office of Substance Abuse Programs, Department of Corrections.

Maddux, J. F. (1988). Clinical experience with civil commitment. In C. G. Leukefeld & F. M. Tims (Eds.), *Compulsory treatment of drug abuse: Research and clinical practice* (NIDA Research Monograph 86, pp. 35-56). Rockville, MD: National Institute on Drug Abuse.

McFarland, K. (1991). *Women Offenders Program/De Paul Treatment Centers, Inc.: Progress report for July 1, 1990-March 31, 1991.* Portland, OR: De Paul Treatment Center.

McGlothlin, W. H., Anglin, M. D., & Wilson, B. D. (1977). *An evaluation of the California Civil Addict Program* (NIDA Services Research Monograph Series, DHEW Pub. No. [ADM] 78-558). Rockville, MD: National Institute on Drug Abuse.

Mental Health Systems, Inc. (1990). *Female offender substance abuse demonstration project, California Institution for Women.* Unpublished proposal.

National Institute of Corrections. (1991). *Intervening with substance-abusing offenders: A framework for action.* Washington, DC: Department of Justice.

Petersilia, J., & Turner, S. (1990). Comparing intensive and regular supervision for high-risk probationers: Early results from an experiment in California. *Crime and Delinquency, 36*(1), 87-111.

Reed, B. G., Beschner, G. M., & Mondanaro, J. (1982). *Treatment services for drug dependent women (Vol. II)* (Treatment Research Monograph Series, DHHS Pub. No. [ADM] 82-1219). Rockville, MD: National Institute on Drug Abuse.

Simpson, D. D. (1979). The relation of time spent in drug abuse treatment to posttreatment outcome. *American Journal of Psychiatry, 136*(11), 1449-1453.

Simpson, D. D. (1981). Treatment for drug abuse: Follow-up outcomes and length of time spent. *Archives of General Psychiatry, 38*(8), 875-880.

The view from behind bars. (1990, Fall). *Time* (Special Issue: Women: The road ahead), pp. 20-23.

Washington State Department of Corrections. (1988). *Substance abuse treatment program: Evaluation of outcomes and management.* Seattle, WA: Planning and Research Section, Washington State Department of Corrections.

Wisconsin Department of Corrections. (1988). *Passages program description.* Madison, WI: Wisconsin Department of Corrections.

Wisconsin Department of Corrections. (1989). *Strategy briefs.* Madison, WI: Wisconsin Department of Corrections.

Wellisch, J., Anglin, M. D., & Prendergast, M. L. (1991). Treatment for chemically dependent women. DAIMP White Paper Series. Los Angeles, CA: UCLA Drug Abuse Research Center, Drug Abuse Information and Monitoring Project.

Wexler, H. K., Blackmore, J., & Lipton, D. S. (1991). Project REFORM: Developing a drug abuse treatment strategy for corrections. *Journal of Drug Issues, 21*(2), 469-491.

Wexler, H. K., Falkin, G. P., & Lipton, D. S. (1990). Outcome evaluation of a prison therapeutic community for substance abuse treatment. *Criminal Justice and Behavior, 17*(1), 71-92.

Wexler, H. K., Lipton, D. S., & Foster, K. (1985). Outcome evaluation of a prison therapeutic community for substance abuse treatment: Preliminary results. Paper presented at the American Society of Criminology Annual Meeting, San Diego, CA.

Wexler, H. K., Lipton, D. S., & Johnson, B. D. (1988). *A criminal justice system strategy for treating cocaine-heroin abusing offenders in custody.* Washington, DC: National Institute of Justice, Department of Justice.

Wexler, H. K., & Williams, R. (1986). Stay'n Out therapeutic community: Prison treatment for substance abusers. *Journal of Psychoactive Drugs, 18*(3), 221-230.

Women in Jail: Unpaid Justice. (1990, June 4). *Newsweek,* pp. 37-38, 51.

Chapter 3

SOME CONSIDERATIONS ON THERAPEUTIC COMMUNITIES IN CORRECTIONS

HAO PAN

FRANK R. SCARPITTI

JAMES A. INCIARDI

DOROTHY LOCKWOOD

Therapeutic communities for the treatment of drug abuse have been in existence for many decades now, but the term *therapeutic community* (or simply *TC*) is continually misapplied and misunderstood. In late 1991, for example, during the course of recruiting staff for a new TC that was being established by the University of Delaware's Center for Drug and Alcohol Studies under a grant from the National Institute on Drug Abuse,[1] this problem became especially apparent. Advertisements had been placed in newspapers and other media seeking drug abuse counselors with prior experience in therapeutic community settings. Not surprisingly, given the fact that good TC counselors are few in number, most of the applicants did not have the desired experience. But more important, even the most qualified applicants couldn't even begin to accurately describe a TC. Almost all envisioned it as "a drug treatment program that uses therapeutic techniques." Quite obviously, such a definition is rather unspecific and likely encompasses virtually every drug abuse treatment enterprise ever launched.

This lack of understanding on the part of practicing clinicians is compounded by the limited agreement among drug abuse and academic researchers with respect to the exact features and components of a TC. Decades ago, for example, the prominent TC pioneer Maxwell Jones conceded that there was no one model of a therapeutic community. He emphasized the staff-patient relationship and dynamics. The key to understanding

30

TCs, he argued, was to look at how the interest, skills, and enthusiasm of staff and their patients were mobilized so that patients had "sufficient freedom of action to create their own optimal living conditions" (Jones, 1962, p. 73).

Clark (1965), however, distinguished between a "therapeutic community approach" and the "therapeutic community proper." He restricted the use of the latter only to the pioneering experiments conducted by Jones as innovations in institutional psychiatry. He subscribed to the view that the initial Jones-type TC set off the TC movement that eventually included diverse modalities that could be grouped under the "therapeutic community approach."

For a third conception of TCs, Bloor, McKeganey, and Fonkert (1988) focused on new meanings constructed around mundane events in light of some therapeutic paradigm. Ordinary events, such as cleaning toilets or mending a leaking sink, are "invested with new meaning and held up as relevant to the cleaner's recovery or rehabilitation" (p. 5). The TC would appear to be unique, then, in terms of its definition of the therapeutic act rather than the social organization of the community.

EARLY THERAPEUTIC COMMUNITIES

The history of the therapeutic community is reasonably well documented (Biasi, 1972; Casriel, 1966; Glaser, 1981; Jones, 1953; Main, 1946; Sugarman, 1974; Volkman & Cressey, 1963; Wills, 1964; Yablonsky, 1965). Briefly, there were several antecedents. For example:

- In 1907, Homer Lane became the superintendent at a Detroit residential institution for juvenile offenders that was subsequently known as "The Boys' Republic." Lane engaged the boys in the construction and janitorial maintenance of the Republic's building. He also set up the governing structure on the basis of a constitution modeled after that of the United States. Close supervision was replaced by an emphasis on successful task performance and behavioral responsibility. Free choice and self-expression were also promoted with the aim of developing latent capabilities of the young residents of the Republic.
- In 1910, psychiatrist J. L. Moreno recognized the value of patients and ex-patients as co-therapists in small-group process. The inventor of psychodrama and numerous other dimensions of group therapy, Moreno wrote extensively about group therapeutic energy and the

role of the therapist in coordinating patients' efforts to help one another in problem resolution.

- In 1935, Alcoholics Anonymous (AA) began when a stockbroker and a physician, both alcoholics, started a 3-year process of self-recovery. In so doing, they developed the basic tenets of AA, accomplishing a major breakthrough in paraprofessional therapy.

- In the 1940s, two psychiatrists, Dr. Tom Main and Dr. Maxwell Jones, independently developed therapeutic community methods that led to revolutionary changes in institutional psychiatry.[2] They attempted, at separate hospitals, to treat the mentally ill by improving social relationships in the hospitals and by experimenting with newly defined roles and new patterns of interactions among staff and patients.[3]

- In 1958, the first therapeutic community for the treatment of substance abusers was founded by AA graduate Charles E. Dederick in Ocean Park, California. Known as *Synanon*,[4] it was an outgrowth of Dederick's successes with manipulating a variety of different group therapy techniques in discussion groups with local alcoholics and heroin addicts.

Two Synanon offshoots, Daytop Lodge (later known as Daytop Village) and Phoenix House, both established in New York City during the early 1960s, provided the impetus for what evolved into a national, and then international, movement. Today, there are therapeutic communities for substance abusers in a majority of Western and Third World nations.

THE BEGINNINGS OF THERAPEUTIC
COMMUNITIES IN CORRECTIONS

In contrast to the history of hospital or community-based TCs, the story of therapeutic communities *in corrections* is not quite as clear. It appears that the first corrections-based TC was established in 1962 in Nevada State Prison as an extension of Charles Dederick's Synanon program (*Time*, 1963, p. 45). Several more appeared during the latter half of the 1960s. In 1967, the Federal Bureau of Prisons established a therapeutic community in its Danbury, Connecticut, institution (Bol & Meyboom, 1988). As part of Governor Nelson A. Rockefeller's Narcotic Addiction Control Commission and its ill-fated civil commitment program for heroin addicts, a small TC program was piloted in New York's Green Haven Prison, a maximum security facility some 90 miles north of Manhattan. At about the same time, the New York City Addiction Services Agency organized TC units patterned after Phoenix House in Rikers Island and Hart Island penitentiaries.

From the early 1970s through the mid-1980s, prison-based TCs seemed to come and go—in Arkansas, Connecticut, Georgia, Michigan, Nebraska, New York, Oklahoma, South Carolina, Virginia, the federal system, and elsewhere. Along with the prison TCs established in the 1960s, almost all were closed, the result of prison crowding, state budget deficits, staff burnout, and changes in prison leadership. In a few instances, shut-downs were precipitated by inmate residents smuggling drugs and alcohol into the TC units. In others, custodial officers distrusted TC staff and operations and deliberately sabotaged the programs (Camp & Camp, 1990; Smith, 1977; Toch, 1980; Weppner, 1983). And not to be forgotten was Professor Robert Martinson's notorious paper, "What Works? Questions and Answers About Prison Reform," published in *The Public Interest* in the Spring of 1974 (Martinson, 1974). In it, Martinson reviewed the literature on hundreds of correctional treatment efforts and concluded that with few and isolated exceptions, nothing worked! His paper created a sensation and helped to usher in an "abolish treatment" era, characterized by a "nothing works" philosophy. This did little to help the cause of therapeutic communities in corrections.

In the midst of the distrust and skepticism of the period, there seemed to be a few bright spots. Somewhat visible in this behalf was the *Stay'n Out* therapeutic community, established in the New York State correctional system in 1974 (Frohling, 1989). Having one component in a men's institution and another in a women's facility, Stay'n Out was the joint effort of state agencies responsible for substance abuse, correctional services, and parole supervision. Program residents came from other state correctional institutions—they had to be at least 18 and have a history of drug abuse but no mental illness or sex crime involvement. In addition, each client had to demonstrate positive involvement in prior prison programs.

Stay'n Out helped define the model structure for prison-based therapeutic communities. Units were established away from the rest of the prison population, staffed with ex-addicts and other personnel capable of providing positive role models. Along with individual counseling, confrontation and support groups played important roles in the therapeutic process. Clients were expected to prove themselves through work and participation in the therapeutic community, achieving greater status and more responsible positions as they succeeded. Strict rules were enforced, however, and penalties were seen as learning opportunities. In various ways, the prosocial values of honesty, responsibility, and accountability were emphasized and reinforced.

Follow-up studies of Stay'n Out provided evidence that prison-based TC treatment could produce reductions in recidivism rates for both male and female offenders with histories of serious drug use (Wexler, Falkin, & Lipton, 1990; Wexler & Williams, 1986). Of the 1,626 men who spent an optimal 9 to 12 months in the program, for example, 77% successfully completed parole. Women who spent that amount of time in the program fared even better, with 92% completing parole. Both men and women spending 9 to 12 months in the TC were three times less likely to become recidivists than those spending less time in the program. Along with other TC evaluations (DeLeon, 1984; DeLeon, Wexler, & Jainchill, 1982; Field, 1989), the Stay'n Out experience significantly contributed to the initiation of a new therapeutic community movement in corrections.

The factor that ultimately launched this movement, however, was the allocation of funds for prison-based treatment by the Anti-Drug Abuse Act of 1986. The Bureau of Justice Assistance was designated as the lead agency, and the effort became known as *Project Reform* (see Wexler, Chapter 10 of this volume). The TC was selected as the key treatment modality for the Project Reform effort because of its positive track record. Yet there were other reasons as well for adopting the TC modality. There are many phenomena in the prison environment that make rehabilitation difficult. Not surprisingly, the availability of drugs is a problem (Inciardi, Lockwood, & Quinlan, 1992). In addition, there is the violence associated with inmate gangs, often formed along racial lines for the purposes of establishing and maintaining status, "turf," and unofficial control over certain sectors of prison ecology and activity. Finally, there is the prison subculture—a system of norms and values that tend to militate against rehabilitation. In contrast, the TC is separated from the rest of the prison population—sequestered from the drugs, the violence, and the negative rules and attitudes that tend to perpetuate antisocial thinking and acting.

By the close of the 1980s, Project Reform had supported the establishment of prison-based TCs in eight states. In 1991, the Reform effort was continued under the rubric of Project Recovery, a treatment demonstration initiative supported by the Department of Health and Human Services' Office of Treatment Improvement. In addition, the National Institute on Drug Abuse began supporting treatment demonstration and treatment evaluation projects involving therapeutic communities in correctional settings.

The emerging momentum with which the TC modality is increasingly applied in corrections for the objective of rehabilitation heightens the need to spell out the assumptions and implications associated with the TC. It also points to the need to consider some difficulties of implementation.

THE THERAPEUTIC COMMUNITY PROCESS

The therapeutic community is a total treatment environment that provides a residential 24-hour-per-day learning experience in which a drug user's transformations in conduct, attitudes, values, and emotions are introduced, monitored, and mutually reinforced as part of the daily regime (DeLeon, 1986). The primary clinical staff of the TC are typically former substance abusers who themselves were resocialized in therapeutic communities. The treatment perspective is that drug abuse is a disorder of the whole person, that the problem is the *person* not the drug, and that the *addiction* is but a *symptom* and not the essence of the disorder. In the TC's view of recovery, the primary goal is to change the negative patterns of behavior, thinking, and feeling that predispose drug abuse. As such, the overall goal is a responsible, drug-free life-style.

Recovery through the TC process depends on positive and negative pressures to change, and this is brought about through a self-help process in which relationships of mutual responsibility to every resident in the program are built. As the eminent TC researcher George DeLeon has put it:

> The essential dynamic in the TC is mutual self-help. Thus, the day-to-day activities are conducted by the residents themselves. In their jobs, groups, meetings, recreation, and personal and social time, it is the residents who constantly transmit to each other the main messages and expectations of the community. (DeLeon, 1986, p. 10)

As in many other drug treatment modalities, individual and group counseling are common vehicles used to bring about change. However, the *peer encounter* is the cornerstone of group process in the TC. The encounter group uses vigorous confrontational procedures as a mechanism for heightening a resident's awareness of the images, attitudes, and conduct that need to be modified. As such, the focus of the encounter is on behavior, with material drawn from peer and staff observations of the resident's daily conduct.

Beyond individual and group counseling, the TC process has a system of explicit rewards that reinforce the value of earned achievement. Privileges are *earned*. In addition, TCs have their own specific rules and regulations that guide the behavior of residents and staff. The purposes of these principles are to maintain the safety and health of the community and to train and teach residents through the use of discipline (Inciardi, 1990, p. 597). TC rules and regulations are numerous, the most conspicuous of which are total prohibitions against violence, theft, possession and use of drugs and alcohol, possession of weapons, and sexual activity. Any infringement of these cardinal rules typically results in immediate expulsion from a TC.

In short, the principal aim of therapeutic community treatment is a global change in life-style: abstinence from alcohol and illicit drugs, elimination of antisocial conduct, and achievement of employability and prosocial attitudes and values. This approach can be distinguished from other treatment modalities in three broad ways:

First, the TC coordinates a comprehensive rehabilitative offering in a single setting, composed of vocational counseling, work therapy, recreation, group and individual therapy, and medical, legal, family, and social services.

Second, the primary therapist and teacher in the TC is the community itself—a community of peers and staff who role model successful personal change and serve as rational authorities and guides in the recovery process.

Third, and as already noted above, TCs have an approach to behavioral change based on an explicit perspective of the drug abuse disorder, the client, and the recovery process (DeLeon & Rosenthal, 1989). Implicit in this view is that the drug abuse disorder affects most of the user's areas of functioning.

THERAPEUTIC COMMUNITIES IN CORRECTIONS

Therapeutic communities in corrections present several distinctive advantages. First, as indicated earlier, drug addiction is understood by the TC approach as a manifestation of deep and personal problems that result from the accumulation of deficits in the areas of values, thinking ability, social skills, cognition, and behavior. The TC's concern is curative rather than punitive. Thus, prison TCs serve to reorient prevailing assumptions about inmates and offer a positive alternative conception.

Second, a prison TC's daily regime derives from the general view on drug addiction and rehabilitation. It includes programs and activities that are based on mutual self-help, therapeutic counseling, recreation, and social skill training. Such programs and activities not only promote meaningful social interactions and social relationships but also set off a process of socialization oriented toward a productive and responsible way of life. Above all, TC strategies and techniques embody positive values. Over the course of treatment, residents begin to understand and see the beneficial effects of such values as honesty, caring, helpfulness, and responsibility that are integral to the TC experience.

Third, staff supervision in prison TCs is qualitatively different than regular prison supervision. Staff supervision can be performance oriented, or it can stress individual or group responsibility. Most important, since TC counselors consist chiefly of recovering addicts who were former residents of TCs and/or were prison inmates, they provide positive role models and change agents.

Fourth, prison TCs are particularly significant and useful for those inmates facing the immediate prospect of release. As reiterated, the TC approach does not aim at a specific area of deficits in exclusion of other problems that a person also exhibits. It aims at the global changes of the person. Put differently, it targets the general enhancement of the person— one's thinking, values, skills, and overall social functioning. Such objectives naturally fit the transitional phase from prison to society. Thus conceived, TCs in corrections—in both prisons and work-release centers— have the potential capacity to bridge the gap that is otherwise missing.

One recent attempt to extend the TC beyond the prison walls but still within the correctional setting is the University of Delaware's establishment of a therapeutic community in a work-release setting. This facility located in Wilmington, Delaware, and known as CREST Outreach Center, recognizes the need for comprehensive rehabilitation of prison releasees with histories of drug abuse and the special problems of transition from incarceration to freedom. This experimental program thus combines the essential features of a TC with the structure of a residential work-release program (Inciardi, Lockwood, Martin, & Wald, 1991; Lockwood, 1992; Martin, 1992).

The treatment model at CREST follows a five-phase design. Phase I is a 2-week orientation, involving induction into the TC, assessment, and evaluation. Phase II is an 8-week component emphasizing involvement in the TC community, such as participation in morning meetings, community jobs, group therapy, individual counseling, confrontation, and nurturing.

Phase III stresses role modeling and supervision of other clients with the assistance of staff. This phase lasts about 5 weeks. Phase IV is a 2-week preparation for transition from the TC community to the outside community, with mock job interviews, resume preparation, and seminars on job seeking. Phase V is reentry, including obtaining and maintaining employment outside the TC. During this phase, which lasts about 7 weeks, clients remain at the facility but begin the transition back to the community by retaining gainful employment, finding appropriate housing, and initiating the recovery stage of their treatment.

SOME CONSIDERATIONS

Veteran therapeutic community researchers have recognized the significance of prison TCs. As Harry Wexler enthusiastically noted:

> Prisons are depressing environments and the inmates' culture engenders survival concerns, pessimism and cynical attitudes. In contrast, the TC communicates a sense of optimism; for example, if participants work hard and develop competencies there are few limits to ambition. There is a strong implicit (staff role models) and explicit message that it is possible to rise out of the mire of social deprivation, prejudice and personal inadequacies. (1986, p. 228)

However, the setting-up and administration of prison TCs can also involve challenging difficulties. It is imperative to recognize that prisons are totally controlled and heavily guarded environments with elaborate custodial arrangements. In many aspects, TCs implement techniques and strategies that challenge the routines of highly organized prisons. Naturally bureaucratic resistance may arise either from willful and suspicious individuals or from sheer organizational rigidity—or both at the same time. Such resistance on the part of the criminal justice bureaucracy is very difficult to overcome unless the TC modality is supported by high-level staff. Enthusiastic support is best secured when the TC modality presents itself to the senior administration as a highly attractive philosophy of rehabilitation. But even if high-level commitment of support is obtained, great effort is needed to ensure that lower-level cooperation is dependable.

Hans Toch (1980) has also pointed to a number of vulnerabilities associated with prison TCs. Negative publicity has threatened the viability of many. Self-defined values, such as autonomy of operation and integrity of program, can also damage the success of TCs if they become excessive and blind to other equally important objectives of the prison routine. In other words, the corrections-based TC holds great promise, but it is not without its detractors and structural weaknesses.

Thus far, the discussion has focused on issues related to TCs and their applications in correctional settings. These are pressing issues because of the renewed interest in TCs in corrections and several significant research projects that are under way. However, given the diversity of TC models and practices, it is important to acknowledge seeming inconsistencies in the appraisal of TCs and the lack of theoretical underpinnings for TC practices.

The general idea of TCs has translated into worldwide practices for decades, with widely varying appraisals. The innovations associated with Maxwell Jones at the old Belmont unit in the 1940s were appraised as a "veritable revolution" in social psychiatry (Carr-Gregg, 1984, p. 14). Another therapeutic community, Matrix, was revealed, however, to be scandalous and short-lived (Weppner, 1983). The metamorphosis of the well-publicized Synanon is also striking. Founded as a therapeutic community, Synanon soon gained the reputation for being an innovative and effective treatment center for drug and alcohol abusers (Casriel, 1966; Yablonsky, 1965). Yet, the subsequent development of Synanon into a permanent "protective" community and eventually into a cult associated with reportedly bizarre practices and events raises questions about the TC process that are not yet fully answered (Anson, 1978; Ofshe, 1980).

Although the development of therapeutic communities continues and is now aided by national and international associations, there are few studies that aim at clarifying conceptual confusions and illuminating therapeutic practices. The prominent trend in the literature seems to be empirical studies of treatment outcome and documentation of ethnographic details followed with tentative and discrete summary statements. It is sometimes difficult to see the logical and consequential connections among components of TCs deemed significant for the particular program under discussion.

A more solid theoretical grounding is needed for TCs than is now available, so as to (1) render the past experience of successes and failures more explainable and (2) to guide the application of TCs in differing social contexts. Otherwise, TC practices become little more than a compilation of individual and disconnected stories.

Take the coverage of Synanon as an example. Many people, including mental health professionals, visited Synanon during its early years. They wrote approvingly about it and helped establish its international reputation. Indeed, the major evolution and development of the TC movement involved the replication of Synanon-like therapeutic communities in other locations by Synanon graduates and some professionals who believed in the Synanon system. For some researchers, Synanon represents a "true" TC (Yablonsky, 1989). Yet, no discussions were produced at that time that allow us to understand the authoritarian orientation of Synanon and the reduction of authoritarianism that characterized Maxwell Jones's TC innovations.

Synanon and its subsequent transformation also provides the ideal occasion to examine the role of charismatic leaders in TCs and their relation to TC process and structure. If charismatic leaders are an integral part of the TC structure, the replication of effective TCs would be extremely difficult to achieve, since charisma is unique and idiosyncratic. If, however, particular TC structures generate charismatic leaders as an unavoidable feature of the TC experience, the objective would shift to copying those structures with charismatic leaders (Almond, Keniston, & Boltax, 1968). The options are not one or the other, of course. The point is that these are significant issues, yet discussions that explicitly address them are scarce.

The lack of theoretical grounding also leads to sharply divergent perceptions of TCs by researchers. Perceptions of TCs range from a treatment method for a specific problem to an instrument of social change that seeks to restore communitarianism to modern society. Hans Toch's introductory article (1980) in his edited book on therapeutic communities in corrections is a case in point. It begins with a call to interpret TCs in terms of a traditional community with certain sociological traits, continues by viewing TC building in prison as a reaction to a repressive institution, and concludes with the suggestion that TCs be exported to achieve social reform and "to expand participatory roles in society at large" (Toch, 1980, p. 14). Although this might be considered an extreme case of multiple usage of TCs, it does represent the general lack of consensus regarding the precise nature and purpose of therapeutic communities. At least part of the confusion found in the extant TC literature derives from the lack of sound theoretical explanations of the TC process.

Theoretically grounded explanations of the TC process would also support assertions and predictions that might otherwise seem arbitrary and spontaneous. In introducing new directions for TCs in the 1990s, Lewis Yablonsky has identified 10 emerging trends, including the increasing involvement of professionals, changing leadership roles, and greater democracy in decision making (Yablonsky, 1989, pp. 44-48). Yet, we are at a loss to understand why these changes are taking place or what is behind these new trends of development. Similarly, Maxwell Jones has come up with a list of 21 "principles essential in putting together a therapeutic community in a prison setting" (1980, pp. 34-35). No explanations are given, however, as to why these principles are essential, or whether his list is a complete one.

As the therapeutic community becomes more popular as an instrument of behavior change, especially for substance abusers in correctional settings, the need for a better understanding of the therapeutic process also increases. An important step in achieving this understanding is the development of a theory of therapeutic communities, a rational and logical context within which the unique features of this treatment modality may be explained and comprehended. Until that is developed, our knowledge of TCs will remain incomplete and their success in modifying the behavior of substance abusers and other clients will continue to be a matter of conjecture.

NOTES

1. This research was supported, in part, by HHS Grant No. R18-DAO6948, "A Therapeutic Community Work Release Center for Inmates," from the National Institute on Drug Abuse.
2. Tom Main (1946) also coined the term *therapeutic community.*
3. Jones's work at the Belmont Industrial Neurosis Unit (now Henderson Hospital) is particularly well known. Jones himself produced a stream of publications about it. It was also the topic of a pioneering study by the American anthropologist Robert Rapoport (1960), which eventually became a sort of textbook of hospital therapeutic community practices.
4. It is said that the name *Synanon* was born when a recovering alcoholic, who was trying to say "seminar" and "symposium" at the same time, slurred the words into "synanon." See Yablonsky (1989, p. 17).

REFERENCES

Almond, R, Keniston, K., & Boltax, S. (1968). The value system of a milieu therapy unit. *Archives of General Psychiatry, 19,* 545-561.
Anson, R. (1978, November 27). The Synanon horrors. *New York Times,* p. 11.
Biasi, D. Vincent. (1972). Phoenix Houses: Therapeutic communities for drug addicts. In W. Keup (Ed.), *Drug abuse: Current concepts and research* (pp. 375-380). Springfield, IL: Charles C Thomas.
Bloor, M., McKeganey, N., & Fonkert, D. (1988). *One foot in Eden: A sociological study of the range of therapeutic community practice.* London: Routledge.
Bol, W. W., & Meyboom, M. L. (1988, Spring). Penitentiary-related drug program in the U.S., Sweden, Switzerland, Austria, and the Federal Republic of Germany. National Institute of Justice. *International Summaries,* pp. 1-6.

Camp, George M., & Camp, Camille G. (1990). *Preventing and solving problems involved in operating therapeutic communities in a prison setting.* South Salem, NY: Criminal Justice Institute.

Carr-Gregg, Charlotte. (1984). *Kicking the habit: Four Austrian therapeutic communities.* Queensland, Australia: University of Queensland Press.

Casriel, Daniel. (1966). *So fair a house: The story of Synanon.* Englewood Cliffs, NJ: Prentice Hall.

Clark, D. (1965). The therapeutic community: Concept, practice, and future. *British Journal of Psychiatry, 111*, 947-954.

DeLeon, George. (1984). *The therapeutic community: Study of effectiveness.* Rockville, MD: National Institute on Drug Abuse.

DeLeon, George. (1986). The therapeutic community for substance abuse: Perspective and approach. In George DeLeon & James T. Ziegenfuss (Eds.), *Therapeutic communities for addictions: Readings in theory, research and practice* (pp. 5-18). Springfield, IL: Charles C Thomas.

DeLeon, George, & Rosenthal, Mitchell S. (1989). Treatment in therapeutic communities. In T. B. Karasu (Ed.), *Treatment of psychiatric disorders* (pp. 1379-1396). New York: American Psychiatric Press.

DeLeon, George, Wexler, Harry F., & Jainchill, Nancy. (1982). The therapeutic community: Success and improvement rates five years after treatment. *International Journal of the Addictions, 17*, 703-747.

Field, Gary. (1989). The effects of intensive treatment on reducing the criminal recidivism of addicted offenders. *Federal Probation, 53*, 51-56.

Frohling, Robert. (1989). *Promising approaches to drug treatment in correctional settings.* Criminal Justice Paper No. 7. Paper presented at the National Conference of State Legislatures, Washington, DC.

Glaser, Fred B. (1981). The origins of the drug-free therapeutic community, *British Journal of Addiction, 76*, 13-25.

Inciardi, James A. (1990). *Criminal justice.* New York: Harcourt Brace Jovanovich.

Inciardi, James A., Lockwood, Dorothy, Martin, Steven S., & Wald, Bruce M. (1991). *Therapeutic communities in corrections and work release: Some clinical and policy considerations.* National Institute on Drug Abuse Technical Review Meeting on Therapeutic Community Research, Bethesda, MD, May 16-17.

Inciardi, James A., Lockwood, Dorothy, & Quinlan, Judith. (1992, Winter). Drug use in prison: Patterns, processes, and implications for treatment. *Journal of Drug Issues, 23*, 119-129.

Jones, Maxwell. (1953). *The therapeutic community: A new treatment method in psychiatry.* New York: Basic Books.

Jones, Maxwell. (1962). *Social psychiatry in the community.* Springfield, IL: Charles C Thomas.

Jones, Maxwell. (1980). Desirable features of a therapeutic community in a prison. In H. Toch (Ed.), *Therapeutic communities in corrections.* New York: Praeger.

Lockwood, Dorothy. (1992, March 10). *Modeling a modified TC design for work release.* Annual Meeting of the Academy of Criminal Justice Sciences, Pittsburgh, PA.

Main, Tom F. (1946). The hospital as a therapeutic institution. *Bulletin of the Menninger Clinic, 10*, 27-37.

Martin, Steven S. (1992, March 10). *Strategies for implementing TCs in prison settings: What has been learned from recent research.* Annual Meeting of the Academy of Criminal Justice Sciences, Pittsburgh, PA.

Martinson, Robert. (1974). What works? Questions and answers about prison reform. *The Public Interest, 35*, 22-54.

Ofshe, R. (1980). The social development of the Synanon cult: The managerial strategy of organizational transformation. *Sociological Analysis, 41*, 103-124.

Rapoport, Robert. (1960). *Community as doctor*. London: Tavistock.

Smith, Roger. (1977). *Drug problems in correctional institutions*. Washington, DC: Law Enforcement Assistance Administration.

Sugarman, Barry. (1974). *Daytop Village: A therapeutic community*. New York: Holt, Rinehart & Winston.

Time. (1963, March).

Toch, Hans (Ed.). (1980). *Therapeutic communities in corrections*. New York: Praeger.

Volkman, Rita, & Cressey, Donald R. (1963). Differential association and the rehabilitation of drug addicts. *American Journal of Sociology, 69*, 129-142.

Weppner, Robert S. (1983). *The untherapeutic community: Organizational behavior in a failed addiction treatment program*. Lincoln, NE: University of Nebraska Press.

Wexler, Harry K. (1986). Therapeutic communities within prision. In G. DeLeon & J. T. Ziegenfuss (Eds.), *Therapeutic communities for addictions: Readings in theory, research, and practice*. Springfield, IL: Charles C Thomas.

Wexler, Harry K., Falkin, Gregory P., & Lipton, Douglas S. (1990). Outcome evaluation of a prison therapeutic community for substance abuse treatment. *Criminal Justice and Behavior, 17*, 71-92.

Wexler, Harry K., & Williams, Ronald. (1986). The Stay'n Out therapeutic community: Prison treatment for substance abusers. *Journal of Psychoactive Drugs, 18*, 221-229.

Wills, W. D. (1964). *Homer Lane—A biography*. London: Allen & Unwin.

Yablonsky, Lewis. (1965). *The tunnel back: Synanon*. New York: MacMillan.

Yablonsky, Lewis. (1989). *The therapeutic community: A successful approach for treating substance abusers*. New York: Gardner Press.

Chapter 4

DRUG TREATMENT IN JAILS AND DETENTION SETTINGS

ROGER H. PETERS

INTRODUCTION

The development of substance abuse treatment programs within the criminal justice system can be traced to the opening of U.S. Public Health Service hospitals to treat narcotics addicts in federal prisons during the 1930s and more recently to the Narcotic Addict Rehabilitation Act (NARA), which provided for civil commitment of addicts to federal prisons. Public support and funding for substance abuse treatment within the criminal justice system has fluctuated considerably in the past 20 years, influenced in part by reports questioning the efficacy of offender treatment programs (Lipton, Martinson, & Wilks, 1975), the perceived relationship between drug use and crime, and the continuing debate concerning the role of rehabilitation in correctional settings.

Several events have focused attention on the need for substance abuse treatment within jails and prisons. Studies sponsored by the National Institute on Drug Abuse (Inciardi, 1981; NIDA, 1991) have helped to document the relationship between heroin use and street crime. The recent crack cocaine epidemic and associated street violence, property crime, prostitution, and open drug dealing in metropolitan areas has increased public alarm and interest in addressing drug problems, and it has strengthened the belief that drug use augments serious criminal behavior. The drug use epidemic has profoundly influenced the criminal justice system, as evidenced by overloaded court dockets, spiralling numbers of incarcerated offenders and community corrections populations, soaring costs for construction of jail and prison facilities, and early release of many violent

44

felons. Federal, state, and local responses to the drug epidemic have focused on reducing the supply of drugs through enhanced law enforcement efforts, minimum mandatory sentences for drug offenses, and unprecedented construction of new jails and prisons. Efforts aimed at drug suppliers and users have not succeeded in reducing the availability of drugs in most communities. As jail and prison populations have risen during the past several years, efforts have intensified to identify alternative strategies within the criminal justice system to address the drug crisis, including use of intermediate sanctions and substance abuse treatment.

THE PREVALENCE OF SUBSTANCE ABUSE
AMONG JAIL INMATES

The population of U.S. jail inmates has grown from 223,551 in 1983 to 405,320 in 1990 (Bureau of Justice Statistics, 1991a, 1991b), reflecting a significant increase in drug-related arrests. Results from the Drug Use Forecasting (DUF) program (National Institute of Justice, 1992) indicate that over half of recent arrestees have tested positive for drugs, including over 60% for cocaine in some areas. A recent survey conducted by the Bureau of Justice Statistics (Bureau of Justice Statistics, 1991c) indicated that 78% of inmates had a history of drug use and that over half were under the influence of drugs or alcohol at the time of their most recent offense. Interviews conducted with a large sample of metropolitan jail inmates (Abram, 1990) revealed that 59% of inmates had a diagnosable substance abuse disorder, including a significant number who were alcoholics (11%), who had a drug abuse disorder (4%), and who had a dual disorder involving both a substance abuse disorder and either depression or antisocial personality disorder (45%). Rates of drug abuse among jail inmates have increased significantly over the past several years (Bureau of Justice Statistics, 1991d). The prevalence of substance abuse among jail inmates is currently about twice as high as in the general U.S. population (Bureau of Justice Statistics, 1991c; NIDA, 1991).

Inmates referred for substance abuse treatment in a metropolitan jail (Peters & Kearns, 1992) indicate a pattern of severe cocaine, alcohol, and polysubstance abuse in the month prior to incarceration and a history of unsuccessful attempts to achieve abstinence. Findings from a Bureau of Justice Statistics survey (1991d) indicate that the most frequently reported drugs of abuse among jail inmates include marijuana (71%), cocaine (50%), amphetamines (22%), LSD (19%), heroin (18%), barbiturates (17%), and PCP (14%). In addition to prolonged exposure to the debilitating effects of drugs and alcohol, substance-involved jail inmates have a history of severe disruption in social, vocational, and psychological functioning (Peters & Kearns, 1992; Peters, Kearns, Murrin, & May, 1991). Despite the prevalence of concurrent substance abuse and vocational, educational, psychological, and other psychosocial problems among jail inmates, few inmates report a history of involvement in drug or alcohol treatment programs. A survey conducted by the Bureau of Justice Statistics (1991d) found that only 24% of inmates reported prior participation in substance abuse programs and that only 5% were currently receiving substance abuse services.

THE RATIONALE FOR JAIL
SUBSTANCE ABUSE TREATMENT

The primary function served by jails in the past has been to detain inmates who are awaiting trial or serving short sentences. Jails have served to provide secure confinement, screening, and classification and to facilitate movement of inmates who are released to the community on bond or recognizance or who must attend court hearings or trial. The role of jails has expanded in the past 20 years to address the needs of special inmate populations, including substance abusers, the mentally ill, and individuals with educational and vocational deficits. These changes have been affected in part by the recognition that jails frequently serve as the repository for socially disadvantaged populations (e.g., mentally ill, substance abusers, the homeless) that move somewhat fluidly from one community institution to another. Identification of psychosocial problems among these individuals while incarcerated is seen as a preventive strategy to attenuate further needs for services in the community following release from custody. Other factors influencing the expansion of jail programs include the development of jail standards (Steadman, McCarty, & Morrissey, 1989), accreditation, and staff credentialing, encouraged in part by the establishment of organizations such as the American Association of Correctional Psychologists (AACP), the American Correctional Association (ACA), the American Jail Association (AJA), and the National Commission on Correctional Health Care (NCCHC). State and federal class-action lawsuits have also led to augmentation of basic inmate services.

Jails provide an opportune time to intervene with offenders who have often experienced little contact with community mental health or substance abuse services. Distrust of social service agencies, lack of funds, or unfamiliarity with community treatment agencies often deter inmates from seeking substance abuse treatment. The severity of substance abuse problems is often not acknowledged among these individuals, their family members, and peers. The initial period of incarceration often serves to focus an inmate's attention on the negative consequences of substance use and can mobilize internal motivation to address long-standing life-style problems through treatment. As many as 43% of new arrestees to metropolitan jails indicated a need for treatment in a recent survey (National Institute of Justice, 1989).

Involvement in jail treatment programs provides an important opportunity to encourage participation in community substance abuse services following discharge from jail. Retention of offenders in community treatment is likely to reduce recidivism to the criminal justice system (Hubbard, Collins, Rachal, & Cavanaugh, 1988). In the absence of involvement in substance abuse treatment, inmates are likely to relapse and to return to jail or prison (Wexler, Lipton, & Johnson, 1988). Participation in jail-based treatment also provides an opportunity for triage with other agencies in the community to help reduce vocational, emotional, and family problems that may be associated with substance abuse.

THE SCOPE OF JAIL SUBSTANCE ABUSE TREATMENT PROGRAMS

Several surveys have been conducted to examine the scope of mental health and substance abuse services in jails. Newman and Price (1977) identified 118 jail systems that reported substance abuse treatment services in response to a survey of local jails conducted by the U.S. Department of Justice (National Criminal Justice Information and Statistics Service, 1972). The original Justice Department survey found that 26% of jails reported substance abuse services. Site visits and extensive interviews were conducted at each of the jails examined in the Newman and Price study. Results indicated that few jails had comprehensive drug treatment services. Of the 118 jails surveyed, researchers identified 9 therapeutic communities, 16 programs with specialized drug counseling, and 27 programs with general counseling available to drug-involved inmates. Most jails did not have an organized system of substance abuse screening, substance abuse treatment services, or linkage to community agencies.

Through a project funded by the National Institute of Mental Health (Steadman, McCarty, & Morrissey, 1989), 43 jails throughout the country were surveyed to examine treatment services for mentally ill inmates. Jails identified for the study had been represented at national correctional training workshops or had developed model mental health programs and thus were likely to have a disproportionately high rate of mental health or other inmate program services. Although 26 of 43 jails (60%) surveyed reported substance abuse services, treatment often consisted of self-help groups such as Alcoholics Anonymous (AA). Jail administrators sometimes relied on community groups to organize these group meetings, and in many cases a general strategy had not been articulated to guide substance abuse treatment programs. Only 37% of jails provided case management services to drug-involved inmates at the time of release from jail. The study found that in-jail substance abuse programs frequently received less attention and were provided lower funding relative to mental health programs and in some cases were not supported by jail administrators. Of all jail services surveyed, substance abuse treatment programs were subject to the greatest change and were more likely to deteriorate over time or to be discontinued in comparison to mental health services.

Through a recent grant project funded by the Bureau of Justice Assistance, the American Jail Association conducted a nationwide survey to examine the extent of jail substance abuse treatment services in 1987 (Peters & May, 1992; Peters, May, & Kearns, 1992). Over 1,700 survey responses were received, representing 57% of all U.S. jails. Among the jails surveyed, 468 (28%) indicated that substance abuse services were available, including 18% that provided funded programs. Only 107 (7%) of jails responding to the survey provided a comprehensive level of services that included drug education, group counseling, transition planning, and referral to community treatment agencies. Fewer than 1% of jails offered at least 10 hours per week of drug treatment services.

Drug treatment programs were more likely to be reported in Northeastern jails, in jails of larger than 250 inmates, and in jails using direct supervision approaches. Jails with substance abuse programs were more likely to have educational services, detoxification services, employee assistance programs, and AIDS and drug testing, in comparison to other facilities. The vast majority of in-jail substance abuse treatment programs offered drug education, individual and group counseling, and follow-up referral to community agencies. However, only 44% of programs reported transition planning prior to release from incarceration. Substance abuse programs had an average capacity of 42 inmates ($SD = 69$), and had an average inmate/staff ratio of 12 to 1. Approximately 52% of inmates participating in jail substance abuse programs were unsentenced and 48% were sentenced. Two thirds of inmates participating in treatment programs were Caucasian, 23% were African American, 8% were Hispanic, and 3% were of other racial/ethnic backgrounds.

Survey findings indicate that a small fraction of jail inmates in need of substance abuse treatment were receiving services. The absence of treatment programs was particularly evident in smaller jails. Results reflect the need for more comprehensive examination of substance abuse treatment needs and for development of screening, assessment, and counseling services, transition planning, and efforts to facilitate placement in aftercare services. It was beyond the scope of the survey to determine specific treatment needs of jail inmates. Nor did the survey examine the quality of substance abuse services provided in jails. Further research is urgently needed in these areas.

TREATMENT APPROACHES

Jail substance abuse programs are characterized by considerable diversity in treatment approaches, program environment, involvement of correctional staff, level of funding, and the scope of services provided. Recent initiatives sponsored by the U.S. Department of Justice, Bureau of Justice Assistance and the U.S. Department of Health and Human Services, Center for Substance Abuse Treatment (formerly the Office for Treatment Improvement) have helped to develop several model demonstration jail programs that are likely to contribute to an understanding of effective treatment approaches and interventions. However, there have been few research efforts examining the effectiveness of jail substance abuse treatment that would provide guidance to administrators interested in implementing new programs.

In-jail programs often combine elements of several types of treatment approaches. For example, several programs have developed psychoeducational approaches within therapeutic community settings. Factors that influence the type of treatment approach implemented in jails include the program budget, anticipated length of stay of the inmate population selected for treatment, perceived level of treatment needs among jail inmates, levels of staff experience and training, facility program space, and treatment approaches used by community substance abuse agencies. The following section reviews several substance abuse treatment approaches used within jails. Examples of existing jail treatment programs are provided to illustrate how these substance abuse treatment approaches have been implemented.

Chemical Dependency/Self-Help Approaches

Chemical dependency (CD) programs often provide a short-term (3-6 week) treatment program and include an emphasis on self-help strategies employed in Alcoholics Anonymous, Narcotics Anonymous, and Cocaine Anonymous groups. These approaches are also referred to as 28-day, 12-step, "medical model," or "Minnesota model" treatment. The CD approach views the development of addictive disorders as a product of physiological, psychological, and social factors. Inmates are taught that drug dependence is a lifetime disorder. During periods of abstinence, the "disease" is in remission, but the individual must always be concerned with reoccurrence of symptoms. Continued contact with community and social supports, including 12-step groups, is encouraged in order to prevent relapse.

The CD treatment regimen is highly structured and often includes initial psychiatric and psychosocial assessment and drug education focusing on the development of the addictive "disease," stages of the disease, and health-related consequences of substance abuse. Participants involved in CD programs are assigned to help in developing a recovery plan, including significant work through the 12 steps of Alcoholics Anonymous. Other adjunctive treatment activities often include individual counseling, psychiatric services, recreation, and family counseling. Chemical dependency approaches share with psychoeducational programs a reliance on didactic and educational activities. The primary objective of the CD approach is total abstinence, with the recognition that recovery requires ongoing involvement in self-help groups and return to residential treatment in the event of a relapse. Staff in CD programs include both recovering addicts and professional counselors. Aftercare activities are encouraged but are not provided the same emphasis as in TC or psychoeducational approaches (Gerstein & Harwood, 1990).

Program Models. Chemical dependency programs have been implemented successfully in the King County Jail and North Rehabilitation Facility, in Seattle, Washington (Peters, 1992a), and in the Jail Substance Abuse Treatment Program (JSAP) within the Washington County Detention Center, in Hagerstown, Maryland (Messmer & Brown, 1991). An innovative CD program has also been recently implemented in the Addiction, Corrections, and Treatment Unit (ACT) within the Arlington Detention Center, in Arlington, Virginia. Substance abuse services in the King County Jail and North Rehabilitation Facility include a 5-week program for 44 inmates in the central jail facility and a 3-week program for 49 inmates in a medium security facility. Treatment services are coordinated by the King County Division of Alcoholism and Substance Abuse Services. Program services include seminars on the disease concept, progression of drug and alcohol addiction, orientation to the 12-step program, health-related consequences of substance abuse, family issues, anger and stress management, AIDS prevention, relapse prevention, and aftercare planning. Other program interventions include involvement in GED and literacy training, development of job-readiness skills, self-help groups, vocational training, mental health assessment, and drama therapy. Indigent participants in jail treatment services are eligible for additional follow-up services through the Alcohol and Drug Addiction Treatment and Support Act (ADATSA), an innovative state-funded program that provides up to 6 months of treatment and financial support. Financial support through ADATSA, such as housing subsidies, are contingent on participation in community substance abuse treatment.

The JSAP program provides 6 weeks of treatment services within the Washington County, Maryland, Detention Center. The program has a capacity of 17 inmates, of whom approximately 90% are sentenced. Treatment services are based on principles of the chronic disease model and are provided by the Washington County Health Department. Program interventions include drug and health education, 12-step groups, group and individual counseling, AIDS education, group assignments, and recreation activities. The daily treatment regimen include four major activities: "task groups," education, group counseling, and "wrap up" and individual counseling sessions. Structured group assignments are provided to develop group cohesion and greater awareness of substance abuse problems. Lectures, outside speakers, and group discussions are provided to assist inmates in understanding the disease process, to develop self-assessment skills, and to identify strategies for maintaining abstinence following discharge from the program. Group counseling provides a supportive environment to review recovery goals, to develop an aftercare plan, and to identify community treatment services to be utilized following release from jail. Participants in the program are eligible to have their sentence modified to allow for early release from jail and for court-supervised participation in intensive aftercare services.

Pharmacological Approaches

Several types of pharmacological agents have been found to be useful in the treatment of offenders who are addicted to opiates. These include narcotic agonists such as methadone, which replace the physiological need for opiates, and narcotic antagonists such as naltrexone, which block the euphoric effects of opiates. Methadone treatments have been researched extensively and have been shown to be effective in reducing withdrawal symptoms and drug cravings (Anglin & Hser, 1990). Methadone can be administered orally, with dosages usually reduced over a period of several weeks to 6 months with minimal side effects. Treatment goals are to provide abstinence from drug use or to provide long-term methadone maintenance. Use of this approach is usually reserved for individuals who have not been able to achieve abstinence in drug-free programs. Use of methadone is governed by federal regulations that require narcotic dependency for at least 1 year prior to the onset of treatment and previous involvement in treatment. Other federal guidelines require drug testing, counseling, and development of individualized treatment plans (Office of Technology Assessment, 1990). Several states have also adopted regulations governing dosage levels and quality assurance monitoring.

Limitations of methadone treatment include the development of dependence on the drug, with concomitant withdrawal symptoms on termination of treatment. Methadone programs have also experienced difficulties with premature dropout from treatment (Craig, 1980; Fisher & Anglin, 1987), although higher dosage levels have been found to increase retention rates. Methadone has been used infrequently in jail settings, because, in part, of a reluctance by administrators to provide narcotics to inmates and related issues of medical supervision and concerns of compromising institutional security (Magura, Rosenblum, & Joseph, 1992).

Program Models. In-jail methadone maintenance has been used successfully in the Key Extended Entry Program (KEEP) within the New York City central jail facility at Rikers Island. Both pretrial detainees and sentenced inmates are treated in the Keep program, which provides methadone maintenance to approximately 3,000 inmates per year. The average length of stay in the program is 45 days, at which time inmates are referred to a KEEP clinic in the community. A review of participants discharged from the KEEP program (Magura, Rosenblum, & Joseph, 1992) found that inmates involved in methadone treatment at the time of arrest were more likely to report to post-incarceration community treatment programs (89%), in comparison to other inmates involved in the jail program (51%). Rates of attrition from community treatment over a 5-month follow-up period exceeded 40% for several groups of KEEP participants and were somewhat higher for inmates who were not in methadone treatment at the time of arrest.

Psychoeducational Approaches

Psychoeducational approaches are often used to address the treatment needs of jail inmates who are incarcerated for relatively short periods of time (1-3 months). These approaches are premised on the belief that substance abuse disorders develop as a result of multiple biopsychosocial factors. Recognition of these factors (e.g., individual predispositions, personal risk factors) and development of strategies to compensate for individual deficits are thought to be essential to achieving and maintaining long-term abstinence. Psychoeducational approaches assist inmates in developing individualized responses to common problems (e.g., coping with high-risk situations faced following release from jail) through modeling, role play, rehearsal, and homework, which frequently involves use of self-monitoring skills. A variety of theoretical approaches are employed in these programs, developed from disciplines of psychiatry, clinical psychology, counseling psychology, and social work and from therapeutic community and self-help settings. An emphasis is placed on development of individualized treatment goals and self-management strategies, enabling participants to initiate and sustain significant life-style changes. Psychoeducational programs are sometimes conducted in isolated jail treatment units but may be conducted on an outpatient basis, with inmates drawn from general housing units to attend daily treatment activities.

Major objectives of psychoeducational approaches include the following: (1) development of motivation and commitment to treatment through recognition of the addiction history, stages of recovery, and the impact of drug use on physical health and vocational and social functioning; (2) enhancement of life skills (e.g., managing a checkbook, time management) and communication skills; (3) AIDS education and prevention activities; (4) relapse prevention skills, including recognition of signs and symptoms of relapse, avoidance of active drug users, identification of high-risk situations, and strategies for managing a lapse or relapse; and (5) development of an aftercare plan that incorporates use of community treatment resources. Treatment is provided through a combination of group and individual counseling and includes use of lectures, group exercises, homework, and other instructional materials. Activities are intended to encourage cohesion among program participants and to develop honesty and openness regarding the past history of addiction and interactions within the treatment community.

Psychoeducational approaches are designed to promote self-awareness of biopsychosocial factors contributing to the development of drug addiction, including the family history of substance abuse, cognitive, behavioral, and environmental antecedents to substance abuse, and positive and negative consequences of use. Inmates are provided an understanding of the level of involvement required to complete treatment and the need for self-management strategies to prevent relapse following release from incarceration. At the conclusion of in-jail treatment, efforts are made to identify problem areas (e.g., family counseling, vocational training) requiring further attention during aftercare, to develop a treatment plan to guide aftercare services, and to develop a contract for involvement in community substance abuse treatment. Triage with community agencies to provide substance abuse, vocational, educational, mental health, and other social services following release from jail is an important function of psychoeducational programs.

Jail-based programs utilizing psychoeducational approaches often provide "closed" groups of inmates who enter and complete treatment at approximately the same time. Program staff may include professional counselors and ex-addicts. A range of adjunctive treatment activities are used to supplement psychoeducational material, including involvement in self-help groups, GED classes, vocational training, mental health counseling, and work assignments.

Program Models. Psychoeducational approaches have been successfully implemented by the DEUCE program in the Contra Costa Jail in Martinez, California (Christiansen, 1988), and by the Hillsborough County Sheriff's Office Substance Abuse Treatment Program in Tampa, Florida (National Institute of Corrections, 1991; Peters & Dolente, 1990). The DEUCE program provides voluntary treatment services for approximately 200 inmates who have at least 30 days remaining on their jail sentence. The program includes two concurrent tracks, involving substance abuse treatment and employability skills. Inmates participate in three phases of treatment over a maximum of 12 weeks: (1) Phase I, Informational Acquisition, using primarily didactic techniques to review drug education, the disease model of addiction, the recovery process, the 12-step program, and basic employability skills; (2) Phase II, Attitude Assessment, using didactic and experiential techniques to address self-esteem and other emotional issues related to recovery, the role of the family in the recovery process, and employment goal setting; (3) Phase III, Behavioral Change, focusing on rehearsal of relapse prevention and employability skills and development of individual relapse prevention and employment plans.

The Hillsborough County Sheriff's Office Substance Abuse Treatment Program provides 6 weeks of treatment to primarily sentenced inmates within a medium- to high-security jail facility. The program offers a range of skills-based interventions, including a focus on relapse prevention. A comprehensive assessment is provided at program intake to review substance abuse history, current psychosocial functioning, mental health status, and personal antecedents to relapse. Inmates are taught to use cognitive restructuring techniques to identify and modify irrational thoughts and rationalizations that contribute to substance abuse. An individualized behavior chain is developed by each inmate to help explore high-risk situations, thoughts, emotions, cues, and urges that precede substance abuse relapse. A range of cognitive-behavioral techniques are provided to help inmates manage these relapse antecedents and to deal with an initial slip to drug or alcohol use or with a full-blown relapse. Staff from a Treatment Alternatives to Street Crime (TASC) program work with the program counselor and inmate to develop an aftercare plan and to assist in the transition to community treatment. Evaluation results from the Hillsborough County Jail program are reviewed later in this chapter.

Therapeutic Communities

Residential therapeutic communities (TCs) were developed to treat severely drug dependent individuals and are predicated on the belief that recovery from addictive disorders is a long-term process involving significant changes in values and behaviors. Treatment reflects the need to adopt major life-style changes and to provide habilitation in social, vocational, and psychological functioning. Many TCs have utilized approaches developed in the Synanon program, started in 1958. TCs provide a highly structured treatment approach that includes strict community norms governing appropriate participant behavior, an often elaborate system of rewards and punishments sanctioning community behaviors, opportunities for development of responsibilities and privileges through completion of assigned activities, and client participation in community management.

Significant differences exist between different TCs in the length of treatment and treatment regimens employed. Several types of TCs are differentiated by the length of client participation (Office of Technology Assessment, 1990). These include a traditional TC (usually 9-15 months in duration), a modified TC (6-9 months), and a short-term TC (3-6 months) program. Clients involved in TCs are generally expected to complete several phases of treatment, including orientation to the system of rules, sanctions, and activities, participation in community activities, and reentry. Strategies such as confrontation and peer pressure are used to encourage motivation and commitment to maintain a drug-free life-style and development of prosocial behaviors. This social learning approach emphasizes regular feedback from peers and staff to identify deficits in interpersonal behaviors, motivation, and social responsibility. Educational and vocational skills development are encouraged during the reentry phase of treatment. Staff within TCs are often ex-offenders and frequently include graduates of the treatment program.

Therapeutic communities have been frequently used in correctional settings (Lipton, Falkin, & Wexler, 1992), reflecting the multiple needs for habilitation, resocialization, and modification of antisocial behaviors and values among offenders. A dedicated treatment unit is typically developed in which TC participants are isolated from other general population inmates. This tends to foster a sense of community identity and to reduce the negative peer influence of inmates who are not involved in treatment. Jail TCs frequently provide services for sentenced inmates or pretrial inmates with a lengthy anticipated period of incarceration. Development of TC approaches in jails have been limited in some cases by a reluctance to provide long-term treatment services, by philosophical opposition to the use of ex-offender staff and to coercive treatment strategies, and by the need for specialized staff training and technical assistance. Premature dropout from treatment has been a common problem faced by TC programs (DeLeon, 1986).

Program Models. Several TC programs have been successfully implemented in jails. The Integrated Multiphase Program of Assessment and Comprehensive Treatment (IMPACT) program in the Cook County Jail in Chicago, Illinois, provides services for approximately 360 pretrial inmates (Bush, Hecht, LaBarbera, & Peters, in press[b]). The program is a collaborative effort between Cermak Health Services, the Gateway Foundation, Inc., the Illinois Department of Alcoholism and Substance Abuse (DASA), and a local TASC program. Inmates spend an average of

6-8 months in the treatment program, including initial involvement in an orientation unit. Treatment services are provided by a community agency, Gateway, Inc., in a modified TC that utilizes a 12-step approach and significant peer involvement in directing treatment activities. Following completion of orientation, inmates are placed in 3 months of TC treatment and are then placed in a 4-month transition treatment program designed to assist in community reentry. The IMPACT program targets high-risk inmates and provides a multi-focal approach that includes AIDS prevention, educational, vocational, medical, and mental health services. The TASC program provides court liaison services, intake assessment, and follow-up of program participants in the community.

The Pima County Sheriff's Office provides treatment for approximately 50 sentenced inmates in the medium-security Adult Detention Center in Tucson, Arizona (Arbiter, 1988; National Institute of Corrections, 1991). The average length of stay in the treatment program is 4 months. Treatment services are provided by a community agency, Amity, Inc., and include educational and counseling services within a modified therapeutic community setting. The program is designed to promote self-investigation to explore the causes of prior substance abuse and criminal behavior and the related alienation from family, friends, and self. Major interventions include encounter group therapy, individual counseling, and seminars on health-related issues, family relationships and dynamics, relapse prevention, and other topics. Inmates are also provided regular work assignments and participate in educational programs. One unique aspect of the program involves the use of video playback to assist inmates to recognize changes in verbal and nonverbal interactions occurring over the course of treatment. Several coed activities are also offered within the treatment unit.

Other TC programs based in jails include the Addictive Disease Treatment Program (ADTP) within the Philadelphia Prison system (Raddock, 1990), the Criminal Justice Substance Abuse Treatment Program (CJSATP) in Jacksonville, Florida, and the Jail Addiction Services (JAS) program, in Rockville, Maryland (Peters, 1992a). Each of these programs offer multi-tiered educational and treatment interventions within modified TC settings. The ADTP program provides services for 138 inmates, for a period of up to 24 months. Inmates involved in Phase I of the program participate in 12-step meetings and intensive group therapy focusing on family relationships, parenting skills, personal growth, and relapse prevention. Following completion of Phase I, inmates are placed in a therapeutic community. Inmates released from the program are supervised by a specialized intensive county probation and parole unit to monitor involvement in aftercare treatment.

The CJSATP program provides drug education programs and a modified TC within the Community Corrections Division of the Jacksonville jail. The TC provides an average of 3 months of treatment services to approximately 48 male inmates and 12 female inmates. The majority of these participants are sentenced to the program under conditions of probation, with community follow-up treatment stipulated after completion of the in-jail program. Both 12-step and CD concepts are integrated within the treatment program. Following release from jail, all TC participants are required to take part in aftercare meetings provided by CJSATP case managers and are placed in a range of inpatient and outpatient community substance abuse treatment services.

The JAS program provides services for approximately 46 pretrial inmates in the Montgomery County Jail. Program participants are initially placed in a 2-week psychoeducational program that includes a review of the stages of addiction, the recovery process, and physiological and psychological effects of addiction. This is followed by involvement in a 4-week intensive treatment program that uses a disease model approach. Group treatment is designed to develop awareness of the addictive lifestyle and to take responsibility for behavior change. Techniques include use of autobiographies, journals, homework, and development of self-management skills. Inmates completing intensive treatment are placed in an aftercare program within the jail, at which time they may serve as peer counselors in educational and 12-step groups. A local TASC program assists in providing court liaison and case management for JAS program participants, in preparation for the transition to placement in community services. Program graduates are eligible for placement in the Community Accountability and Treatment Services (CATS) program, operated by the Montgomery County Department of Correction and Rehabilitation, or for other follow-up treatment services.

TREATMENT INTERVENTIONS

A range of treatment interventions is provided by jail substance abuse programs. These interventions reflect the wide array of needs among drug-involved inmates and the availability of other important nonprogram resources within the jail.

Detoxification

Detoxification is an important first step in the treatment of substance abuse for individuals experiencing acute effects of drugs or alcohol. Goals of detoxification are to provide stabilization of the inmate and to manage withdrawal symptoms while toxic substances are eliminated from the body. Major activities include observation and medical treatment to reduce symptoms of withdrawal. The most common drug used in detoxification from opiates is methadone, although clonidine has also been used effectively for this purpose (Gerstein & Harwood, 1990). Several agents, including desipramine, have been used to reduce withdrawal symptoms among cocaine addicts (Office of Technology Assessment, 1990). Although most larger jails provide detoxification, nonviolent offenders are often referred to community agencies for these services.

Drug Testing

A small proportion of jails provide regular drug testing of inmates (Peters, May, & Kearns, 1992), although 37% of jails with treatment programs provide testing on suspicion of drug use and 13% provide random urinalysis. Drug testing can provide useful information to supplement an initial drug history assessment and can reduce denial of drug use during this first stage of treatment. Random drug testing also is useful in monitoring compliance with treatment guidelines in the jail setting and during placement in follow-up treatment services. Random drug testing has also been found to be effective in reducing substance abuse within correctional institutions.

Assessment

Comprehensive assessment should be conducted for each inmate admitted to jail substance abuse treatment. Assessment should be provided prior to development of a treatment plan and should include use of standardized instruments whenever possible (National Institute of Corrections, 1991). In addition to basic demographic and background information, content areas frequently examined within assessment should include the following: (1) substance abuse history; (2) current evidence of drug or alcohol dependency; (3) history of substance abuse treatment; (4) current psychosocial functioning, including social and family relationships, physical health, mental health symptoms, and prior treatment; (5) criminal justice history, including prior criminal behavior related to substance abuse; and (6) history of AIDS risk behavior. One of the most commonly used assessment instruments in jail programs is the Addiction Severity Index (ASI; McLellan, Luborsky, Woody, & O'Brien, 1980). Results of assessment should be summarized or otherwise made available for aftercare treatment providers, case managers, or probation officers working with the offender in the community. Assessment results should be compiled in a cumulative file to assist in program evaluation and research.

Drug Education

Drug education was provided in only 14% of jails responding to a recent survey (Peters, May, & Kearns, 1992). These services are typically provided during the early stages of a jail substance abuse treatment program. Drug education is particularly useful in developing inmate motivation and encouraging retention in treatment through identification of individual antecedents to past drug use, recognition of drug-related consequences to psychosocial functioning, and developing commitment to the recovery process. Drug education efforts are designed to help inmates to understand the following areas: (1) the physical and psychological effects of cocaine, amphetamines, heroin, and other commonly abused drugs, including withdrawal effects (e.g., cocaine cravings) that can be expected during participation in the jail treatment program; (2) the development of addictive behaviors, including compulsive patterns of use and denial; (3) the stages of recovery from drug addiction; (4) the dysfunctional aspects of the addictive life-style; and (5) the relapse warning signs and how the relapse affects the recovery process.

AIDS Education and Prevention

AIDS education and prevention activities are extremely important within jail substance abuse programs, in which large numbers of inmates report IV drug use or unprotected sex with high-risk partners (Magura, Rosenblum, & Joseph, 1992; National Institute of Justice, 1990; Peters & Kearns, 1992). AIDS interventions within jails should address the following: (1) the need for basic information regarding methods of transmission and the effects of the virus to compromise the immune system; (2) health promotion strategies, including identification and reduction of unsafe sexual and drug abuse behaviors, and implementation of positive health habits (e.g., nutrition, exercise); and (3) examination of attitudes and behaviors associated with drug use, including denial and rationalization supporting IV use, exchange of sex for drugs, or other high-risk sexual behaviors. AIDS education and prevention activities should be conducted in group settings. Peer feedback should be used to challenge perceptions that there are no alternatives to AIDS risk behaviors and to develop strategies for interacting assertively with sexual partners to use safe sexual practices. Repeated exposure to AIDS prevention concepts and techniques should be provided in order to counteract denial among inmates who are unwilling or afraid to confront their own high-risk behaviors.

Life Skills Training

Many jail inmates referred for substance abuse treatment have skills deficits in areas of managing finances, cooking, or maintenance of health and personal hygiene. These deficits are sometimes quite pronounced at the time of incarceration because of neglect of basic needs associated with recent drug binges. Inmates often tend to deny the absence of life skills out of embarrassment.

Educational and Vocational Training

Many jail inmates referred for substance abuse treatment have not completed high school and have had an unstable pattern of employment prior to incarceration. Development of educational and vocational skills tends to support other treatment activities in reducing drug use and criminal recidivism. Educational and vocational interventions are designed to develop marketable skills and to improve educational skills essential for employment and continued involvement in treatment. Specific objectives include development of basic literacy skills, progress toward completion of the GED, and participation in employability skills and vocation training.

Interpersonal Skills Training

Inmates entering jail substance abuse treatment programs have a history of conflict with family members, spouses, and co-workers (Peters, Kearns, Murrin, & May, 1991). Difficulties in social relationships often lead to frustration, depression, and anger that are frequent precursors of relapse. Interpersonal skills that have been found to be particularly useful for drug-involved jail inmates include stress management, anger management (involving identification of "trigger" events preceding anger and destructive consequences of anger such as drug use and development of cognitive restructuring strategies), problem-solving skills to help inmates develop a range of alternatives when facing difficult situations, and communication skills to encourage development of support and intimacy in primary relationships. Parenting skills are useful for inmates from single-parent or dysfunctional families to help resolve difficulties associated with discipline within the home and other child care issues. Development of assertiveness skills is particularly useful among female inmates or others who have a history of dependent relationships or difficulties in disengaging from drug-using family members, friends, or lovers.

Group Counseling

Group counseling is the preferred method of treatment for drug-involved offenders. Group sessions provide a forum to discuss and review core treatment issues related to drug and alcohol use and criminality. Participation in group counseling is designed to help inmates learn new skills through support received for prosocial behaviors and confrontation of antisocial behaviors. Group sessions serve as an important vehicle for inmates to take responsibility for behavior and to develop a shared commitment to change. Most "core" treatment groups include between 8 and 15 participants.

Individual Counseling

Individual counseling sessions provide an important opportunity to review an inmate's treatment plan and to address problems in adjusting to the jail environment or to the treatment program. Mental health counseling should be provided to address depression, excessive anxiety, or other symptoms that may inhibit participation in treatment activities and other personal problems that may contribute to substance abuse. Individual sessions should be conducted in facilities that are segregated from other program areas.

Family Counseling

The family structure—including extended family members, spouse or girlfriend, and children—represents a critical source of support in the inmate's recovery. Interventions include family support groups that meet in the community or family counseling activities within the jail. Major objectives of family support and counseling interventions include the following: (1) awareness by the family of the severity of an inmate's addiction, including recognition of the signs and symptoms of drug and alcohol dependency; (2) recognition of the effects and consequences of substance abuse on the family unit, and identification of community resources to provide support to family members and to help restore life-style balance; (3) awareness by family members of how they may have unwittingly supported ongoing substance abuse and development of strategies to take a more assertive role in confronting addictive behaviors and in obtaining assistance for the substance-involved family member; (4) enlisting the support of family members in identifying and responding to warning signs of relapse.

Psychiatric Services

Prevalence rates for mental illness among jail inmates are two to three times higher than in the general population (Teplin, 1990). Many inmates referred for in-jail substance abuse treatment have preexisting mental health problems or experience emotional or psychological difficulties related to drug withdrawal or incarceration. Among inmates examined in a recent study (Peters, Kearns, Murrin, & Dolente, 1992a) who were enrolled in jail substance abuse treatment, over half reported a history of depression, 45% reported serious anxiety or tension, and 19% had a history of suicidal thoughts. Jail substance abuse treatment programs often include regular psychiatric consultation to review the need for medication and to monitor use of and compliance with medication.

Treatment of Criminal Thinking Errors

The development of drug abuse and dependence is closely associated with long-standing criminal thinking patterns and values. Similar to the distorted thought patterns used by addicts, criminal thinking is characterized by denial, minimalization, and self-centeredness. Among inmates involved in jail treatment programs, criminal behavior is often perceived as the result of drug use, to which the individual has fallen victim (Yochelson & Samenow, 1986). However, for many inmates referred for treatment, development of criminal thought patterns and values has preceded involvement with drugs. Treatment interventions that address patterns of criminal thinking include the reorienting of the inmate's value system through self-monitoring and the restructuring of distorted thoughts. Other treatment techniques consist of didactic presentations, completion of thinking logs, exercises designed to explore the connection between criminal thinking errors and substance abuse, and group treatment focusing on identification and modification of criminal thought patterns. These interventions require regular feedback to alert inmates to recurrent patterns of criminal thinking or behavior. Inmates must have a high degree of motivation to accept and integrate feedback from other program participants in order to fully benefit from this type of treatment.

Relapse Prevention

Inmates referred for in-jail substance abuse treatment often have a history of multiple prior relapses and unsuccessful attempts to maintain abstinence. Despite their relapse history, most inmates typically have little understanding of how this process occurs. Most inmates have few strategies other than the use of drugs for dealing with interpersonal conflict, negative emotions, and other high-risk situations, which lead to relapse. According to the relapse prevention model (Marlatt & Gordon, 1985), progressive psychosocial difficulties contributing to life-style imbalance often lead to a desire for indulgence or immediate gratification. This may precipitate frequent urges and cravings that are mediated by expectations of pleasurable short-term effects of drug or alcohol use. Relapse prevention efforts assist inmates to develop an awareness of the chronic relapsing nature of their addiction. Other major objectives include the development of confidence in managing high-risk situations through successful use of drug coping skills and the maintenance of a prolonged period of abstinence in the community.

Relapse prevention strategies have become increasingly popular within criminal justice settings during the past several years (Peters, 1992b), reflecting the need for interventions to address the high rate of relapse and recidivism among offenders. These techniques combine elements of cognitive therapies, behavioral skill training, and life-style change to assist inmates in developing greater control during the maintenance stage of recovery. Program participants are encouraged to take responsibility for their recovery through development of self-management strategies. These strategies include assessment of prior relapse episodes, development of individual coping skills for counteracting relapse antecedents (e.g., high-risk situations, rationalizations, negative emotions, cues, cravings) that are likely to occur following release from jail, and rehearsal of strategies for dealing with lapses and relapses. Inmates also participate in mock relapse episodes in order to rehearse potential coping responses to high-risk situations that are likely to occur following release to the community. Another important strategy is the development of drug refusal skills relevant to the inmate's home environment. This is accomplished through role play and rehearsal of refusal strategies. Carefully detailed plans are often developed to guide the inmate's activities during the first few days following release from jail, to help participants avoid or successfully cope with salient cues for relapse, such as drug neighborhoods or dealers.

Self-Help Groups

Self-help groups based on the principles of AA are particularly effective in reducing self-centered and exploitive behaviors and in encouraging more altruistic values among drug-involved offenders. As described in a previous section, AA, NA, and CA groups employ peer role models to encourage motivation and commitment to treatment and to provide practical information and advice about the recovery process. Self-help groups can provide a valuable source of support as inmates make the transition from the jail program to involvement in community treatment. Many jails provide regular 12-step meetings that are led by staff from the community. Jail substance abuse programs often arrange for 12-step meetings to be held within the treatment unit.

Case Management and Transition Planning

In most jail treatment programs, inmate participants receive regular feedback from counselors regarding progress toward successful completion of treatment plan goals. Counselors also review with the inmate any critical incidents that may arise during treatment. Another important case management function is to develop an aftercare plan, describing key problem areas to be addressed during involvement in community treatment, the location of these services, and the need for other ancillary services. Several jail programs encourage staff from community treatment agencies to meet with the inmate prior to release to help develop an aftercare plan. Staff from TASC programs or from other similar agencies may also work with inmates and treatment counselors in developing an aftercare plan. TASC staff provide valuable assistance to jail programs in coordinating exchange of information regarding continued treatment needs to probation officers and community treatment staff services and in monitoring the offender's involvement in aftercare treatment. Specialized probation or parole units are available in some jurisdictions to supervise drug-involved offenders released to the community. Case management services have been found to enhance retention in community treatment among drug-involved offenders (Hubbard, Collins, Rachal, & Cavanaugh, 1988), an outcome that is closely linked to reduction in recidivism.

Aftercare Services

Involvement in jail substance abuse treatment provides an important first step towards successful recovery, but in the absence of aftercare it is often insufficient to maintain abstinence following release from jail. Drug-involved inmates are the most vulnerable to relapse during the first several months following release, when they leave the supportive and insulated treatment environment and are exposed to high-risk situations, cues, and urges associated with prior substance abuse. On release from jail, many program participants have an unwarranted sense of optimism and confidence in their abilities to avoid active drug users and to resist initial use of drugs or alcohol. Involvement in aftercare substance abuse treatment (and other ancillary services) serves as an important bridge to assist the offender's reintegration to the community. In addition to strengthening coping skills learned during in-jail treatment, involvement in aftercare assists the offender in adjusting to major life-style changes, in rehearsing relapse prevention skills, in monitoring employment and living arrangements, and in coping with family, social, and professional difficulties.

PRINCIPLES OF EFFECTIVE TREATMENT

Reviews of the correctional substance abuse treatment literature and substance abuse treatment programs within the criminal justice system (Andrews & Kiesling, 1980; Bush, Hecht, LaBarbera, & Peters, in press[a]; Falkin, Wexler, & Lipton, 1990; Gendreau & Ross, 1984; Leukefeld & Tims, 1992; Wexler, Lipton, & Johnson, 1988) indicate several key principles associated with successful treatment of offenders. These principles are drawn from experiences in implementing both jail and prison treatment programs and are briefly summarized below.

1. Develop commitment from jail administrators to support the substance abuse treatment program and to provide adequate staff and technical resources.

2. Use a coordinated approach in the design and implementation of the in-jail substance abuse program, involving both substance abuse and custody staff.

3. Conduct cross-training for substance abuse treatment staff, custody staff, and key administrators to review the program philosophy, inmate management techniques, policies and procedures, and other common areas of interest.

4. Provide a treatment unit that is isolated from general population inmates. This strategy tends to remove participants from the corrosive influences of the jail subculture and encourages development of prosocial behaviors and group cohesion.

5. Provide incentives and sanctions to encourage inmates to enter and complete in-jail treatment programs.

6. Develop a sequence of in-jail treatment services that is consistent with the expected length of incarceration.

7. Provide comprehensive assessment examining an inmate's treatment needs, risks presented to the institution (e.g., suicidal or aggressive behavior), and level of supervision required. Match inmates to treatment services according to results of this assessment.

8. Develop a structured treatment environment. An intensive array of in-jail program services tends to encourage self-discipline and commitment to treatment and is necessary to address the many skills deficits and areas of psychosocial dysfunction among this population.

9. Provide clear consequences for inmate behavior within the jail treatment program. Positive and negative consequences for inmate behaviors should be clearly indicated. Program rules and guidelines are reinforced through a system of formal and informal sanctions.

10. Encourage sustained participation in substance abuse treatment. Jail programs of less than 3 months duration should develop procedures to insure that inmates are placed in supervised aftercare treatment within the community.

11. Provide multimodal treatment services. Treatment activities should address the range of psychosocial problems and areas of skills deficits that may inhibit successful recovery from drug and alcohol dependence.

12. Encourage identification and modification of criminal thinking patterns, values, and behaviors. Program counselors systematically model and reinforce prosocial behaviors within the treatment unit. Clearly defined sanctions are provided for antisocial behaviors.

13. Employ cognitive-behavioral treatment techniques. Self-management strategies such as cognitive restructuring and self-monitoring should be addressed in treatment programs. Opportunity should be provided for modeling, rehearsal, and overlearning of these techniques.

14. Involve inmates in skills-based interventions. Programs should encourage the acquisition and rehearsal of drug-free and prosocial skills to deal with interpersonal problems, stress, anger, and other personal, parental, and professional challenges faced during recovery.

15. Provide training in relapse prevention techniques. Exercises should promote awareness of individual relapse patterns, including warning signs, high-risk situations, and covert setups. A range of coping skills should be provided to anticipate the high rate of relapse among drug-involved offenders. Opportunities should be provided to rehearse these skills in the jail treatment program and during aftercare.

16. Involve inmates in "core" group treatment experiences. Involvement in a primary treatment or therapy group provides a catalyst for behavior change that is achieved through reinforcement of progress toward recovery and confrontation of denial and resistance. Group treatment also provides a cost-effective vehicle for educational and skills-based interventions.

17. Provide pre-release planning and assist program participants in the transition to aftercare services. Successful jail substance abuse treatment programs help to coordinate placement in follow-up treatment services. Most jail program participants are in need of at least 1 year of follow-up treatment and regular drug testing that is provided within the context of probation or parole supervision. TASC-like agencies have proven to be particularly useful in linking offenders to community treatment and in monitoring compliance with aftercare treatment.

18. Develop measures to insure accountability to short- and long-term program objectives. Evaluation strategies are implemented in the early stages of program development and include process, impact, and outcome measures.

SELECTION OF INMATES FOR TREATMENT

Identification of eligibility criteria for inmates involved in jail substance abuse treatment is one of the most important tasks completed during early stages of program design and implementation. This decision will affect the subsequent development of a referral and screening system, court liaison activities, pre-release planning, procedures for monitoring and reporting on inmate progress, the length and type of treatment to be offered, and expected outcomes during follow-up (Peters, 1992a). Key issues to be resolved in selecting inmate participants include whether to provide services for pretrial detainees or sentenced inmates (or some mixture of both groups) and determination of program admission and exclusion criteria. Resolution of these issues often reflects the composition of the jail population, existing jail policies and procedures, and goals and objectives of the treatment program.

Although most jails include large numbers of unsentenced inmates, this population presents several problems in designing a treatment program. The relatively short period of detention for unsentenced inmates in many jails limits the scope and intensity of treatment services offered and may discourage the implementation of therapeutic communities or other approaches requiring lengthy involvement in treatment. The sudden and unpredictable release of pretrial inmates on bond or personal recognizance often requires considerable staff time for monitoring inmate detention status and insuring that the court is informed of follow-up treatment needs.

Programs involving sentenced inmates generally have a smaller population from which to sample but have a longer period in which to conduct screening, assessment, and treatment. Problems may arise when sentenced inmates are referred directly by the court to the treatment program, without preliminary screening by staff counselors. Court referrals may include drug dealers, casual drug users, or other offenders with significant behavior problems who may be inappropriate for treatment. In sentencing offenders to participate in jail treatment, the court may also neglect to order involvement in aftercare services. These problems may be addressed through coordination with the court to (1) refer sentenced inmates for program screening rather than for participation in treatment and to (2) develop model sentences used by the court that require participation in both jail and aftercare treatment.

Jail substance abuse treatment programs often select inmate participants who have a history of steady drug or alcohol use, significant impairment in psychosocial functioning related to substance abuse, and a history of crime associated with substance abuse (Peters, 1992a). Casual drug users are sometimes referred for in-jail treatment but are thought to be most appropriately placed in community outpatient settings. A separate screening for program admission is usually conducted by classification and program staff. Several common elements of screening include the following: (1) motivation and commitment to receive treatment, including recognition of a substance abuse problem; (2) history of substance abuse and drug or alcohol treatment; (3) mental health symptoms; and (4) evidence of aggressive behavior or other risks to institutional security.

Several types of inmates should receive additional assessment prior to admission for in-jail substance abuse treatment. Inmates with mental health problems should be assessed for suicide risk and for symptoms that may interfere with treatment, although individuals who are stabilized on psychotropic medication may be able to effectively participate in jail substance abuse treatment. Many mentally ill inmates require psychiatric monitoring and intensive individual counseling services that may not be available within the substance abuse program.

Although many incarcerated sex offenders report a history of drug and alcohol abuse, involvement in substance abuse treatment may serve as a vehicle to direct attention away from the development of deviant behavior patterns or to rationalize this behavior. Inmates whose primary contact with drugs is through dealing and who deny substance abuse problems may also be inappropriate for treatment. Dealers often elicit powerful memories of relapse episodes among other program participants and may serve to undermine motivation and commitment to treatment. Inmates who have an established criminal life-style, a chronic history of drug and alcohol abuse, or an unsuccessful history of prior involvement in treatment may require more lengthy and intensive substance abuse services, such as those received in a traditional therapeutic community (Field, 1986).

EVALUATION OF JAIL SUBSTANCE ABUSE PROGRAMS

With the advent of new in-jail substance abuse programs in the past several years, there has been a corresponding need for evaluation to examine the effect of treatment on criminal recidivism, substance abuse relapse, and other indicators of community adjustment. These efforts have become increasingly important within the context of local budget shortfalls and ongoing skepticism regarding the efficacy of correctional treatment. Major steps in developing an evaluation of in-jail services include these: (1) establishing evaluation goals that recognize the needs of policymakers and administrators, and that are consistent with available evaluation resources; (2) selection of evaluation measures, following an assessment of current criminal justice, classification, and program-level data available in the jail, and potential follow-up measures obtained in the community; (3) development of a data coordination system, involving identification of staff to collect and compile data, development of procedures for merging diverse sources of data, and design of software to compile and analyze data; and (4) completion of an evaluation report and dissemination of results to administrators and policymakers.

Key elements of evaluation data collected within jail substance abuse treatment programs include the following:

1. *Intake assessment and description of inmate population characteristics.* This information is useful in identifying characteristics of inmates selected for treatment, unsuccessfully terminated from treatment, successfully completing treatment, and making a successful adjustment to the community during follow-up. Areas assessed often include demographic characteristics, criminal justice history, substance abuse history, family relationships, social adjustment, living arrangements, vocational status, mental health history, medical history, HIV risk behaviors, history of physical or sexual abuse, and attitudes toward treatment.

2. *Participation in treatment.* This information assists in tracking an inmate's involvement in the jail program. Areas examined include inmate admission and discharge dates, types of interventions received, completion status, incident or disciplinary reports, drug testing results, criminal justice status at discharge, service needs at discharge, and discharge referrals initiated by the in-jail program.

3. *Progress in treatment.* This area of evaluation examines whether short-term program objectives are achieved. Key evaluation elements may include assessment of skills acquisition, knowledge in specific areas of the treatment program (e.g., relapse prevention strategies, drug or AIDS education), psychological functioning, cognitive functioning (e.g., expectancies related to substance abuse, self-efficacy, motivation for treatment), counselor ratings of inmate participation or progress, and inmate satisfaction with the treatment program. Pre- and post-treatment evaluation measures are often obtained to identify changes occurring over the course of treatment.

4. *Changes in the treatment program over time.* Interpretation of evaluation results may be hindered by an inability to identify the type of program services provided and significant changes occurring within the treatment program during the evaluation period. In addition to describing the array of jail treatment services offered, it is important to log changes in administrative and fiscal policies, referral and screening procedures,

intake and assessment procedures, characteristics of the inmate population and program census, the length of program interventions offered, coordination and linkages within the jail and with the court, probation, and community agencies, program facilities and resources, and public policy affecting the criminal justice or social services system.

  5. *Follow-up evaluation and tracking.* Jail treatment programs that are able to compile evaluation information in the areas described above, that provide a comprehensive level of services, and that have sufficient evaluation resources may choose to examine the impact of treatment on community adjustment following release from custody. Key evaluation components include dates of follow-up arrests, convictions, and incarcerations, the type of criminal charges, evidence of substance abuse relapse, including results of drug testing, participation in follow-up treatment, probation or parole status, and employment. Follow-up tracking of program participants requires a considerable investment of resources relative to other types of evaluation and often involves individual interviews with offenders and probation officers. Follow-up evaluation designs are strengthened by the inclusion of a comparison group of untreated jail inmates. This strategy enables evaluators to determine the extent to which follow-up outcomes are attributable to jail treatment interventions.

  Few controlled studies have been conducted to examine the effectiveness of jail substance abuse treatment programs. A recent evaluation was conducted of the Hillsborough County Sheriff's Office Substance Abuse Treatment Program in Tampa, Florida, as part of the model jail demonstration program developed by the Bureau of Justice Assistance and administered by the American Jail Association (Peters, Kearns, Murrin, & Dolente, 1992b; Peters & May, 1992). The study examined a sample of 168 inmates who completed a 6-week jail substance abuse treatment program and included a comparison group ($N = 252$) of inmates who requested treatment at the time of booking or while incarcerated. Treatment and comparison groups were quite similar across demographic variables, although treated inmates had a slightly higher number of arrests during the year prior to incarceration.

  A survival analysis was conducted to examine the cumulative proportion of individuals in both groups who were arrested during a 1-year follow-up period. Participants in the Hillsborough County Sheriff's Office Substance Abuse Treatment Program were found to remain significantly longer in the community until rearrest ($M = 221$ days, $SD = 131$) in comparison to the group of untreated offenders ($M = 180$ days, $SD = 144$).

Program participants were arrested significantly less frequently ($M = 1.1$, $SD = 1.1$) during follow-up in comparison to untreated inmates ($M = 1.5$, $SD = 1.6$). No major differences were detected among groups in the number of drug-related offenses. However, inmates participating in substance abuse treatment spent significantly less time in jail ($M = 32$ days, $SD = 46$) in comparison to untreated inmates ($M = 45$, $SD = 58$). Repeated evaluation measures administered during the treatment program indicated that jail program participants gained considerable knowledge in use of relapse and recovery skills. Participants also demonstrated significant improvement in use of coping skills during simulated high-risk situations involving interpersonal pressures or temptations to use drugs or alcohol.

Although results from the Hillsborough County Sheriff's Office provide preliminary evidence for the effectiveness of jail substance abuse treatment, additional research is needed to clarify characteristics of inmates who respond most favorably to various types of treatment approaches and interventions, the optimal length of jail treatment programs, the effect of ancillary services such as educational and vocational training on treatment outcomes, and strategies for matching inmates to jail treatment programs and to follow-up programs. Several jail demonstration projects funded through the U.S. Department of Health and Human Services, Center for Substance Abuse Treatment are currently providing follow-up evaluations. These include the IMPACT program in Chicago, Illinois, the Jail Addiction Services (JAS) program in Rockville, Maryland, and the King County Jail Substance Abuse Treatment Program in Seattle, Washington. The Criminal Justice Substance Abuse Treatment Program (CJSATP) within the Community Corrections Division facility in Jacksonville, Florida, and Project Challenge in the Humboldt County Jail in Eureka, California, are also developing coordinated follow-up evaluation strategies to examine inmates completing in-jail treatment. The National Institute of Justice has also funded a recent evaluation of five jails that will include examination of follow-up arrests, drug involvement, and participation in aftercare treatment.

FUNDING STRATEGIES

More than 70% of jails reporting a substance abuse treatment program receive funding from the county, 62% received support from U.S. Department of Health and Human Services block grant programs, and 43% were supported by state funds (Peters, May, & Kearns, 1992). Jail substance abuse treatment programs are eligible to receive funding through several block grant programs. The Block Grant for Prevention and Treatment of Substance Abuse, authorized by the ADAMHA Reorganization Act of 1992, is administered by the U.S. Department of Health and Human Services, Center for Substance Abuse Treatment. Grant funds flow through the state alcohol and drug abuse agencies and support a range of alcohol and drug treatment and prevention initiatives. Although several states, such as Colorado, Ohio, and Texas, have chosen to support jail treatment programs through this block grant program, there are no specific guidelines requiring states to fund criminal justice treatment activities. Jail staff interested in this program should work through county or regional drug and alcohol administrators to explore with the state substance abuse coordinating agency the possibility of prioritizing jail treatment initiatives within the state plan for block grant funding.

A second block grant program providing funding for jail substance abuse programs was authorized by the Anti-Drug Abuse Act of 1988, and is administered through the U.S. Department of Justice, Bureau of Justice Assistance. This program provides local "pass through" funds that flow through state criminal justice coordinating agencies. The program also provides discretionary state funds to support law enforcement, correctional, and prevention and treatment initiatives within the criminal justice system. Substance abuse treatment services within prisons and jails are specifically identified as priorities for funding through this block grant program. Jail staff interested in this funding source should work through the county criminal justice planning agency and state criminal justice coordinating agency to include jail treatment programs within the state plan as a priority for funding.

A variety of competitive criminal justice grant programs are also administered by the Center for Substance Abuse Treatment, designed to develop substance abuse treatment services in jails, prisons, and in non-incarcerated settings. These are provided through the Grants for Substance Abuse Treatment in State and Local Criminal Justice Systems program. Several comprehensive model demonstration jail programs have been funded through this program in the past. A range of training and technical assistance activities are provided by the Center for Substance Abuse Treatment to support development of substance abuse treatment in jails and other criminal justice settings. Funding for construction of treatment facilities has been available in the past through the U.S. Department of Housing and Urban Development, Community Development Program. These funds are subject to annual goals and guidelines developed by the Department.

Several innovative funding strategies employed by local jails include reimbursement for psychoeducational substance abuse treatment services through state adult education funding, court supervised reimbursement of treatment costs by probationers who have completed in-jail treatment, and use of consortium arrangements between local agencies. The DEUCE program in Contra Costa County, California, has worked with the California Department of Education to develop alternative funding sources for their jail treatment program. The program qualified for state education funds through inclusion of employability and life skills within the jail treatment curriculum. Linkages with the Department of Education were instrumental in establishing eligibility of jail treatment programs for funding within the state education plan.

Inmates participating in the JSAP program in Washington County, Maryland, are sentenced to complete in-jail treatment, and are supervised by probation following release from custody. While under community supervision, program graduates are required to pay for treatment services received in jail. Terms of repayment are adjusted according to a sliding fee schedule, with probationers typically paying $65-per month for six months following completion of the JSAP program. Probationer fees are expected to generate $40,000 in fiscal year 1992.

Treatment program services planned for the Solano County Jail in Fairfield, California, will be funded through the Jail-Based Treatment/ Education Consortium, consisting of four community agencies. Members of the consortium include the Solano County Sheriff's Office, the Solano County Health Services, Alcohol and Drug Administration, the City of Vallejo-Fighting Back Project (supported by the Robert Wood Johnson Foundation), and the Fairfield-Suisun Adult School. Additional funding for specialized women's treatment groups and aftercare educational programs will be provided by the March of Dimes and the Solano Community College. Through pooling resources of member agencies, the program will offer a full range of jail and aftercare services, including case management in the community. The consortium provides an important measure of program stability, and insures that no single agency will have to carry the burden for program funding.

SUMMARY

Jails throughout the country have been inundated with large numbers of drug-involved arrestees. Many of these offenders are likely to relapse or to commit additional drug-related crimes in the absence of community supervision and involvement in substance abuse treatment. Although some jails have responded to this newly emerging inmate population by developing substance abuse treatment programs, the vast majority of inmates in need of treatment are not receiving substance abuse services. Several recent demonstration programs developed by the Bureau of Justice Assistance and the Center for Substance Abuse Treatment provide exemplary models of comprehensive jail treatment services. These programs have served a dual role in assisting other jails to implement similar treatment approaches and in facilitating outcome research examining the effectiveness of jail treatment. Further initiatives are greatly needed to identify jail substance abuse treatment approaches and interventions that will successfully reduce relapse and recidivism following release from custody.

As observed by Newman and Price (1977), there is a critical need for additional work to define the parameters of jail substance abuse treatment. Recent surveys need to be updated and expanded to define the scope of jail initiatives, and to identify key characteristics of programs (e.g., inmate characteristics, length of stay, treatment approaches and interventions, staffing patterns), innovative treatment strategies, methods of linkage and coordination with treatment and criminal justice agencies, and models of jail program funding. Concurrent efforts need to address development of standards for jail treatment programs. Standards should attempt to define minimally acceptable criteria for: (1) education and training of jail program counselors, (2) treatment interventions, (3) physical characteristics of jail treatment units, and (4) other key areas related to program implementation. These standards should be developed collaboratively by organizations representing jail professionals (e.g., AJA, ACA), associations of treatment professionals (e.g., AACP, NCCHC), and federal and local agencies working to improve treatment within the criminal justice system (e.g., Center for Substance Abuse Treatment, National Association of Criminal Justice Planners). Training and technical assistance should be provided to jails in implementing standards for substance abuse treatment, in implementing various treatment approaches and interventions shown to be effective, and in development of evaluation strategies.

Research examining jail substance abuse treatment is still in the early stages of development. Further work is needed to determine the effectiveness of major treatment approaches and to identify the most important features of these approaches that contribute to cognitive and behavior change. Once the efficacy of treatment approaches has been determined, research is needed to identify the most effective sequence of treatment interventions and to examine the length of in-jail treatment required to affect differences in follow-up outcomes. Subsequent work should also examine the marginal utility of adding ancillary services to in-jail treatment programs, such as interventions to prevent relapse and to restructure patterns of criminal thinking, case management following release from custody, and involvement in aftercare services. An innovative example of this type of research initiative was recently funded through the collaborative efforts of the U.S. Department of Justice, the Casey, Ford, Robert Wood Johnson, and Rockefeller Foundations, and the Pew Charitable Trusts, and is administered by the Center on Addiction and Substance Abuse (CASA) at Columbia University. Other jail-based research should attempt to identify effective substance abuse treatment approaches and interventions for special inmate populations (e.g., female addicts, the dually diagnosed, the homeless, and AIDS-risk inmates), cocaine-involved inmates, and inmates who have an established criminal life-style. Complimentary efforts will help to refine assessment instruments for use in identifying inmates with specialized substance abuse treatment needs. Finally, research efforts should examine the utility of various service delivery models (e.g., use of community treatment agencies versus in-house staff), and models to enhance stable program funding and support.

REFERENCES

Abram, K. M. (1990). The problem of co-occurring disorders among jail detainees. *Law and Human Behavior, 14*(4), 333-345.

Andrews, D. A., & Kiesling, J. (1980). Program structure and effective correctional practices: A summary of CaVIC research. In R. Ross & P. Gendreau (Eds.), *Effective correctional treatment.* Toronto: Butterworth Press.

Anglin, M. D., & Hser, Y. (1990). Treatment of drug abuse. In M. Tonry & J. Wilson (Eds.), *Drugs and crime.* Chicago: University of Chicago Press.

Arbiter, N. (1988). Drug treatment in a direct supervision jail: Pima County's Amity Jail Project. *American Jails, 22*(2), 35-40.

Bureau of Justice Statistics. (1991a). *Bulletin: Jail inmates, 1990.* Washington, DC: U.S. Department of Justice.

Bureau of Justice Statistics. (1991b). *Correctional populations in the United States, 1989.* Washington, DC: U.S. Department of Justice.

Bureau of Justice Statistics. (1991c). *Drugs and crime data. Fact sheet: Drug data summary.* Washington, DC: U.S. Department of Justice.

Bureau of Justice Statistics. (1991d). *Special report: Drugs and jail inmates. 1989.* Washington, DC: U.S. Department of Justice.

Bush, D., Hecht, F. R., LaBarbera, M. J., & Peters, R. H. (in press[a]). *Design and implementation issues for drug treatment in the jail setting.* Washington, DC: Bureau of Justice Assistance.

Bush, D., Hecht, F. R., LaBarbera, M. J., & Peters, R. H. (in press[b]). *Drug treatment in the jail setting: A national demonstration program.* Washington, DC: Bureau of Justice Assistance.

Craig, R. J. (1980). Effectiveness of low-dose methadone maintenance for the treatment of inner city heroin addicts. *International Journal of the Addictions, 15*(5), 701-710.

Christiansen, P. H. (1988). Contra Costa County, California, jail school program. *American Jails, 2*(1), 30-35.

DeLeon, G. (1986). Therapeutic community research: Overview and implications. In G. DeLeon & J. Ziegenfuss (Eds.), *Therapeutic communities for addictions.* Springfield, IL: Charles C Thomas.

Falkin, G. P., Wexler, H. K., & Lipton, D. S. (1990). *Establishing drug treatment programs in prisons* (Draft). New York: Narcotic and Drug Research, Inc.

Field, G. (1986). The psychological deficits and treatment needs of chronic criminality. *Federal Probation, 50*(4), 60-66.

Fisher, D. G., & Anglin, M. D. (1987). Survival analysis in drug program evaluation: Part I. Overall program effectiveness. *International Journal of the Addictions, 22*(2), 115-134.

Gendreau, P., & Ross, R. (1984). Correctional treatment: Some recommendations for successful intervention. *Juvenile and Family Court Journal, 22,* 31-40.

Gerstein, D. R., & Harwood, H. J. (Eds.). (1990). *Treating drug problems: Volume 1.* Institute of Medicine, Committee for the Substance Abuse Coverage Study, Division of Health Care Services. Washington, DC: National Academy Press.

Hubbard, R. L., Collins, J. J., Rachal, J. V., & Cavanaugh, E. R. (1988). The criminal justice client in drug abuse treatment. In C. Leukefeld & F. Tims (Eds.), *Compulsory treatment of drug abuse: Research and clinical practice.* National Institute on Drug Abuse, Research Monograph Series, No. 86. Washington, DC: U.S. Government Printing Office.

Inciardi, J. A. (Ed.). (1981). *The drugs-crime connection.* Beverly Hills: Sage.

Leukefeld, C. G., & Tims, F. M. (Eds.). (1992). *Drug abuse treatment in prisons and jails.* National Institute on Drug Abuse, Research Monograph Series, No. 118. Washington, DC: U.S. Government Printing Office.

Lipton, D. S., Falkin, G. P., & Wexler, H. K. (1992). Correctional drug abuse treatment in the United States: An overview. In C. Leukefeld & F. Tims (Eds.), *Drug abuse treatment in prisons and jails.* National Institute on Drug Abuse, Research Monograph Series, No. 118. Washington, DC: U.S. Government Printing Office.

Lipton, D. S., Martinson, R., & Wilks, J. (1975). *The effectiveness of correctional treatment: A survey of treatment evaluation studies.* New York: Praeger Press.

Magura, S., Rosenblum, A., & Joseph, H. (1992). Evaluation of in-jail methadone maintenance: Preliminary results. In C. Leukefeld & F. Tims (Eds.), *Drug abuse treatment in prisons and jails.* National Institute on Drug Abuse, Research Monograph Series, No. 118. Washington, DC: U.S. Government Printing Office.

Marlatt, G. A., & Gordon, J. R. (1985). *Relapse prevention.* New York: Guilford Press.

McLellan, A. T., Luborsky, L., Woody, G. E., & O'Brien, C. P. (1980). An improved diagnostic evaluation instrument for substance abuse patients. *Journal of Nervous and Mental Disease, 168*(1), 26-33.

Messmer, C. R., & Brown, H. A. (1991). Beyond the '80s: The emergence of a model substance abuse treatment program within the correctional setting. *American Jails, 4*(5), 114-120.

National Criminal Justice Information and Statistics Service. (1972). *Survey of local jails, 1972.* U.S. Department of Justice, Law Enforcement Assistance Administration, Advance Report. Washington, DC: U.S. Government Printing Office.

National Institute of Corrections. (1991). *Intervening with substance-abusing offenders: A framework for action.* Report of the National Task Force on Correctional Substance Abuse Strategies. Washington, DC: U.S. Department of Justice.

National Institute of Justice. (1989). *Research in action. Drug Use Forecasting (DUF). Cocaine use: Arrestees in Washington. D.C.* Washington, DC: U.S. Department of Justice.

National Institute of Justice. (1990). *Research in action. Drug Use Forecasting (DUF). First DUF findings from arrestees in San Jose.* Washington, DC: U.S. Department of Justice.

National Institute of Justice. (1992). *Research in brief. Drug Use Forecasting (DUF). Marijuana use measured at alternate detection levels.* Washington, DC: U.S. Department of Justice.

National Institute on Drug Abuse. (1991). *National household survey on drug abuse: Highlights 1990* (DHHS Publication No. ADM 91-1789). Rockville, MD: U.S. Department of Health and Human Services.

Newman, C. L., & Price, B. P. (1977). *Jails and drug treatment.* Beverly Hills: Sage.

Office of Technology Assessment. (1990). The effectiveness of drug abuse treatment: Implications for controlling AIDS/HIV infection. Washington, DC: U.S. Government Printing Office.

Peters, R. H. (1992a). Referral and screening for substance abuse treatment in jail. *Journal of Mental Health Administration, 19*(1), 53-75.

Peters, R. H. (1992b). Relapse prevention approaches in the criminal justice system. In T. Gorski, J. Kelly, L. Havens, & R. Peters (Eds.), *Relapse prevention and the substance abusing criminal offender.* Rockville, MD: Office for Treatment Improvement.

Peters, R. H., & Dolente, A. S. (1990). Relapse prevention for drug-dependent inmates in the Hillsborough County Jail. *American Jails, 3*(4), 107-110.

Peters, R. H., & Kearns, W. D. (1992). Drug abuse history and treatment needs of jail inmates. *American Journal of Drug and Alcohol Abuse, 18*(3) 355-366.

Peters, R. H., Kearns, W. D., Murrin, M. R., & Dolente, A. S. (1992a). Psychopathology and mental health needs among drug-involved inmates. *Journal of Prison and Jail Health, 11* (1), 3-25.

Peters, R. H., Kearns, W. D., Murrin, M. R., & Dolente, A. S. (1992b). Effectiveness of in-jail substance abuse treatment: Evaluation results from a national demonstration program. *American Jails, 6,*(1), 98-104.

Peters, R. H., Kearns, W. D., Murrin, M. R., & May, R. L. (1991). *Evaluation findings from the National Model Demonstration In-Jail Drug Treatment Program: Final Report.* American Jail Association, Hagerstown, Maryland.

Peters, R. H., & May, R. L. (1992). Drug treatment services in jails. In C. Leukefeld & F. Tims (Eds.), *Drug treatment in prisons and jails.* National Institute on Drug Abuse, Research Monograph Series, No. 118. Washington, DC: U.S. Government Printing Office.

Peters, R. H., May, R. L., & Kearns, W. D. (1992). Drug treatment in jails: Results of a nationwide survey. *Journal of Criminal Justice, 20,* 283-297.

Raddock, D. (1990). Substance abuse treatment programming in the Philadelphia prisons. *American Jails, 4*(3), 22-27.

Steadman, H. J., McCarty, D. W., & Morrissey, J. P. (1989). *The mentally ill in jail: Planning for essential services.* New York: Guilford Press.

Teplin, L. A. (1990). The prevalence of severe mental disorder among male urban jail detainees: Comparison with the Epidemiologic Catchment Area Program. *American Journal of Public Health, 80*(6), 663-669.

Wexler, H. K., Lipton, D. S., & Johnson, B. D. (1988). *A criminal justice system strategy for treating cocaine-heroin abusing offenders in custody.* National Institute of Justice: Issues and Practices. Washington, DC: U.S. Department of Justice.

Yochelson, S., & Samenow, S. E. (1986). *The criminal personality. Volume III: The drug user.* Northvale, NJ: Jason Aronson.

Chapter 5

CASE MANAGEMENT APPROACHES FOR CRIMINAL JUSTICE CLIENTS

STEVEN S. MARTIN
JAMES A. INCIARDI

Criminal justice clients with histories of chronic drug abuse face numerous difficulties in reentering the community, regardless of whether their justice mandate involves court ordered diversion, probation, or return to the free community through work release, parole, or some other form of supervised custody. In addition to the complications associated with reestablishing ties with family, finding stable employment, and providing for life's necessities, former users face the likelihood of relapse to drugs and active users must deal with the obstacles associated with a continuing addiction career. And with renewed or enduring drug use comes criminal activity and a high probability of rearrest. In 1990, for example, Drug Use Forecasting (DUF) data from the National Institute of Justice found that at least 30% and as many as 78% of arrestees in its 21 city sites tested positive for an illicit drug (National Institute of Justice [NIJ], 1990). Similarly, over half of the admissions to the Federal Bureau of Prisons in 1990 were diagnosed as users of illegal drugs (Murray, 1991). The odds of breaking the drugs/crime connection are even more problematic for those who inject drugs or who trade or sell sex for drugs because of the associated risks for HIV/AIDS.

The costs to society from the failure of so many criminal justice clients to avoid relapse and recidivism are rapidly increasing. Moreover, the associated costs in human, social, health, and economic terms have expanded

AUTHORS' NOTE: This work was supported, in part, by grants DA-06124 and DA-06948 from the National Institute on Drug Abuse.

dramatically in recent years (Hubbard, Collins, Rachal, & Cavanaugh, 1988). In addition to the social and economic costs of the criminal activity, there are those associated with incarcerating greater numbers of offenders each year. In 1989, for example, the expense to house a single inmate in a correctional facility averaged $25,000 (Abel, 1989), and that figure has likely risen since then. Furthermore, there is the rather costly matter of providing health care to an expanding population of HIV-positive inmates. Given these exigencies, criminal justice policymakers have been examining the efficacy of treatment in reducing relapse to drug use and recidivism.

Even the community supervision of drug-involved offenders has become a major correctional cost. Among federal probationers, for example, those identified as in need of drug abuse aftercare services swelled threefold between 1984 and 1990 (Chavaria, 1992). Since it is apparent for economic reasons that the majority of drug-involved offenders must be supervised in the community rather than in the penitentiary, community-based treatment alternatives have become attractive. These range from a few days of chemical detoxification, to several months of drug-free outpatient counseling, to a year or more in a therapeutic community, to a multi-year commitment to methadone maintenance (Anglin & Hser, 1990). In each of these modalities the focus is on providing the client with medical, counseling, and psychological services. Medical and psychological services are primary. However, as case studies have repeatedly pointed out, such stressful life events as divorce or loss of employment can play a critical role in precipitating a relapse to drug use (Weppner, 1983; Wexler, Falkin, Lipton, Rosenblum, & Goodloe, 1988). Integrating educational, vocational, and life skills management with standard counseling more comprehensively addresses drug abuse symptomatology. Providing aftercare resources to assist and buffer the client from life stressors may be a more effective means of preventing relapse. And for many women, addressing such matters as child care and physical security are basic to a successful treatment experience.

Yet few treatment programs have the resources for educational and vocational development, and an even smaller number offer vocational counseling (Hubbard & Harwood, 1981). In fact, Anglin and Hser (1990) report that relapse prevention training is atypical in most programs, that educational and vocational services are rarely provided, and that assistance in securing social and community support beyond referrals to self-help programs such as Alcoholics Anonymous (AA) and Narcotics Anonymous

(NA) is minimal. As for child care during treatment, the possibilities are almost nonexistent.

Traditional drug-free outpatient treatment programs vary widely— from drop-in "rap" centers to highly structured arrangements that offer counseling or psychotherapy as the treatment mainstay (O'Brien, 1987). Simpson and Sells (1982) reported that after outpatient treatment, opiate abusers reduced their daily use, arrest rates reflected significant declines, and employment rates increased. Although these results suggest some efficacy for traditional, counseling-focused outpatient treatment, other research has suggested that treatment outcome is more likely to be successful when drug use is viewed as having a multitude of symptom patterns involving various dimensions of the individual's life (Lipton, 1989; McLellan, Luborsky, Woody, O'Brien, & Kron, 1981).

This perspective is remarkably akin to the rationale for the "case management" approach to rehabilitation found in both the social work and mental health fields to improve the delivery of health and social services. The basic case management approach is to assist clients in obtaining needed services in a timely and coordinated manner. The key components of the approach are assessing, planning, linking, monitoring, and advocating for clients within the existing nexus of treatment and social services (Bagarozzi & Pollane, 1984). As a treatment tool, case management has been increasingly employed in these fields for clients who have chronic, multiple problems and whose treatment and service needs are quite complex. This is particularly the case in situations where the available social service delivery systems are highly bureaucratized and the services provided are fragmented and scattered across both geographical and social service "turf."

However, until recently there have been few efforts to extrapolate the application of case management to the treatment of drug abusers and, most pointedly, to linking drug abuse treatment and primary care services. This omission seems to be changing rapidly, and several large scale research and evaluation projects are currently assessing the application of case management in drug abuse treatment (Greenhouse, 1992; Schlenger, Kroutil, & Roland, 1992). With the exception of the Treatment Alternatives to Street Crime (TASC) initiatives and a few independent demonstration projects (Buddress, 1992; Inciardi, Isenberg, Lockwood, Martin, & Scarpitti, 1992), application of case management to criminal justice clients with histories of drug abuse has received little attention.

Within this context, this chapter reviews the origins and principles of case management as it developed in the mental health and social work fields. In addition, it examines the analogies and the differences in the application of case management to drug abuse treatment, considering both the promise and the problems for expanded use with drug-involved offenders. Finally, it extends the application to the treatment of criminal justice clients under supervision in the community. Existing case management applications in criminal justice settings are briefly reviewed, with particular attention to the potential strengths of compulsory supervision and the practical problems of large case loads and recalcitrant clients.

ORIGINS OF THE CASE MANAGEMENT APPROACH

Case management has its roots in early 20th century social work models of providing services to clients in need. The range of services has varied, from case managers offering referral information only, to others acting as brokers and advocates for the community services needed by clients, to still others directly providing services. All three levels of intervention continue in contemporary case management applications. The current concept of case management grew out of a recognition in the 1960s of a need to coordinate the burgeoning and fragmented services offered by the new social programs of Kennedy's "New Frontier" and Johnson's "Great Society,"[1] coupled with the desire of the Nixon administration to reduce inefficient service delivery (Dybal, 1980).

A recent definition from the social work field is offered by Austin and Caragonne (1988) who see case management as a "systematic problem-solving process consisting of a series of sequentially related tasks aimed at delivering a variety of services to a client." As noted earlier, Bagarozzi and Pollane (1984) delineate five defining services encompassed in the balanced service system model of case management, at least from the point of view of the case manager: assessment, planning, linking, monitoring, and advocacy.

Others have extended the definition to include the goal for the client—independent living—as well as the case manager's means to reach it. As Roberts-DeGennaro (1987, p. 470) puts it:

> A successful case manager enables clients to control their lives to the fullest extent possible. The case manager must develop or have access to an existing network of available resources to use on behalf of a client.

As such, the process of "linking" consumer to services becomes the most salient characteristic of case management. Cohen and his colleagues (Cohen, Nimec, Cohen, & Farkas, 1988) note in a major training package for case management:

> The heart of case management is the linking activity. When linking clients to services, the case manager arranges for the client's use of preferred service providers. The linking activity is more than referring and forgetting. The case manager presents the client's assets and overcomes objections to ensure the service provider's acceptance of the client. After the client has been accepted for services, the case manager monitors whether or not the client is being assisted and, if not, implements action steps to remove any barriers to service use. (p. 223)

In this manner case management moves beyond a passive referral system to emphasize the need to follow the client's progress and intervene on the client's behalf when necessary.

In many ways the linkages between treatment and other primary services needed by the client can best be accomplished when case management takes on both functions. Recently, case management has come to recognize the potential advantage of combining treatment and managerial elements in the same program. Harris and Bergman (1987) present this rationale of case management:

> The role of a case manager is generally seen as one of coordinating and overseeing a patient's overall treatment. In this sense, case management, although integrally related to it, is a set of functions independent of the treatment itself. . . . [In contrast] we are suggesting that the process of effective case management can enhance patients' own capacities to cope and function in the world. . . . The emphasis is thus shifted from the managerial functions onto those aspects of the process which make case management a potential vehicle for intrapsychic growth. (p. 296)

An important elaboration of Harris and Bergman's call to provide case management and treatment services in the same context is the continuity of care model for the community treatment of the chronically mentally ill that originated in Madison, Wisconsin, during the early 1970s (Test, Knoedler, & Allness, 1985). Often referred to as "assertive case management," the program's focus is proactive—to go out to help the client reenter the community by providing "*in vivo* treatment" in small client staff ratios (Bond, Witheridge, Dincin, & Wasmer, 1991). Treatment goes beyond counseling to include material, interpersonal, and moral support in the areas of education, vocational training, use of leisure time, and self-care in dealing with the stresses and pressures of interpersonal living. Basic components of the approach (Anthony & Margules, 1974; Cutler, Terwillinger, Faulkner, Field, & Bray, 1984; Thompson, Griffith, & Leaf, 1990) include the following:

- Counselors actively keeping track of their clients with numerous face-to-face contacts, rather than waiting for problems to arise
- Staff being available to clients at all times
- Staff treating clients normatively
- Counselors having access to instrumental support for clients (e.g., job training, rent and food money, tools for work, transportation, child care)
- The program providing the more traditional forms of treatment, rehabilitation, and support group services

Although evaluations of case management approaches with the mentally ill are limited (Fisher, Landis, & Clark, 1988), the results are generally positive. Studies demonstrate that, when compared with matched control patients who are discharged from inpatient psychiatric and other mental health settings *without* some form of case management program, those who are case managed tend to (a) have better occupational functioning, (b) live in residential situations requiring some level of independence, (c) be less socially isolated, and (d) be rehospitalized less often and remain in the community longer before rehospitalization (Bond, Miller, Krumwied, & Ward, 1988; Goering, Farkas, Wasylenkl, Lancee, & Ballantyne, 1988; Olfson, 1990; Rapp & Chamberlain, 1985; Stein & Test, 1980; Test, 1981).

CASE MANAGEMENT AND
DRUG-INVOLVED TREATMENT CLIENTS

The great majority of existing out-patient drug programs provide treatment to clients who are living and working in the community. Treatment usually involves some combination of group and individual counseling. Out-patient treatment interventions vary in the intensity and length of treatment, but regardless of the duration of the regimen, the majority of programs are "self-contained" in that they do not access the nontreatment services a client may require. At most they rely on referrals to other human resource agencies to provide assistance with primary care and such social service needs as educational and vocational training, employment counseling, and physical and mental health services.

There are, however, striking similarities between chronic mentally ill persons and drug users, which suggest the potential value of case management in the drug abuse field. Both populations require treatment and a comprehensive network of continuing support in order to interrupt the relapse cycle and allow the client to remain stabilized in the community. The prevention of relapse has challenged the addiction treatment field despite several decades of research (Marlatt & Gordon, 1985; Vaillant, 1988).

Mental health clients and substance abusers in treatment both may require a variety of rehabilitative services in order to "treat" the multiple areas of their lives affected by their disorders. Both groups are likely to have problems accessing and negotiating on their own to get the services they need. It seems natural, therefore, to apply to both types of clients an approach that stresses multimodal and holistic methods of assessment, and managerial and treatment services. Although relapse prevention can be and usually is addressed in the treatment context (for example, using a psychoeducational, skill development approach [Daley, 1986]), other problem dimensions can also be treated effectively when properly integrated in a comprehensive rehabilitation program that provides reinforcement and support in the community (Brekke & Test, 1987). The assertive framework of the continuity of care model may be particularly appropriate for substance abusers who are not likely to be self-starters in seeking treatment.

Until very recently, however, there have been few attempts to exploit the similarities by applying case management directly to substance abusers. Ogborne and Rush (1983) discussed the potential for case management linkages in providing treatment and related social services for problem drinkers. More recently, Graham and Birchmore-Timney (1990) have laid the groundwork for the application of case management techniques in substance abuse treatment.

A more consequential reason for the increased attention being paid to substance abuse treatment and case management of services through primary care systems is the realization of the impending need for primary and social services for drug users at high risk for HIV/AIDS. To foster improved linkages between drug treatment and the provision of primary care, two federal agencies with lead responsibilities in the area—the Alcohol, Drug Abuse and Mental Health Administration (now known as the Substance Abuse and Mental Health Services Administration) and the Health Resources Service Administration—initiated a demonstration program involving 21 projects in 15 states across the country in 1989. All of these projects include both community-based drug treatment and primary care components, and all use case management as a mechanism for making the treatment and primary care linkage.

Preliminary findings from the national evaluation of these projects suggest that clients have a wide variety of health care needs as well as social and life adjustment problems in addition to their substance abuse (Schlenger et al., 1992). Given the opportunity, clients generally make use of linkage and referral services to provide family counseling and assistance with employment, transportation, housing, child care, and benefit entitlements. Most encouraging, those who receive more case management get more assistance of all kinds, including drug treatment, health care, and other social services.

Another major federal initiative in applying case management to drug abuse treatment is a group of the Applied Evaluation Demonstration Projects funded by the National Institute on Drug Abuse (NIDA). In a Chicago study, for example, case managers do not provide treatment. Rather, they assess client needs, then assist them to negotiate through the obstacles of limited availability of publicly funded services by referral, linking, and advocacy (Bokos, Mejta, Mickenberg, & Monks, 1992). Preliminary findings suggest that case managed clients were significantly more likely to get into treatment than those who were not case managed and that the length of time between intake and beginning treatment was significantly shorter (6 days versus 32 days). In a Los Angeles project, building on recent evidence that providing service enhancements to methadone programs increases treatment compliance (Dolan, Black, Perk, Rabinowitz, & DeFord, 1986), case management services have been added to a methadone maintenance program (Anglin, Miller, Mantius, & Grella, 1993). A third study in Dayton, Ohio, based on the advocacy focused strengths approach developed by Rapp and Chamberlain (1985), seeks to help veterans work their way through the drug treatment social service nexus (Rapp, Siegal, & Fisher, 1992). The aim is to build the client's internal resources, then support the veteran in developing and negotiating personal treatment and service needs.

Despite the promise of these federal demonstration programs, there are also major differences in translating the case management model from the mental health field and applying it to treating chronic drug abusers. Most obvious is the expectation that, although drug use may be considered a chronic relapsing syndrome, drug users can improve, and eventually may cease to need the case management assistance. As such, with the exception of programs for the dually diagnosed, most existing case management applications in the drug field have time limits and success goals, rather than the continuous availability of help envisioned for the mentally ill.

A second major difference is the difficulty of getting treatment staff to leave the confines of their offices and clinics. The more traditional "passive" convention of waiting for clients to visit counselors in treatment programs is in sharp contrast to the more proactive and even assertive procedures of delivering treatment and support to clients directly in the community. This was a difficult barrier to overcome in the mental health field. It is even more arduous in dealing with drug users where there is the perception, by service providers, that the clients are more responsible for the situation they are in. Unfortunately, there is some evidence that substance abusers are less likely to receive the array of rehabilitative services available to the chronically mentally ill person (Solomon, 1986).

CASE MANAGEMENT AND DRUG-INVOLVED CRIMINAL JUSTICE CLIENTS

Drug-involved criminal justice clients often face a wider spectrum of problems than other populations targeted by case management, including the life disruptions associated with police and court processing, the perceived stigma of a criminal record, the possibility of lost freedom through incarceration, and the disruptions caused in work, school, and family activities. The likelihood of relapse and recidivism from the failure of these clients to find support for their dual problems of recovery and reentry into society creates the circumstances for a more complex, problematic, and costly treatment conundrum both for the individual and for the community. Given the individual needs of these clients and the correctional mandate to monitor and supervise criminal justice clients in community settings, the application of case management techniques would seem an important component of treatment for drug involved offenders.

There is some evidence that treatment perspectives for offenders are moving to incorporate nontreatment services in community-based programs. This is part of a general movement in correctional treatment toward community oriented programs. Sometimes as a corollary and sometimes as an alternative to prison-based treatment, drug treatment in community-based correctional settings has emerged in the United States over the past two decades. These programs developed as part of the widespread interest in early criminal justice diversion projects, and have experienced renewed attention since the late 1980s as they relate to the growing trend toward "alternatives to incarceration" and "intermediate sanctions."

The most visible and enduring of these programs is the Treatment Alternatives to Street Crime (TASC) program. Under TASC, community-based supervision is made available to drug-involved offenders who would otherwise burden the justice system with their persistent drug-associated criminality. Specifically, TASC identifies, assesses, and refers drug-involved offenders to community treatment and social services as an *alternative* or *supplement* to existing justice system sanctions and procedures. In the more than 100 jurisdictions where TASC currently operates, it serves as a court diversion mechanism or a supplement to probation or parole supervision.

After referral to community-based treatment, TASC monitors client progress and compliance, including expectations for abstinence, employment, and improved personal and social functioning. It then reports treatment results back to the referring justice system agency. Clients who violate the conditions of their justice mandate, TASC contract, or treatment agreement are typically returned to the justice system for continued processing or sanctions (Inciardi & McBride, 1991; Swartz, Chapter 7 of this book).

Although the TASC model incorporates elements of assessment, planning, linking, and monitoring, little or no emphasis is placed on the advocacy functions of case management. By contrast, the assertive/advocacy capacities of some case management initiatives have been incorporated into a new treatment demonstration project funded by the National Institute on Drug Abuse. This research demonstration effort seeks to apply an "assertive community treatment" (ACT) model for parolees released from the Delaware prison system (Inciardi et al., 1992). Clients must have a previous history of chronic drug use that has placed them at increased risk for HIV infection.

After classification to parole status, and selection for the program, each ACT client ideally proceeds through drug treatment and case management in five stages: (1) intake assessment; (2) intensive drug treatment (e.g., group counseling, AIDS education, individual counseling, family assessment therapy); (3) moderate treatment, where education/vocation sessions come more to the forefront in group counseling and life skills planning; (4) relapse prevention; and (5) case management, where clients who have completed their active involvement in the treatment oriented parts of ACT transfer into a case management phase, designed to support their transition into normal community life. Although the project has put into place all of the necessary components of an assertive case management initiative, preliminary evaluative efforts have identified a significant shortcoming. Since the project was funded under a federal research demonstration effort, special protections for prisoners as research subjects were mandated. Among these was the requirement that participation in treatment was voluntary. As such, clients could not be offered treatment as either a means for early parole or as a *condition* of parole. This inability to require participation in treatment severely impacted on retention (Martin & Scarpitti, 1993).

The ACT study illustrates that, despite some potential advantages, there remain a number of practical problems with applying case management to criminal justice clients. The first is the issue of retention in treatment. As mentioned above, ACT clients are free to leave the program at any time; no form of coercion and only the benefit of treatment can be offered to induce prolonged participation. Some of the clients assigned to the program never make contact with it, others fail to fully connect and engage with it, while many others drop out prematurely.

A second problem is the potential for the intervention to be less "assertive" than planned. At the outset of the ACT project, counselors and case managers were less willing to reach out to clients who, because of the selection process, were not actively seeking treatment (Scarpitti & Pan, 1992). Moreover, and as noted earlier, treatment and managerial personnel often experience more difficulty in dealing with drug users as compared with the mentally ill or the homeless. It is even more problematic for case managers to work with criminal justice clients because of fears of greater physical risk and pronounced feelings that clients are in great part responsible for the precarious situations they are in.

On the whole, the ACT experience suggests the need for restructuring to better retain criminal justice clients in treatment. The one consensual finding from drug treatment research is that the longer a client stays in treatment, the better the outcome in terms of declines in drug use and criminality. This is an often replicated finding (Anglin & Hser, 1990; DeLeon, 1984; Simpson, Savage, & Lloyd, 1979). One of the few advantages of dealing with criminal justice clients is the potential to support compulsory and coerced treatment. Studies have demonstrated that success in treatment is a function of length of stay, and that those coerced into treatment do at least as well as, and often better than, voluntary commitments. that is, those coerced into treatment tend to remain longer than their voluntary counterparts (Collins & Allison, 1983; DeLeon, 1988; Gerstein & Harwood, 1990; Hubbard et al., 1989; Leukefeld & Tims, 1990; Platt, Buhringer, Kaplan, Brown, & Taube, 1988).

DISCUSSION

Case management is a problem-solving mechanism for clients who cannot effectively deal with diverse, bureaucratic, and non-user friendly treatment and social service organizations and structures. Case management seeks to link the client with "a network of caring and responsible people committed to assisting vulnerable clients to meet their needs and develop their potentials without being unnecessarily isolated or excluded from the community" (National Institute of Mental Health, 1977, p. 2). Turner and Shifren (1979) have suggested that this general concept could be adapted to other vulnerable populations. Certainly drug users (many of whom are at high risk for HIV/AIDS because of unsafe injection practices) with past and current involvement in criminal activity present a complex array of service needs. Vulnerability to relapse, HIV and other infections, overdose, and return to illegal activity and exposure to the violence associated with the street drug scene are possible without a comprehensive approach to treatment.

Case management has been shown to encourage substance abusers to stay in treatment and reach treatment goals (Kofoed, Tolson, Atkinson, Toth, & Turner, 1986). If case management is combined with legal sanctions to enforce participation and monitoring, perhaps in combination with parole and probation conditions, supervision, and reporting, the potential for retention in treatment and provision of necessary services can be greatly increased. TASC programs have accomplished this to a very great extent (Collins & Allison, 1983; Inciardi & McBride, 1991). A case management program that incorporates the features of TASC or a TASC-like model, provides the assertiveness and continuity of care of an ACT model, and offers court- or parole-ordered treatment to enhance retention would appear appropriate for criminal justice clients. At the same time, the general premises of case management can facilitate relationship building and trust, elements crucial to assisting client skills enhancement, empowerment, and self-sufficiency (Rapp & Chamberlain, 1985).

NOTE

1. The "New Frontier" was the legislative program of President John F. Kennedy that emphasized domestic social programs and increased foreign aid. It was met with mixed reactions in Congress and was only in part effected. In May 1964, President Lyndon B. Johnson called for a "Great Society," in which the quality of life would be improved for all. The Great Society incorporated and soon extended Kennedy's New Frontier, especially with

the Economic Opportunity Act of 1964, which carried into legislation Kennedy's vision of a "war on poverty" (see Matusow, 1984; White, 1982).

REFERENCES

Abel, R. (1989). Beyond Willie Horton: The battle of the prison bulge. *Corrections Today, 51,* 158-164.

Anglin, M. D., & Hser, Y. (1990). Treatment of drug abuse. In M. Tonry & J. Q. Wilson (Eds.), *Drugs and crime* (pp. 93-460). Chicago: University of Chicago Press.

Anglin, M. D., Miller, M. D., Mantius, K., & Grella, C. (1993). Enhanced methadone maintenance treatment: Limiting the spread of HIV among high risk Los Angeles narcotics addicts. In J. A. Inciardi (Ed.), *Innovative approaches to the treatment of drug abuse: Program models and strategies.* New York: Greenwood Press.

Anthony, W., & Margules, A. (1974). Toward improving the efficacy of psychiatric rehabilitation: A skills training approach. *Rehabilitation Psychology, 21,* 101-105.

Austin, D., & Caragonne, P. (1988). A comparative analysis of twenty-two settings using case management components. In *The Case Management Research Project.* Austin, TX: University of Texas School of Social Work. Cited in G. O'Connor, Case management system and practice, *Social Casework, 69*(2), 97-106.

Bagarozzi, D. A., & Pollane, L. P. (1984). Case management in mental health. *Health and Social Work, 9,* 201-211.

Bokos P., Mejta, C., Mickenberg, J., & Monks, R. (1992, February 4-5). Case management: An alternative approach to working with IV drug abusers. National Institute on Drug Abuse Technical Review Meeting on Case Management. Rockville, MD.

Bond, G. R., Miller, L. D., Krumwied, R. D., & Ward, R. S. (1988). Assertive case management in three CMCHs: A controlled study. *Hospital and Community Psychiatry, 39,* 411-418.

Bond, G. R., Witheridge, T. F., Dincin, J., & Wasmer, D. (1991). Assertive community treatment: Correcting some misconceptions. *American Journal of Community Psychology, 19,* 41-51.

Brekke, J. S., & Test, M. A. (1987). An empirical analysis of services delivered in a model community support program. *Psychosocial Rehabilitation Journal, 10*(4), 51-61.

Buddress, L. A. N. (1992). Cost management and effectiveness of treatment alternatives with a substance abuse offender population: A systems approach to longitudinal outcome analysis. Unpublished paper, U.S. District Court, Northern District of California, Probation Office, San Francisco, CA.

Chavaria, F. R. (1992, March). Successful drug treatment in a criminal justice setting: A case study. *Federal Probation Quarterly,* 48-52.

Cohen, M. R., Nimec, P. B., Cohen, B. F., & Farkas, M. (1988). *Psychiatric rehabilitation trainer package: Case management.* Boston: Boston University Center for Psychiatric Rehabilitation.

Collins, J. J., & Allison, M. (1983). Legal coercion and retention in drug abuse treatment. *Hospital and Community Psychiatry, 34,* 1145-1149.

Cutler, D. L., Terwillinger, W. , Faulkner, L., Field, G., & Bray, D. (1984). Disseminating the principles of a community support program. *Hospital and Community Psychiatry, 35,* 51-55.

Daley, D. (1986). *Relapse prevention workbook*. New York: Learning Publications.

DeLeon, G. (1984). Program based evaluation research in therapeutic communities. In F. M. Tims & J. P. Ludford (Eds.), *Drug abuse treatment evaluation: Strategies, progress, and prospects* (pp. 69-87). National Institute on Drug Abuse Research Monograph No. 51. Rockville, MD: National Institute on Drug Abuse.

DeLeon, G. (1988). Legal pressure in therapeutic communities. *Journal of Drug Issues, 18,* 625-640.

Dolan, M. P., Black, J. L., Perk, W. E., Rabinowitz, R., & DeFord, H. A. (1986). Predicting the outcome of contingency contracting for drug abuse. *Behavior Therapy, 17,* 470-474.

Dybal, L. (1980). Case management in selected Wisconsin counties. *Wisconsin Department of Health and Social Services report,* Human Services Development Series. Madison, WI.

Fisher, G., Landis, D., & Clark, K. (1988). Case management service provision and client change. *Community Mental Health Journal, 24,* 134-142.

Gerstein, D. R., & Harwood, H. J. (1990). *Treating drug problems: Volume 1. A study of the evolution, effectiveness, and financing of public and private drug treatment systems.* Washington, DC: National Academy Press.

Goering, P. N., Farkas, M., Wasylenkl, D. A., Lancee, W. J., & Ballantyne, P. (1988). Improved functioning for case management clients. *Psychosocial Rehabilitation Journal, 12,* 3-17.

Graham, K., & Birchmore-Timney, C. (1990). Case management in addictions treatment. *Journal of Substance Abuse Treatment, 7,* 181-188.

Greenhouse, C. M. (1992, July/August). Case management may be the wave of the future for drug abuse treatment. *NIDA Notes,* 6-7.

Harris, M., & Bergman, H. C. (1987). Case management with the chronically mentally ill. *American Journal of Orthopsychiatry, 57,* 296-302.

Hubbard, R. L., Collins, J. J., Rachal, J. V., & Cavanaugh, E. R. (1988). The criminal justice client in drug abuse treatment. In C. G. Leukefeld & F. M. Tims (Eds.), *Compulsory treatment off drug abuse: Research and clinical practice* (pp. 57-81), National Institute on Drug Abuse Research Monograph No. 86. Rockville, MD: National Institute on Drug Abuse.

Hubbard, R. L., & Harwood, H. J. (1981). Employment related series in drug treatment programs. *Treatment Research Report.* Rockville, MD: National Institute on Drug Abuse.

Hubbard, R. L., Marsden, M. E., Rachal, J. V., Harwood, H. J., Cavanaugh, E. R., & Ginzburg, H. M. (1989). *Drug abuse treatment: A national study of effectiveness.* Chapel Hill, NC: University of North Carolina Press.

Inciardi, J. A., Isenberg, H., Lockwood, D., Martin, S. S., & Scarpitti, F. R. (1992, February 4-5). Assertive community treatment with a parolee population: An extension of case management. National Institute on Drug Abuse Technical Review Meeting on Case Management, Rockville, MD.

Inciardi, J. A., & McBride, D. C. (1991). *Treatment Alternatives to Street Crime (TASC): History, experiences, and issues.* Rockville, MD: National Institute on Drug Abuse.

Kofoed, L., Tolson, R., Atkinson, R., Toth, R., & Turner, J. (1986). Outpatient treatment of patients with substance abuse and coexisting psychiatric disorders. *American Journal of Psychiatry, 143,* 867-872.

Leukefeld, C. G., & Tims, F. M. (1990). Compulsory treatment for drug abuse. *International Journal of the Addictions, 25,* 621-640.

Lipton, D. S. (1989, October). The theory of rehabilitation as applied to addict offenders. Paper presented at the *What Work's* Conference, New York City.

Marlatt, G. A., & Gordon, J. R. (Eds.). (1985). *Relapse prevention: Maintenance strategies in addiction behavior change*. New York: Guilford Press.

Martin, S. S., & Scarpitti, F. R. (1993). An intensive case management approach for paroled IV drug users. *Journal of Drug Issues, 23*(1), 43-59.

Matusow, A. J. (1984). *The unraveling of America: A history of liberalism in the 1960s*. New York: Harper & Row.

McLellan, A. T., Luborsky, L., Woody, G. E., O'Brien, C. P., & Kron, R. (1981). Are the "addict-related" problems of substance abusers really related? *Journal of Nervous and Mental Disease, 169*, 232-239.

Murray, D. W. (1991, June). New initiatives in drug treatment in the federal bureau of prisons. *Federal Probation Quarterly*, pp. 35-41.

National Institute of Justice. (1990). *Drug use forecasting 1990 annual report*. Washington, DC: U.S. Department of Justice.

National Institute of Mental Health, Community Support Section. (1977). *Request for proposals No. NIMH-MH-77-0080-0081*. Rockville, MD: National Institute of Mental Health.

O'Brien, C. P. (1987). Treatment research, drug abuse and drug abuse research. In *The Second Triennial Report to Congress from the Secretary*, Department of Health and Human Services. Rockville, MD: National Institute on Drug Abuse.

Ogborne, A. C., & Rush, B. R. (1983). The coordination of treatment services for problem drinkers: Problems and prospects. *British Journal of the Addictions, 78*, 131-138.

Olfson, M. (1990). Assertive community treatment: An evaluation of the experimental evidence. *Hospital and Community Psychiatry, 41*, 634-641.

Platt, J. J., Buhringer, G., Kaplan, C. D., Brown, B. B., & Taube, D. O. (1988). The prospects and limitations of compulsory treatment for drug addiction. *Journal of Drug Issues, 18*, 505-525.

Rapp, C. A., & Chamberlain, R. (1985). Case management services for the chronically mentally ill. *Social Work, 30*, 417-422.

Rapp, R. C., Siegal, H. A., & Fisher, J. H. (1992). A strengths-based model of case management/advocacy: Adapting a mental health model to practice work with persons who have substance abuse problems. In R. Ashery (Ed.), *Case management in drug abuse treatment*. National Institute on Drug Abuse Research Monograph. Rockville, MD: National Institute on Drug Abuse.

Roberts-DeGennaro, M. (1987). Developing case management as a practice model. *Social Casework, 68*(8), 466-470.

Scarpitti, F. S., & Pan, H. (1992). Preliminary report: Process evaluation of the ACT program. Unpublished paper. Newark, NJ: University of Delaware.

Schlenger, W. E., Kroutil, L. A., & Roland, E. J. (1992). Case management as a mechanism for linking drug abuse treatment and primary care: Preliminary evidence from the ADAMHA/HRSA linkage demonstration. In R. Ashery (Ed.) *Case management in drug abuse treatment*. National Institute on Drug Abuse Research Monograph. Rockville, MD: National Institute on Drug Abuse.

Simpson, D. D., Savage, J., & Lloyd, M. R. (1979). Follow-up evaluation of treatment of drug abuse during 1969 to 1972. *Archives of General Psychiatry, 36*, 772-780.

Simpson, D. D., & Sells, S. B. (1982). Effectiveness of treatment for drug abuse: An overview of the DARP research program. *Advances in Alcohol and Substance Abuse Treatment, 2*, 7-29.

Solomon, P. (1986) Receipt of aftercare services by problem types: Psychiatric, psychiatric/substance abuse and substance abuse. *Psychiatric Quarterly, 58*(3), 180-188.

Stein, L. I., & Test, M. A. (1980). Alternative to mental hospital treatment. *Archives of General Psychiatry, 37*, 392-412.

Test, M. A. (1981). Effective community treatment of the chronically mentally ill: What is necessary? *Journal of Social Issues, 37*, 71-86.

Test, M. A., Knoedler, W. H., & Allness, D. J. (1985). The long-term treatment of young schizophrenics in a community support program. In L. I. Stein & M. A. Test (Eds.), *Training in community living—Ten years later* (pp. 17-27). San Francisco: Jossey-Bass.

Thompson, K. S., Griffith, E. E., & Leaf, P. J. (1990). A historical review of the Madison Model of community care. *Hospital and Community Psychiatry, 41*, 625-634.

Turner, J. E. C., & Shifren, I. (1979). Community support systems: How comprehensive? *New Directions for Mental Health Services, 2*, 1-13.

Vaillant, G. E. (1988). What can long-term follow-up teach us about relapse and prevention of relapse in addiction? *British Journal of Addiction, 83*, 1147-1157.

Weppner, R. S. (1983). *The untherapeutic community: Organizational behavior in a failed addiction treatment program.* Lincoln, NE: University of Nebraska Press.

Wexler, H. K., Falkin, G. P., Lipton, D. S., Rosenblum, A. B., & Goodloe, L. P. (1988). *A model prison rehabilitation program: An evaluation of the "Stay'n Out" therapeutic community.* New York: Narcotic and Drug Research.

White, T. H. (1982). *America in search of itself: The making of the president 1956-1980.* New York: Harper & Row.

Chapter 6

ADDRESSING THE PROBLEMS
OF SUBSTANCE ABUSE
IN JUVENILE CORRECTIONS

RICHARD DEMBO

LINDA WILLIAMS

JAMES SCHMEIDLER

INTRODUCTION

Treatment of adolescents for alcohol or other drug abuse problems in the juvenile justice system has become a matter of increasing importance. Two trends of experience are responsible for this development: (1) the rise in youth crime and the growing awareness of the magnitude of these and related problems among various high-risk groups, and (2) increasing evidence that treatment of individuals with alcohol/other drug problems can result in significant decreases in delinquency/crime.

At the same time, the field of adolescent substance abuse treatment is in its infancy. A number of critical issues need to be resolved for the field to mature. First, much of the knowledge that has derived from the experience of treating adults with alcohol/other drug abuse problems cannot be directly applied to adolescents. A knowledge base deriving from experience in treating youths is only beginning to be established. There is limited knowledge about which treatment methods are best for specific

AUTHORS' NOTE: The preparation of this chapter was supported by Grant No. 1 RO1 DA06657-01, funded by the National Institute on Drug Abuse. However, the research results reported and the views expressed in the paper do not necessarily imply any policy or research endorsement by our funding agency.

sociodemographic subgroups of youths or those experiencing different substance abuse difficulties. Second, there is a need to place treatment intervention activities in proper context. There is growing recognition that alcohol/other drug abuse among youths is related to difficulties in a number of areas of experience or functioning—including family relationships, physical abuse/sexual victimization, educational performance, and emotional/psychological functioning. Third, given the experience that juvenile justice agencies focus on specific problems and have limited coordination in many jurisdictions, there is increased recognition that systems of care need to be developed to identify troubled youths, link them with appropriate programs, and provide them with supportive post-treatment, or aftercare, services. Fourth, the high post-treatment relapse rates among adolescents treated for substance abuse problems has highlighted the chronic relapsing nature of these problems, challenging the field to develop services to address this issue.

This paper provides a summary of our knowledge of the needs of troubled youths entering or involved with the juvenile justice system, as well as a review of efforts to address their alcohol/other drug abuse problems. This information is presented in the context of a recommended continuity of care model covering key decision points in identifying and responding to the needs of these youths. The model provides a holistic, integrated approach to organize and inform future efforts in the field, and identifies significant gaps in our knowledge and service delivery systems. The service delivery model we propose consists of the following sequence of interrelated activities: (1) preliminary screening, (2) in-depth assessment, (3) intervention, (4) aftercare, and (5) long-term continuity of service.

VIEWING DELINQUENT YOUTHS IN A HOLISTIC MANNER

Many youths involved with the criminal justice system have serious, multiple problems in the areas of physical abuse (Dembo, Dertke, Borders, Washburn, & Schmeidler, 1988), sexual victimization (Dembo et al., 1989; Mouzakitis, 1981), alcohol and other drug use (Dembo, Williams, Wish, & Schmeidler, 1990; U.S. Department of Justice, 1983a, 1983b) emotional/ psychological functioning (Dembo, Williams, La Voie et al., 1990; Teplin & Swartz, 1989), and educational functioning (Dembo, Williams, Schmeidler, & Howitt, 1991). Many of these youths' difficulties can be traced to family alcohol/other drug use, mental health, or crime problems that began at an early age (Dembo, Williams, Wothke, Schmeidler, & Brown, in press; Garbarino & Gilliam, 1980). These factors place youths at high risk for future drug use and delinquency/crime.

It is important that these youths be seen in holistic terms, not one problem at a time (cf. Steiger & Knobel, 1991). Information needs to be collected on their experience of specific problems so that their service needs can be identified and appropriate interventions developed.

STUDIES OF YOUTHS IN THE GENERAL POPULATION AND JUVENILE JUSTICE SYSTEM

Studies involving youths in the general population have uncovered low rates of serious forms of delinquency, alcohol/other drug use, mental health problems, and the experience of physical abuse and sexual victimization, which place young people at highest risk of becoming involved in personally and socially damaging life styles (Elliott, Huizinga, & Menard, 1989; Lewis, Lovely, Yeager, & Famina, 1989). A number of self-report cross-sectional and longitudinal studies involving youths/young adults in the general population have documented a positive relationship to exist between youths' alcohol/other drug use and their involvement in delinquency/crime (Elliott & Huizinga, 1984; Elliott et al., 1989; Kandel, Simcha-Fagan, & Davies, 1986).

The Tampa Longitudinal Study

In contrast, youths involved with the juvenile justice system have high rates of problems in the areas noted above. This is reflected, for example, in the detention center sample we have been studying. Since 1986, the authors and their associates have been pursuing a longitudinal study of a cohort of 399 juveniles who entered the Hillsborough Regional Juvenile Detention Center (HRJDC) in Tampa, Florida. The study included 286 male and 113 female detainees (average age 15 years). Most of the youths were Caucasian (51%), and 42% were African American. The design of the initial interview and follow-up phase of this study are discussed elsewhere (Dembo, Williams, Berry et al., 1990; Dembo, Williams, Schmeidler, Getreu et al., 1991). The results of this research are discussed at various points throughout this chapter.

RISK FACTORS IN YOUTHS' ALCOHOL/OTHER DRUG USE AND DELINQUENCY/CRIME

Alcohol and Other Drug Use

Urine testing studies have found high rates of drug use to exist among juvenile arrestees in various cities (Dembo, Williams, Wish et al., 1990; National Institute of Justice [NIJ], 1992). Complementing the results of urine test studies involving adults, the findings of research involving juvenile detainees have indicated that drug using youths have higher rates of arrest for various felony offenses than youths who have not recently used drugs (Dembo, Williams, Berry et al., 1990; Dembo et al., 1987).

Urine testing is a necessary supplement to self-reports for identifying drug use among juveniles taken into custody. Research indicates that the more unacceptable the use of a given drug, the more likely youths are to deny its use (Dembo, Williams, Berry et al., 1990). Youths tend to report accurately the use of marijuana but underreport the recent use of cocaine.

Cocaine Use and the Youths' Recidivism

The Tampa longitudinal study has collected official arrest data on seven categories of offenses for a 3½-year period following the youths' initial interviews. By 42 months following the youths' initial interviews, 56% had at least one referral to juvenile court or one adult arrest for a property felony offense, 43% for a property misdemeanor offense, and 26% for a drug felony charge. Recidivism analyses indicated a very consistent predictor of the youths' subsequent arrests was their use of cocaine. Youths found to be EMIT® positive for cocaine use at initial interview had a significantly higher rate of referrals/arrests for property misdemeanor offenses than cocaine-negative youths (Dembo, Williams, Schmeidler, & Christensen, in press).

HIV Infection/Transmission Risk Among Drug-Using Juveniles

Drug-using youths are at high risk for being infected by HIV as a result of injecting drugs or sexual activity (Inciardi, Pottieger, Forney, Chitwood & McBride, 1991; also see Inciardi & Pottieger, 1991). Hence, youths having contact with the juvenile justice system represent an important target group to address the AIDS problem and reduce the spread of AIDS (Wish, O'Neil, Crawford, & Baldau, 1992).

Official Record and Self-Reported Information
on Previous Involvement in Delinquent Behavior

Research has indicated that youth who become involved in delinquent life-styles tend to continue that behavior over time (Nagin & Paternoster, 1991). For example, at the time of their initial interviews, many of the youths in the Tampa study had already had extensive contact with the juvenile court: 67% were referred to juvenile court at least once for a felony property offense, 51% for a felony violence offense, 63% for a misdemeanor property offense, and 47% for a status offense. Further, 23% of the youths were referred to juvenile court four or more times for felony property offenses. Self-report information on the youths' delinquent behavior in the year prior to their initial interviews indicated high rates of delinquency involvement.

Physical Abuse and Sexual Victimization

Youths entering the justice system have high rates of emotional/psychological difficulties, particularly in the areas of physical abuse and sexual victimization (Teplin & Swartz, 1989). Data in the Tampa study indicate that, at initial interview, 60% of the youths reported being physically harmed in one or more of six different ways by an adult (someone over the age of 18) (Dembo, Williams, Berry et al., 1990). These rates of physical abuse are much higher than those reported in the 1985 national survey on family violence (Straus & Gelles, 1986).

Youths in the Tampa longitudinal study were also asked about their sexual victimization experiences. As discussed in more detail elsewhere (Dembo, Williams, Berry, Getreu et al., 1990), 35% of the youths (61% of the females and 25% of the males) were sexually victimized at least once in their lives. These rates should be regarded as conservative estimates of this experience. Although the questions were sensitively asked, some youngsters were reluctant to talk about these painful experiences.

Educational Problems

Studies involving youths from the general population as well as official delinquents have documented the influence of educational factors in their alcohol/other drug use and other delinquent behavior. Youths who perform poorly in school, attend school irregularly, or show a lack of commitment to education are more likely to engage in antisocial activities (Elliott, Huizinga, & Ageton, 1985; Gottfredson, 1988; Hawkins & Lishner, 1987;

Newcomb & Bentler, 1988; Zarek, Hawkins, & Rogers, 1987). Further, youths experiencing problems in one of these areas are likely to experience difficulties in other areas (Jessor & Jessor, 1977).

In the Tampa longitudinal study, the youths' average grade completed (8th) lagged 2 years behind what would be expected based on their age. Moreover, their average standardized test scores lagged 2 years behind their actual grade level! The youths' difficulties in school were first seen in the early school years, and had the effect of separating them from school in a profound way. Forty-six percent of the youths had been retained in grade two or more times, with 37% having been held back in the 1st or 2nd grades. Eighty-five percent of the youths had been expelled or suspended from school one or more times; and the youths had a D– grade average for the academic year prior to their initial interviews. Over a third of the youths stopped going to school prior to their 16th birthday (Dembo, Williams, Schmeidler, & Howitt, 1991). These troubled educational experiences are consistent with what Lazar, Darlington, Murray, Royce, and Snipper (1982) refer to as the "cumulative deficit" problem among inner-city youths—these youths begin school at an academic handicap and lose ground over time.

Family Problems

At-risk youths frequently grow up in troubled families (e.g., experiencing alcohol/other drug use or mental health [ADM] problems, violence between family members and/or involvement with the criminal justice system) (Lewis et al., 1989; Miller, Downs, Gondoli, & Keil, 1987). Studies consistently have found an association between family functioning factors and delinquency/crime. Families that provide emotional/psychological support to their children, supply conventional role models for them, exert social control over children's behavior, and where strong bonds of attachment exist between youngsters and their parents, tend to have lower rates of delinquency (Cernkovich & Giordano, 1987; Laub & Sampson, 1988).

Tampa study youths came from families who experienced a number of difficulties in psychosocial functioning. Most respondents' families experienced ADM problems. Nearly half (45%) reported that at least one member of their family or household family besides themselves had an alcohol abuse problem, 27% noted a family or household family member had another drug abuse problem (most frequently marijuana/hashish or cocaine), and 22% indicated a family or household family member had experienced an emotional or mental health problem.

In addition, large proportions of the youths' families had contact with the juvenile or adult justice systems. Most of the youths (71%) claimed that at least one member of their family or household family besides themselves had been arrested, and from 50% to 65% reported that a member of their family/household family had been in jail or detention, adjudicated delinquent, or convicted of a crime or put on community control or probation. Further, 29% of the youths noted that at least one family member or household family member had been sent to a training school or a prison.

Peer Influences

Peers are a strong influence in the development of patterns of alcohol/other drug use (Kandel, 1975) and delinquency (Elliott, Huizinga, & Ageton, 1985). Thus it is not surprising that many youths entering the juvenile justice system have friends who are involved with alcohol/other drug use or have had contact with the justice system themselves. For example, large proportions of youths in the Tampa longitudinal study indicated one or more of their close friends had used marijuana/hashish (60%) or cocaine (24%) during the previous year. In addition, large proportions of the youths' close friends had some type of contact with the legal system—being arrested (75%), held in jail or detention (67%), adjudicated delinquent or convicted of a crime (53%), been put on community control or probation (60%), or sent to a training school or prison (24%) (Dembo, Williams, Berry et al., 1990).

INTERRELATIONSHIPS AMONG VARIOUS RISK FACTORS AND THE YOUTHS' DRUG USE AND DELINQUENCY OVER TIME: AN EXAMPLE FROM THE TAMPA STUDY

We examined the relationships among the youths' family problems, their abuse/victimization experiences, and their alcohol/other drug use and delinquency over time as shown in Figure 6.1. This prototype model represents the youths' family socioeconomic status (SES), parental presence, family ADM problems and their contact with the justice system factors, and the youths' sexual victimization and physical abuse as interrelated experiences. In turn, these factors are specified to influence the use of alcohol/other drugs and involvement in delinquency at Time 1 (T1). Parallel sets of analyses were performed for (1) the use of alcohol, (2) self-reported use of marijuana/hashish, (3) marijuana/ hashish use as measured by both self-report and EMIT® urine test results, and (4) use of cocaine as measured by EMIT® urine test results. For each of these substance use measures, separate analyses were performed for each of the five self-reported delinquency scales noted in the figure.

Overall, the hypothesized model was consistent with the data, with the fit of the model being especially good in regard to the youths' marijuana/hashish use and self-reported delinquency. The findings highlight that the SES and composition of the youths' families are much less important in understanding their marijuana/hashish use and delinquency than their families' ADM problems and involvement in crime and the youths' experience of sexual victimization or physical abuse (cf. Widom, 1989a, 1989b).

Additional analyses found the youths' family problems and abuse/victimization experiences influenced their initial involvement in drugs and their delinquent behavior. Once these behavior patterns are established, they tend to continue over time (Dembo, Williams, Wothke et al., in press). Early intervention with these youths, and their families, holds promise of addressing more effectively and at lower cost the damaging behavior dynamics we have identified, before drug use and delinquent careers become firmly established.

THE SERVICE DELIVERY MODEL

Preliminary and In-Depth Screening

As the discussion above highlights, it is critical to identify the alcohol/other drug use, mental health, and related problems among youths having contact with the justice system. These youths are at high risk of becoming antisocial adults. Identification of these youths' problems, and involving them in needed services, would benefit them and their families and help reduce the enormous cost to our society of crime, drug abuse, and mental illness (Rice, Kelman, Miller, & Dunmeyer, 1990).

Our experience interviewing and testing urine of juvenile detainees at entry into secure detention has proven valuable in identifying troubled youths. Since 1985, the senior author has developed assessment and referral-placement procedures at the HRJDC (Dembo, Washburn et al., 1987). The triage-screening activities are conducted by counselors employed by Northside Centers, Inc. (a local community mental health center), who are located at the detention center. Following an approximately 30-minute triage-screening interview, youths with apparent mental health or alcohol/

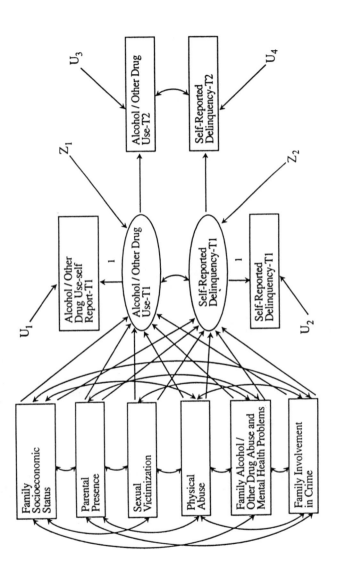

Figure 6.1. Model of the Relationships Among Family Background and Other Factors and Youths' Alcohol/Other Drug Use and Delinquency Over Time

NOTES: Alcohol use was measured by self-reports. Marijuana/hashish use was measured by self-reports. Cocaine use was measured by EMIT® urinalysis results.

The self-reported delinquency scales included (a) general theft crimes, (b) drug sales, (c) index offenses, (d) crimes against persons, and (e) total delinquency.

Because of the autoregressive structure of the model, the separate parameters U and Z, for measurement error and structural residual error, respectively, are identified at Time 1.

other drug abuse problems are referred for further assessment and, where indicated, treatment (Dembo, Williams, Getreu, Schmeidler, & Wish, 1990). Efforts are made to involve both the youths and their families in treatment planning, as well as to work in concert with a local substance abuse treatment program serving adolescents, Florida Department of Health and Rehabilitative Services (DHRS) staff, and juvenile court personnel and processes. Criteria for referral for further assessment have been developed with the assistance of community service providers (Dembo, Washburn, Broskowski, Getreu, & Berry, 1986; Dembo, Williams, Getreu et al., 1990).

Unfortunately, quality assessments of youths entering in the juvenile justice system remains the exception rather than the rule. For example, in Hillsborough County, Florida, between July and November 1991, delinquency petitions were filed on 3,335 youths. Only 1,842 (55%) of these youths were given preliminary screenings to identify alcohol/other drug abuse or mental health problems by Florida DHRS workers, and only 671 (or 20%) of the 3,335 youths were given in-depth assessments for these problems.

Another important methodology, the Adolescent Assessment/Referral System (AARS), has been developed by the National Institute on Drug Abuse (NIDA) (NIDA, 1991a). The AARS consists of three main elements. One is the Problem Oriented Screening Instrument for Teenagers (POSIT). The POSIT probes for difficulties in 10 functional areas: substance use/abuse, physical health status, mental health status, family relationships, peer relations, educational status, vocational status, social skills, leisure and recreation, and aggressive behavior and delinquency. The POSIT is designed to flag whether a problem may exist in any functional area requiring further assessment and perhaps treatment. A personal history questionnaire is also part of the POSIT. Recent studies indicate the discriminant and predictive validity of the POSIT (McLaney, Del Boca, & Babor, 1992).

The second AARS component is the Comprehensive Assessment Battery (CAB), which includes psychometrically validated protocols probing in more depth each problem area tapped by the POSIT. The third element of the AARS is a referral system guide, which assists the case manager or referral agent in placing troubled youths in services to address their medical, psychiatric, educational, or psychosocial needs.

Preliminary screening and in-depth assessments of troubled youths should, ideally, take place in a setting where a comprehensive picture of these youths and their service needs can be gained. We recommend that these important activities occur in community-based centralized receiving and processing facilities, such as the facility being established in Tampa, Florida. Such units can serve as focal points for assessing and processing troubled youths, and linking them and their families with needed services.

Establishing the Tampa Centralized Receiving Facility

The Tampa facility will be operated and staffed with clinicians 24 hours a day by a community-based substance abuse treatment program (the Agency for Community Treatment Services, Inc. [ACTS]). Co-located in the facility will be law enforcement juvenile booking functions, the delinquency intake functions of the Florida DHRS, dropout prevention services of the Hillsborough County School Board, community mental health services, intake staff of the status offender intake program of the Hillsborough County Department of Children's Services (DCS), and the truancy programs of the Tampa Police Department and the Hillsborough County Sheriff's Department. The facility will be located above and supported by the presence of ACTS' 20-bed, 24-hour-a-day adolescent detoxification and stabilization program.

Critical to the successful operation of the centralized receiving unit is the establishment of an *Adolescent Agency Coordinating Work Group*. This group, which will include representatives of key agencies and treatment programs, will identify problems in addressing the needs of youths with alcohol/other drug use or mental health difficulties and develop solutions to them and will create common intake (preliminary screening) and in-depth assessment instruments.

There is also a need to improve the linkages and coordination among various community agencies dealing with high-risk youths—including law enforcement, the courts, schools, human service agencies, and treatment programs. Particular need exists for greater coordination between schools and vocational and employment resources and services addressing the substance abuse and mental health needs of these youths and their families. Such an effort would reduce duplication of effort, reduce barriers to treatment, and respond to these youths in a holistic manner. Greater integration of community agencies would smooth the transition of these youths from program to program and reduce the likelihood that youths will slip through the gaps in the community support system. The Adolescent Agency Coordinating Work Group will make a constructive contribution to these issues.

Developing Preliminary Screening
and In-Depth Assessment Instrument Packages

A major task of the Work Group will involve assisting in the development of preliminary screening and in-depth instrument packages. A subcommittee of the Work Group will coordinate the development of preliminary screening and in-depth assessment instrument packages for use uniformly and systematically by staff in evaluating youths entering the centralized receiving facility. Diversity in the protocols that are used by service agencies prevents meaningful comparison of youths' problems, severity levels, and needs for services.

The preliminary screening and in-depth instrument packages need to be reasonably brief and feasible to administer in the context of the flow rate of youths into the centralized receiving facility and staff time and resources and to strengthen clinical judgment by identifying problem severity levels.

Preliminary Screening Package. On admission to the centralized receiving facility, it is planned that the following information will be collected:

1. Demographic: age, gender, ethnicity, and the SES of the youths' families.

2. Legal history: (a) a record of the youths' contacts with the juvenile court and (b) a record of agency contact as a victim of neglect or physical or sexual abuse/victimization.

3. Self-reported alcohol/other drug use: recency, lifetime, and past-year frequency of use of alcohol, marijuana/hashish, inhalants, LSD or other hallucinogens, cocaine, heroin, other drugs (e.g., MPTP, "China White,"), and the nonmedical use of sedatives, tranquilizers, stimulants, and analgesics.

4. Breathalyzer test and urine test results: the results of breathalyzer tests probing the recent use of alcohol and EMIT® urine tests probing for the recent use of cannabinoids, cocaine (these two drugs are the most frequently identified in urine testing of youths entering the juvenile justice system in Tampa [Dembo, Williams, Wish et al., 1990; Dembo et al., 1991]), amphetamines, and opiates will be completed. The threshold for a positive on the breathalyzer test will be 0.06 blood alcohol level—the legal level of impairment. The threshold for a positive for cannabinoids (THC), cocaine, opiates, and amphetamines will be in line with American Correctional

Association and Institute for Behavior and Health, Inc. guidelines (1991). On-site urine testing involving a Syva ETS R Plus System machine will be completed by staff trained by the Syva Company.

5. Problems in the previously noted 10 functional areas probed by the POSIT (National Institute on Drug Abuse [NIDA], 1991a).

6. A brief locator form: names, addresses, and telephone numbers of relatives and friends who are likely to know the whereabouts of the youth in the future.

In-Depth Assessment Instrument Package. Efforts will be made to ensure that youths who preliminary screening identifies as having alcohol/other drug abuse or mental health problems receive in-depth assessments. The in-depth instruments will consist of protocols included in the AARS, CAB (NIDA, 1991a), or comparable public domain (and, therefore, less costly) instruments. To the degree possible, family members will be included in the assessment process. The following domains will be probed:

1. Medical history: family member alcohol/other drug use or other medical problems, youth's medical history (illnesses/conditions, contagious diseases, physical impairments/deficiencies, neurological conditions).

2. Alcohol/other drug use: consequences of use; alcohol/other drug abuse treatment history. Urine specimens will be obtained from youths refusing to provide same at the time of their preliminary screening and analyzed by the EMIT® procedure. There will be an adequate surveillance window for detecting the recent use of cannabinoids, cocaine, amphetamines, and opiates.

3. A psychosocial history will be completed on each youth using a modified version of the Prototype Screening/Triage Form for Juvenile Detention Centers developed by the senior author and his associates (National Association of State Alcohol and Drug Abuse Directors [NASADAD], 1991); an earlier version of this form is currently being administered to youths entering the Florida juvenile justice system. (A copy of this form is available from the senior author on request.)

4. HIV infection-transmission risk behavior: probed by a modified version of the Risk Behavior Assessment Questionnaire (NIDA, 1991b). Testing for HIV will be free for youths and their significant others. Blood will be drawn for HIV testing by nurses at the receiving facility and analyzed at a state laboratory.

5. Emotional/psychological functioning problems: Brief Symptom Inventory (BSI) (Derogatis & Melisaratos, 1983); psychiatric problem behavior history; self-derogation (Kaplan, 1980).

6. Educational problems: scholastic aptitude test scores, school grades, retention in grade, placement in a special or remedial education program, attendance records, school disciplinary problems (e.g., suspension from school), dropping out of school (supplied by a Hillsborough County school system computer terminal at the receiving facility).

7. Friends' alcohol/other drug use and delinquent behavior.

8. Self-reported involvement in delinquency/crime and gang membership/participation.

9. Family member reporting of the youth's problem behavior in the above areas (Quay & Peterson, 1987).

Intervention

It is important to refer youths who are identified as having a potential substance abuse or mental health problem for additional assessment and, if indicated, placement in needed services. A number of approaches and strategies are discussed in this section.

Early Intervention

Klitzner and his associates (Klitzner, Fisher, Stewart, & Gilbert, 1991) completed a valuable survey of early intervention strategies. Among the problems they identified is a lack of consensus on the definition of early intervention, and how it differs from prevention or treatment. Klitzner et al (1991, pp. 8-9) urge that early intervention services be directed to individuals/groups (1) whose use of alcohol/other drugs puts them at high risk of negative consequences, (2) whose use of alcohol/other drugs has resulted in clinically significant dysfunction or consequences, and (3) who exhibit particular problem behaviors that are precursors to alcohol/other drug problems (e.g., youths failing at school).

Klitzner et al. (1991) found relatively few preadjudication or postadjudication early intervention programs in juvenile justice settings; and most of the identified programs had not been formally evaluated. One promising preadjudication program—the Family Education Program, operated by the Prevention and Intervention Center for Alcohol and Drug Abuse (PICADA) in Madison, Wisconsin—had been subject to preliminary outcome evaluation. PICADA is a diversion program, providing a number of intervention services, including screening, assessment, education and referrals to adolescents and their families. The goals of the program are to (1) increase knowledge about alcohol/other drugs, (2) increase clients' ability to identify and communicate attitudes about alcohol/other drugs, (3) promote attitude change, (4) increase clients' abilities to more accurately assess their substance use/abuse, and (5) increase clients' willingness to accept PICADA's referrals. Program activities include family attendance at an educational lecture and family and adolescent participation in screening for alcohol/other drug abuse problems. A preliminary evaluation, involving pre- and post-test measurements in the absence of a control or comparison group, indicated the program led to intended changes in knowledge, attitudes and feelings regarding substance use when assessed shortly after program participation.

In terms of postadjudication strategies, Hawkins and his colleagues (Hawkins, Jenson, Catalano, & Wells, 1986) assessed the effectiveness of a cognitive-behavioral skills training program among institutionalized juveniles in reducing recidivism and substance abuse. The program was conducted in two phases: (1) a 10-week first phase involving group sessions to develop skills in consequential thinking, self-control, avoiding trouble, social networking, problem-solving negotiation and compliance, and drug and alcohol refusal—and assignment to a case manager; (2) continued contact with the case manager for 6 months following release from the institution. During this aftercare phase, the case manager facilitated reintegration into the family or alternative placement, assisted in the practice of skills, and helped in enrollment in school or finding a job. Results of this experimental study were promising. Short-term improvement in social skills were evidenced in role-playing situations as a result of the cognitive-behavioral skills training.

Klitzner et al.'s (1991) work highlights the need to identify, catalog, and describe the variety of early intervention programs in the juvenile justice system. They stress the need for a nosology and nomenclature for adolescent substance-related problems. Further, improvements in understanding the etiology of these problems are needed, so that more effective and theoretically informed programs can be developed.

Other Early Intervention Approaches for At-Risk Youth. A most effective reduction of drug use and delinquency/crime lies in early intervention. The nature and quality of family life has an influence on youths' drug use and other delinquent behavior. Fragmented and dysfunctional families have high rates of substance misuse and other problem behavior (Garbarino & Gilliam, 1980). Tampa study youths had high rates of neglect, physical abuse, or sexual victimization.

Not all physical abuse or sexual victimization of children occurs in their homes. However, in many cases these traumatizing experiences do take place in the youths' households. In these cases, children and their families should receive early, long-term, deep-reaching, and intensive intervention. Where indicated, children should be separated from these families and raised in more wholesome environments.

Unfortunately, the juvenile justice system generally does not become concerned over the behavior of a youth until he or she has appeared in court several times. At this point, the youngster has probably failed in a number of informal and loosely structured programs and has developed serious problems in school and delinquent behavior, including the use of various drugs. Many have developed a delinquent life-style, and it is often too late to turn them around (Guidry, 1991).

Resources should be placed in assessing and providing needed services to youths and their families at the earliest (ideally the first) point of contact with the juvenile justice system. Services provided at this point are more likely to be effective and cost-efficient than those targeted to youths after repeated contact with the juvenile courts.

A centralized receiving facility represents a useful setting to engage in early intervention efforts. Youth in custody brought to the Tampa receiving facility will fall into three major legal categories: youth referred for delinquent acts; runaway youth, youth in violation of truancy laws, or ungovernable youth (i.e., status offenders); and youth who are perceived by law enforcement to be at risk of harming themselves or others because of intoxication, their mental status, or the lack of appropriate care and supervision. Some youths will be coming to the attention of authorities for the first time; others will have had previous contact with the state's delinquency and/or dependency systems.

It is anticipated that youths charged with serious delinquency offenses will be brought to the receiving facility for formal processing. Youth who commit minor law violations will be handled informally at the discretion of the intervening officer—without the filing of a delinquency petition.

Youth who commit status offenses or Children (or Families) in Need of Services (CINS/FINS), constitute a key target group for early intervention efforts. Few services have been targeted to this population. As a result, to access needed services such youth have historically had to penetrate the dependency or delinquency systems. The receiving facility will provide one avenue for early intervention with this population. For example, the facility will combine the truancy programs of the Tampa Police Department and the Hillsborough County Sheriff's Office and will include a diagnostic classroom. Youth taken into custody for truancy will participate in educational programming for the remainder of that day and will undergo a review of their school performance and educational skills. A report of their participation and skills will be sent to their respective schools. In addition, Hillsborough County DCS CINS/FINS Intake Unit staff co-located in the facility will provide linkage to ongoing case management and counseling services. For habitually truant youth, the receiving facility will serve as a focal point for multi-agency staffings to bring the family, the school system, and service providers together to develop strategies to secure/provide needed assistance. Youth with substance abuse or mental health services will be linked to these services.

Protective custody provides a public safety authority law enforcement to secure appropriate care and protection for persons unable to care for themselves. The receiving facility will back up law enforcement's protective custody efforts with youth by serving as a safe place (with adequate supervision) while appropriate agency staff arrange for more substantive care. Intoxicated youth will be placed downstairs until stabilized. Emotionally disturbed youth will have access to on-site mental health staff and to a mobile crisis team. Youth who lack adequate supervision will be served by DHRS dependency staff.

Providing Quality Treatment

Research has repeatedly found that criminal behavior increases following addiction, and that arrests for drug offenses and property offenses decline with decreasing frequency of drug use (Anglin & Speckart, 1988). These results stress the value of treatment in reducing crime among drug-dependent persons.

There is growing evidence that treatment for drug dependence and related psychosocial difficulties can be effective in reducing criminality. Programs that are based on social learning theories are particularly effective among drug-involved persons who have developed their drug use life-style over a period of years (DeLeon & Ziegenfuss, 1986; Wexler & Williams, 1986). Recent treatment evaluation studies show clear evidence regarding the efficacy and cost-effectiveness of treatment, supplying a strong argument for continuing government support of these efforts (see, e.g., Hubbard et al., 1989; Pickens, Leukefeld, & Schuster, 1991).

Unfortunately, there is a serious lack in substance abuse treatment services—especially for youths (Pickens, Leukefeld, & Schuster, 1991). A recent study of children in custody in 1987 (Thornberry, Tolnay, Flanagan, & Glynn, 1991) found treatment for drug offenders was available in less than 40% of the 3,000 public and private juvenile detention, correctional, and shelter facilities across the United States. Even when some services are available, they may not be sufficient. Very few youths in the Tampa longitudinal study needing treatment to address their substance-use difficulties received such help for any length of time during the follow-up period. In addition, there were very few treatment program slots for adolescents in the community—particularly those in the public sector (Dembo, Williams, Schmeidler, Getreu et al., 1991).

What Is Known About Juvenile Alcohol/Other Drug Abuse Treatment?

As a recent Institute of Medicine report on drug treatment (Gerstein & Harwood, 1990) discusses, the goals of treatment are multiple and include the following: (1) reduce individuals' drug use and the overall demand for illicit drugs, (2) reduce street crime, (3) change users' personal values, (4) develop educational or vocational capabilities, (5) restore or increase employment or productivity, and (6) improve the users' overall health, psychological functioning, and family life. However, an informed perspective on juvenile alcohol/other drug abuse needs to be developed and appropriate treatment strategies implemented and evaluated for this critical target group. An informed perspective on youth alcohol/other drug abuse needs to appreciate the following facts: (1) there is no widely accepted definition of "abuse" in juveniles; (2) the course of youth alcohol/other drug abuse is often different from that of adults; (3) the severity of youth alcohol/other drug use problems needs to take the factor of age into account; and (4) troubled youths tend to have multiple problems—their alcohol/other drug use may not be primary.

What do we know about youth alcohol/other drug abuse treatment and its impact? A recent survey of the field by Catalano, Hawkins, Wells, Miller, and Brewer (1990-1991) indicates that (a) some treatment is better than no treatment; (b) post-treatment relapse rates are high (35% to 85%—depending on the definition of relapse); (c) few comparisons of treatment method have consistently demonstrated the superiority of one method over another—however, there is some indication that the therapeutic community (TC) (DeLeon & Ziegenfuss, 1986) is particularly effective for youths and young adults of the urban underclass who have been the driving force behind the recent, dramatic growth in the number of persons on probation, on parole, in jail, detention centers, or prison (see Wexler & Williams, 1986); and (d) additional controlled studies of adolescent treatment are needed.

There is particular need to identify the factors associated with post-treatment relapse among treated clients, and to design program components to reduce factors associated with higher relapse rates and increase factors associated with lower relapse rates. Such a risk-oriented approach has a lot of merit (Hawkins, Catalano, & Miller, in press). Lipton (1989) has applied this concept to the recovery experience (although developed from experience with adults, these ideas are germane to youths). Critical to his theory of rehabilitation are the ideas that (1) there are certain personal characteristics (or impedimenta—e.g., inadequacy, ill-equipped in social skills, vocational maladjustment, antisocial attitudes) that impede an individual's ability to function at a generally acceptable level in one or more basic social areas; (2) the difficulty in performing at a generally acceptable level in such areas significantly contributes to returning to criminal conduct; and (3) treatment should be directed at overcoming these personal characteristics.

The Institute of Medicine report (Gerstein & Harwood, 1990) reviews five major types of treatment programs for adults. These are summarized in Table 6.1. These treatment modalities have been adapted for youths. However, it is important to recognize that adolescent substance abusers differ from adult abusers and require tailored treatment strategies. A number of important differences have been observed between adolescents and adults in residential treatment. Compared to adults, adolescents (1) use drugs at an earlier age, (2) have less involvement with opiates, shorter abuse histories, and more involvement in alcohol, marijuana, and multiple drug use (DeLeon & Deitch, 1987), (3) have a greater incidence of family deviance and experience of past psychological treatment, (4) tend to be more fascinated with the drug-related life-style and less fatigued with failure and the negative social consequences of their drug use, (5) have an unrealistic sense of their invulnerability, and (6) require a greater emphasis on addressing educational needs and parental/family support in the treatment process.

Factors Relating to Relapse Among Youths. There are variations in the definition of the term *relapse.* Relapse has been defined as a discrete event occurring with the single use of a drug or as a process developing over time (Wesson, Havassy, & Smith, 1986). When defined as a discrete event,

Table 6.1 Major Drug Abuse Treatment Modalities for Adults

Treatment Modality	Description	Demonstrated Effectiveness
Methadone maintenance	Treatment for extended dependence on opiates (usually heroin). Sufficient daily dose of methadone hydrochloride yields a very stable metabolic level of the drug. Stabilized clients are amendable to counseling, environmental changes, and other social services to move them to more socially acceptable life-styles.	Methadone maintained clients have better outcomes in terms of illicit drug use and other criminal behavior than when not treated or detoxified and released or when methadone is tapered down and terminated. Clients who stay in treatment longer have better outcomes than clients with shorter treatment courses.
Therapeutic communities (TCs)	Residential programs (generally involving 9-12 month stays) phasing into independent residence with contact for a variable period. TCs are highly structured, relying on multidisciplinary staffing—including recovering graduates.	TC clients demonstrate better behavior (drug use, criminal activity, social productivity) during treatment and after discharge than before admission and better outcomes than individuals who contacted programs but did not enter treatment or who dropped out of treatment. Treatment length important.
Outpatient nonmethadone programs	Programs differ in treatment processes, philosophies and staffing. Clients generally not opiate dependent and tend to have less serious criminal histories than methadone or TC clients. Programs generally provide 1-2 visits per week for individual or group therapy/counseling for an average of 6 months.	Clients show better performance during and following treatment than before treatment and better outcomes than clients contacting but not entering programs or program dropouts. Outcome at follow-up positively related to length of stay in care.
Chemical dependency (CD) programs	Residential or inpatient programs of 3-6 weeks duration, followed by 2 years of attending self-help groups or a week outpatient therapy group. CD programs are based on an AA (12-step) model of change and the belief that vulnerability to dependence is a permanent but controllable disability. Total abstinence and life-style change are its goals.	The few studies that have been completed indicate that clients whose primary problem involves alcohol have better outcomes than clients who are primarily dependent on other drugs.
Correctional treatment programs	A small number of TCs have become well established in prison settings and have strong linkages to community-based treatment programs.	Prospective studies indicate prison TCs can reduce treated group's rate of rearrest by a worthwhile margin. Length of time in treatment is a key factor in posttreatment success.

SOURCE: D. R. Gerstein & H. J. Harwood (Eds.), *Treating Drug Problems*, Washington, DC: National Academy Press, 1990. Excerpted with permission from *Treating Drug Problems*,

distinction is usually made between first use of the primary drug of abuse or first use of another psychoactive drug. Return to the primary drug holds clear potential for return to abuse (Hubbard & Marsden, 1986); at the same time, drug substitution may also lead to compulsive use of the primary drug. However defined, Catalano et al. (1990-1991) have identified a number of background or pretreatment, during-treatment, and post-treatment factors associated with relapse or failure to complete treatment:

1. *Background or Pretreatment* factors: (1) *Race:* being Caucasian appears to be related to less drug use during treatment and slightly less frequent post-treatment drug use. Race has not been found to be related to completing treatment; (2) *Drug Use:* the younger the age of onset, the more serious the primary drug of abuse and the abuse of multiple drugs is related to not completing treatment; (3) *Criminality:* the amount of lifetime criminal involvement is related negatively to post-treatment outcome; (4) *Educational Level:* this is related positively to completion of treatment and post-treatment outcome.

2. *During-Treatment* factors: (1) *Length of Time in Treatment:* this is related positively to treatment outcome; (2) *Voluntary versus Mandated Treatment Entry:* mandated (often legal sanction) clients fare better than one might expect in completing treatment and in post-treatment outcome—the key is length of treatment (perceived choice regarding treatment is also predictive of positive during- and post-treatment outcomes); (3) *Staff Characteristics:* quality staff, who establish positive role relationships with clients, can improve treatment outcome; (4) *Involvement of Family/Parents in Treatment:* this is positively related to program completion.

3. *Post-treatment* factors: (1) *Thoughts and Feelings About Drugs and Drug Cravings:* these are related negatively to post-treatment outcome; (2) *Involvement in Productive Activities:* activities such as school or work are related positively to post-treatment outcome; (3) *Few and Less Satisfactory Active Leisure Activities:* these are related positively to relapse.

These clusters of factors associated with relapse or failure to complete treatment have important implications for the development of more effective programs. First, pretreatment factors tend to be fixed entities; there is little a treatment program can do to manipulate these factors with a view to reducing post-treatment relapse (Catalano, Wells, Jenson, & Hawkins, in press). Second, in regard to treatment modality, available studies indicate that adolescents reduce their involvement in the use of opiates and non-opiates but not marijuana and alcohol—which are the most often used substances (Sells & Simpson, 1979). Third, drawing on treatment outcome studies involving adults, and the few such inquiries involving youths, pretreatment and during treatment factors combined account for a smaller amount of the variance in post-treatment relapse than post-treatment experiences (Catalano et al., in press). Hence, addressing factors placing youths at risk of relapse while they are in treatment, program transition, or on aftercare is a critical issue to long-term program success. The post-treatment success factors highlight the importance of involving youths in productive roles, providing an environment supporting positive change initiated in treatment, and reducing youths' alcohol/other drug use.

Improving the effectiveness of drug abuse treatment is a critical need and is one of the primary priorities of NIDA. A recent NIDA Five-Year Plan (1992) highlights several priority areas: (1) large-scale, multiple-program treatment evaluation research every 5 years to produce current information on different treatment modalities and their effectiveness for different client populations, (2) research to improve treatment engagement and retention, (3) the development and pilot testing of new treatment interventions—especially new psychotherapies and behavioral therapies, (4) the development and validation of therapy-specific diagnostic procedures—involving better methods of categorizing and defining drug abuse syndromes to be addressed by specific treatments, (5) studies of untreated drug-dependent persons as well as individuals in treatment, (6) research on specific treatment modalities and treatment techniques and strategies—involving controlled clinical trials of appropriately specified and consistently delivered interventions, (7) research on neurobiological, intrapersonal, and environmental factors relating to program entry, engagement, remission, and relapse and on the role played by social networks in these processes, and (8) research to adapt or develop culturally appropriate treatments for racial and ethnic minority groups, women, children, and adolescents, and individuals involved in the criminal justice system. The carrying out of this agenda, together with the results of a recently funded multi-site, longitudinal study of drug abuse treatment of adolescents, promises to have a significant impact on the field.

The Office of Treatment Improvement (OTI) is also focusing attention on the treatment needs of substance-abusing adolescents. OTI has established national consensus panels for (a) the screening and assessment of substance-abusing adolescents and (b) the treatment of substance-abusing adolescents. Among the purposes of these panels is to assess the current state of knowledge in each of these areas, to establish common definitions, standards, and criteria, and to produce manuals and protocols for use by practitioners. Special attention is being given to the needs of youths involved in the justice system.

Aftercare

Aftercare services are a vital link in the service continuum. Although seriously needed, these services are infrequent, underdeveloped, and tend to be narrowly focused on single problem areas—such as school placement or peer networks (Armstrong, 1991). They are perhaps the weakest link in the program service chain. It is counterproductive to treat youths in residential settings, only to return them unassisted to environments that supported their problem behavior in the past (Altschuler & Armstrong, 1991; Catalano et al., in press).

Other factors have increased interest in juvenile aftercare programs. In recent years, youths displaying troubled behavior in the community have been placed in large and frequently crowded residential facilities. These facilities are often intimidating and otherwise stressful environments, where youths' educational and other rehabilitative needs are often ignored or insufficiently addressed. Evidence has been accumulating that these expensive programs serve primarily to isolate youths from the general society, are ineffective, and have no significant impact on recidivism (Altschuler & Armstrong, 1991; Greenwood & Zimring, 1985; U.S. Department of Justice, 1987).

Under the support of the Office of Juvenile Justice and Delinquency Prevention (OJJDP), Altschuler and Armstrong (1991) completed an important review of intensive community-based aftercare programs. Their work included the following steps: (1) a review of relevant theoretical, research, and service program literature; (2) a mail survey of state officials; (3) a telephone survey of directors of aftercare programs considered innovative or promising by the surveyed state officials; and, based on information collected in steps 1, 2 and 3, (4) visits to 20 different programs in Arizona, Colorado, Florida, Maryland, and Pennsylvania. A number of important findings and conclusions emerged from this extensive project:

1. A relatively small proportion of the literature on aftercare programs focuses on programs for juveniles; most of the literature tends to be descriptive, anecdotal, and impressionistic, rather than evaluative and empirical; most evaluation studies involve such nonexperimental designs as case

studies. This literature does not provide a firm basis for developing particular approaches and practices for use in different settings.

2. In many programs, the basic concept and rationale for the design of the program and its operations are not clearly articulated, consistently and logically explained, and implemented in program activities. To address this need, the authors adopt an integrated control-strain social learning theory model as a foundation for an Intensive Aftercare Supervision (IAS) model that involves five underlying principles: (1) preparing youth for progressively increased responsibility and freedom; (2) facilitating youth-community interaction and involvement; (3) working with the youth and targeted community support systems; (4) developing new resources, supports, and opportunities where needed; and (5) monitoring and testing youths and the community on their ability to deal with one another productively.

3. Aftercare programs should include a comprehensive system of services, use graduated sanctions, and place emphasis on incentives and positive reinforcements.

4. The site visits to programs collected descriptive information in a number of important areas (e.g., history, background, and overall context of the aftercare program, organization/structure, number of clients, program philosophy and content). However, Altschuler and Armstrong (1991, p. 180) note that few of the programs had ever "been even haphazardly evaluated . . . [making] . . . it impossible to say with any precision whether the programs were in fact successful."

If behavior change influenced by treatment programs is to be lasting, it needs to be supported following the youths' reentry into the community. The youths often return to stressful environmental circumstances, including austere economic conditions, social or family disorganization, deviant peers, and other social pressures. These stressors, together with the lack of educational or vocational skills and other problems they may be experiencing, present formidable challenges to their involvement in conventional activities. Aftercare programs need to include elements that deal quickly with relapse to substance use, responding to these relapses in a manner that discourages continued drug use and supports a return to abstinence (Catalano et al., in press). It is also important that aftercare programs maintain contact with youth during their transition from institutional to aftercare services—perhaps involving continuity of staff across institutional-community program placement (Altschuler & Armstrong, 1991).

Long-Term Continuity of Care

Juvenile justice agencies tend to have an interest in troubled youth that is episodic. Interest centers around the behavioral reason for the youth's contact with the system and the judicially imposed consequences of that behavior. Once the period of program involvement ends, agency interest in the youth's case ceases—unless he or she comes to the attention of a juvenile justice agency again.

However, this manner of responding to troubled youths fails to incorporate the experience that many youths' problemed lives can be traced to their early years and that their problems become more serious as they proceed through adolescence. The delinquent behavior of these youths frequently reflects a chronic involvement in personally and socially damaging activities (Farrington & West, 1990; Robins & Ratcliff, 1978-1979).

We must give serious consideration to providing long-term assistance to seriously troubled youths. For example, in treating a person for dysfunctional drug use, it is important to appreciate that altering a drug-dependent existence is often a prolonged process involving periodic relapses to drug use. Repeated interventions over a protracted period, which are reinforced by improvements in the social, vocational, and educational skill levels of the individuals in treatment, are most likely to be successful (NIDA, 1992; Pickens, Leukefeld, & Schuster, 1991). Our service delivery systems, and associated support services, must accommodate themselves to this need for repeated intervention.

We must involve troubled youths (many of whom will pursue law-violating activities into adulthood) and, where indicated, their families in long-term, intensive service and supervision programs to remedy their difficulties that find expression in delinquency/crime. Investing in these youth now (particularly the small proportion of youth who are heavily involved in delinquency) will reduce the personal and social harm they will cause themselves and their families and the long-term burden they will present to our country's educational, economic, judicial, and correctional system resources.

CONCLUSIONS

A national commitment to help troubled youths is needed to reduce their substance abuse and delinquency. Adequate resources are needed for this effort to succeed. Youths involved in the juvenile justice system, especially those with alcohol/other drug abuse or mental health problems, consume a large and growing amount of state resources as they grow older; this issue is of critical national concern.

The facts that 52% of the youths in the Tampa longitudinal study had already entered the Florida DOC within 3½ years following their initial interviews, that high rates of recidivism exist for young parolees (U.S. Department of Justice, 1987) and other prisoners (U.S. Department of Justice, 1989), and that many middle-aged prisoners in state prisons can trace their criminal careers to adolescence (U.S. Dept. of Justice, 1983c) stress the importance of investing resources to remedy youths' alcohol/other drug abuse, delinquency, and other problemed behavior. Relatedly, official record data on Tampa study youths for the 3½ years following their initial interviews indicated that $4.4 million in Florida public funds (an average of $11,000 per youth) were spent to keep them in detention centers, jail, and department of corrections facilities—locations where they received little or no treatment.

Beyond these economic estimates is the poignancy of young lives lost to useful purpose and the pain and tragedy this failure causes these youths, their families, and the community. The issues are clear. Do we have the dedication of purpose to rise to the challenge they present?

REFERENCES

Altschuler, D. M., & Armstrong, T. L. (1991). *Intensive community-based aftercare prototype: Policies and procedures.* Submitted to the Office of Juvenile Justice and Delinquency Prevention, U.S. Department of Justice.

American Correctional Association and Institute for Behavior and Health, Inc. (1991). *Drug testing of juvenile detainees.* Washington, DC: Office of Juvenile Justice and Delinquency Prevention, U.S. Department of Justice.

Anglin, M. D., & Speckart, G. (1988). Narcotics use and crime: A multisample, multimethod analysis. *Criminology, 26,* 197-233.

Armstrong, T. L. (Ed.). (1991). *Intensive interventions with high-risk youths: Promising approaches in juvenile probation and parole.* Monsey, NY: Criminal Justice Press.

Catalano, R. F., Hawkins, J. D., Wells, E. A., Miller, J., & Brewer, D. (1990-1991). Evaluation of the effectiveness of adolescent drug abuse treatment, assessment of risks for relapse, and promising approaches for relapse prevention. *The International Journal of the Addictions, 25,* 1085-1140.

Catalano, R. F., Wells, E. A., Jenson, J. M., & Hawkins, J. D. (in press). Aftercare services for drug-using adjudicated youth in residential settings. *Social Service Review.*

Cernkovich, S. A., & Giordano, P. C. (1987). Family relationships and delinquency. *Criminology, 25,* 295-321.

DeLeon, G., & Deitch, D. (1987). Treatment of the adolescent substance abuser in a therapeutic community. In A. S. Friedman & G. M. Beschner (Eds.), *Treatment services for adolescent substance abusers.* Rockville, MD: National Institute on Drug Abuse.

DeLeon, G., & Ziegenfuss, J. T., Jr. (Eds.). (1986). *Therapeutic communities for addictions: Readings in theory, research and practice.* Springfield, IL: Charles C Thomas.

Dembo, R., Dertke, M., Borders, S., Washburn, M., & Schmeidler, J. (1988). The relationship between physical and sexual abuse and tobacco, alcohol and illicit drug use among youths in a juvenile detention center. *International Journal of the Addictions, 23,* 357-378.

Dembo, R., Washburn, M., Broskowski, A., Getreu, A., & Berry, E. (1986, March). Development and evaluation of an innovative approach to identify and engage troubled youths in mental health and substance abuse treatment services at entry into secure detention. Paper presented at the annual meeting of the Academy of Criminal Justice Sciences, Orlando, FL.

Dembo, R., Washburn, M., Wish, E. D., Schmeidler, J., Getreu, A., Berry, E., Williams, L., & Blount, W. R. (1987). Further examination of the association between heavy marijuana use and crime among youths entering a juvenile detention center. *Journal of Psychoactive Drugs, 19,* 361-373.

Dembo, R., Williams, L., Berry, E., Getreu, A., Washburn, W., Wish, E. D., & Schmeidler, J. (1990). Examination of the relationships among drug use, emotional/psychological problems and crime among youths entering a juvenile detention center. *International Journal of Addictions, 25,* 1301-1340.

Dembo, R., Williams, L., Getreu, A., Schmeidler, J., & Wish, E. D. (1990). *Setting up a screening/triage unit at a juvenile detention center.* Tampa, FL: University of South Florida, Department of Criminology.

Dembo, R., Williams, L., La Voie, L., Berry, E., Getreu, A., Wish, E. D., Schmeidler, J., & Washburn, M. (1989). Physical abuse, sexual victimization and illicit drug use: Replication of a structural analysis among a new sample of high risk youths. *Violence and Victims, 4:*121-138.

Dembo, R., Williams, L., La Voie, L., Getreu, A., Berry, E., Genung, L., Schmeidler, J., Wish, E. D., & Kern, J. (1990). A longitudinal study of the relationships among alcohol use, marijuana/hashish use, cocaine use and emotional/psychological functioning problems in a cohort of high risk youths. *International Journal of the Addictions, 25:*1341-1382.

Dembo, R., Williams, L., Schmeidler, J., & Christensen, C. (in press). Recidivism in a cohort of juvenile detainees: A 3½ year follow-up. *International Journal of the Addictions.*

Dembo, R., Williams, L., Schmeidler, J., Getreu, A., Berry, E., Genung, L. Wish, E. D., & La Voie, L. (1991). A longitudinal study of the relationships among marijuana/hashish use, cocaine use and delinquency in a cohort of high risk youths. *Journal of Drug Issues, 21,* 271-312.

Dembo, R., Williams, L., Schmeidler, J., & Howitt, D. (1991). *Tough cases: School outreach for at-risk youth.* Washington, DC: U.S. Department of Education, Office of the Assistant Secretary for Educational Research and Improvement.

Dembo, R., Williams, L., Wish, E. D., & Schmeidler, J. (1990). *Urine testing of detained juveniles to identify high-risk youth.* Washington, DC: U.S. Department of Justice.

Dembo, R., Williams, L., Wothke, W., Schmeidler, J., & Brown, C. H. (in press). The role of family factors, physical abuse, and sexual victimization experiences in high risk youths' alcohol and other drug use and delinquency: A longitudinal model. *Violence and Victims.*

Derogatis, L. R., & Melisaratos, N. (1983). The brief symptom inventory: An introductory report. *Psychological Medicine, 13,* 595-605.

Elliott, D. S., & Huizinga, D. (1984). *The relationship between delinquent behavior and ADM problems.* Boulder, CO: Behavioral Research Institute.

Elliott, D. S., Huizinga, D., & Ageton, S. S. (1985). *Explaining delinquency and drug use.* Beverly Hills: Sage.

Elliott, D. S., Huizinga, D., & Menard, S. (1989). *Multiple problem youth.* New York: Springer-Verlag.

Farrington, D. P., & West, D. J. (1990). The Cambridge study in delinquent development: A long-term follow-up of 411 London males. In H. J. Kerner & G. Kaiser (Eds.), *Criminality: Personality, behavior and life history.* New York: Springer-Verlag.

Garbarino, J., & Gilliam, G. (1980). *Understanding abusive families.* Lexington, MA: Lexington Books.

Gerstein, D. R., & Harwood, H. J. (1990). *Treating drug problems. Vol. 1 (Summary): A study of the evolution and financing of public and private drug treatment systems.* Washington, DC: National Academy Press.

Gottfredson, G. D. (1988). American education—American delinquency. (National Center for Juvenile Justice, Pittsburgh.) *Today's Delinquent, 6,* 5-70.

Greenwood, P. W., & Zimring, F. E. (1985). *One more chance: The pursuit of promising intervention strategies for chronic delinquent offenders.* Santa Monica, CA: Rand.

Guidry, J. (1991, June 18). Cloak of evil not worn by adults alone. *Tampa Tribune* (Florida).

Hawkins, J. D., Catalano, R. F., & Miller, J. Y. (in press). Risk and protective factors for alcohol and other drug problems in adolescence and early adulthood: Implications for substance abuse prevention. *Psychological Bulletin.*

Hawkins, J. D., Jenson, J. M., Catalano, R. F., & Wells, E. A. (1986). Effects of a skills training intervention with juvenile delinquents. *Research on Social Work Practice.* Newbury Park, CA: Sage.

Hawkins, J. D., & Lishner, D. M. (1987). Schooling and delinquency. In Elmer H. Johnson (Ed.), *Handbook on crime and delinquency prevention* (179-221). Westport, CT: Greenwood Press.

Hubbard, R. L., & Marsden, M. E. (1986). Relapse to use of heroin, cocaine, and other drugs in the first year after treatment. In E. R. Rahdert & J. Grabowski (Eds.), *Adolescent drug abuse. Analyses of treatment research* (NIDA Research Monograph DHHS ADM 88-1523). Rockville, MD: National Institute on Drug Abuse.

Hubbard, R. L., Marsden, M. E., Rachal, J. V., Harwood, H. J., Cavanaugh, E. R., & Ginzburg, H. M. (1989). *Drug abuse treatment. A national study of effectiveness.* Chapel Hill, NC: The University of North Carolina Press.

Inciardi, J. A., & Pottieger, A. E. (1991). Kids, crack, and crime. *Journal of Drug Issues, 21,* 257-270.

Inciardi, J. A., Pottieger, A. E., Forney, M. A., Chitwood, D. D., & McBride, D. C. (1991). Prostitution, IV drug use, and sex-for-crack exchanges among serious delinquents: Risks for HIV infection. *Criminology, 29,* 221-235.

Jessor, R., & Jessor, A. L. (1977). *Problem behavior and psychological development: A longitudinal study of youth.* New York: Academic Press.

Kandel, D. B. (1975). Stages in adolescent involvement in drug use. *Science, 190,* 912-914.

Kandel, D. B., Simcha-Fagan, O., & Davies, M. (1986). Risk factors for delinquency and illicit drug use from adolescence to young adulthood. *Journal of Drug Issues, 16,* 67-90.

Kaplan, H. B. (1980). *Deviant behavior in defense of self.* New York: Academic Press.

Klitzner, M., Fisher, D., Stewart, K., & Gilbert, S. (1991). *Report to the Robert Wood Johnson Foundation on strategies for early intervention with children and youth to avoid abuse of addictive substances.* Bethesda, MD: Pacific Institute for Research and Evaluation.

Laub, J. H., & Sampson, R. J. (1988). Unraveling families and delinquency: A reanalysis of the Gluecks' data. *Criminology, 26,* 355-380.

Lazar, I., Darlington, R., Murray, H., Royce, J., & Snipper, A. (1982). Lasting effects of early education: A report from the consortium for longitudinal studies. *Monographs of the Society for Research in Child Development,* Serial No. *195, 47,* 2-3.

Lewis, D. O., Lovely, R., Yeager, C., & Famina, D. D. (1989). Toward a theory of the genesis of violence: A follow-up study of delinquents. *Journal of the American Academy of Child and Adolescent Psychiatry, 28,* 431-436.

Lipton, D. S. (1989). *The theory of rehabilitation as applied to addict offenders.* New York: Narcotic and Research, Inc.

McLaney, M. A., Del Boca, F. K., & Babor, T. F. (1992, April). *A validation study of the Problem Oriented Screening Instrument for Teenagers (POSIT).* Storrs, CT: University of Connecticut School of Medicine, Department of Psychiatry, Alcohol Research Center.

Miller, G. A., Downs, W. R., Gondoli, D. M., & Keil, A. (1987). The role of childhood sexual abuse in the development of alcoholism in women. *Violence and Victims, 2,* 157-172.

Mouzakitis, C. M. (1981). Inquiry into the problem of child abuse and juvenile delinquency. In R. J. Hunner & Y. E. Walker (Eds.), *Exploring the relationship between child abuse and delinquency.* Montclair, NJ: Allenheld, Osmum.

Nagin, D. S., & Paternoster, R. (1991). On the relationship of past to future participation in delinquency. *Criminology, 29,* 163-189.

National Association of State Alcohol and Drug Abuse Directors (NASADAD). (1991). *Drug offender assessment monograph.* Washington, DC: NASADAD.

National Institute of Justice (NIJ). (1992). *Drug use forecasting* (Second Quarter 1991). Washington, DC: U.S. Department of Justice.

National Institute on Drug Abuse (NIDA). (1991a). *The adolescent assessment/referral system manual* (U.S. Department of Health and Human Services. Public Health Service. Alcohol, Drug Abuse, and Mental Health Administration.) Rockville, MD: National Institute on Drug Abuse.

National Institute on Drug Abuse (1991b). *Risk behavior assessment questionnaire: Final version.* Rockville, MD: National Institute on Drug Abuse.

National Institute on Drug Abuse (1992). *Drug abuse treatment research: A five year plan.* Rockville, MD: National Institute on Drug Abuse.

Newcomb, M. D., & Bentler, P. M. (1988). *Consequences of adolescent drug use. Impact on the lives of young adults.* Newbury Park, CA: Sage.

Pickens, R. W., Leukefeld, C. G., & Schuster, C. R. (Eds.). (1991). *Improving drug abuse treatment.* Rockville, MD: National Institute on Drug Abuse.

Quay, H. C., & Peterson, D. R. (1987). *Manual for the behavior problem checklist.* Coral Gables, FL: University of Miami.

Rice, D. P., Kelman, S., Miller, L. S., & Dunmeyer, S. (1990). *The economic costs of alcohol and drug abuse and mental illness.* San Francisco: Institute for Health and Aging, University of California.

Robins, L. N., & Ratcliff, K. S. (1978-1979). Risk factors in the continuation of childhood antisocial behavior into adulthood. *International Journal of Mental Health, 7,* 96-116.

Sells, S. B., & Simpson, D. D. (1979). Evaluation of treatment outcome for youths in the drug abuse reporting program (DARP): A follow-up study. In G. M. Beschner & A. S.

Friedman (Eds.), *Youth drug abuse: Problems, issues, and treatment.* Lexington, MA: D. C. Heath.

Steiger, J. C., & Knobel, D. (1991). *Profiles of juvenile offenders in Washington State Division of Juvenile Rehabilitation Facilities: Results from a 1990 survey of youth in residence.* Olympia, WA: Washington Department of Social and Health Services, Children's Administration Management Services Division, Juvenile Offender Research Unit.

Straus, M. A., & Gelles, R. J. (1986). Societal change and change in family violence from 1975 to 1985 as revealed by two national surveys. *Journal of Marriage and the Family, 48,* 465-479.

Teplin, L. A., & Swartz, J. (1989). Screening for severe mental disorder in jails. The development of the referral decision scale. *Law and Human Behavior, 13,* 1-18.

Thornberry, T. P., Tolnay, S. E., Flanagan, T. J., & Glynn, P. (1991). *Children in custody 1987: A comparison of public and private juvenile custody facilities.* Washington, DC: U.S. Department of Justice. Office of Juvenile Justice and Delinquency Prevention.

U.S. Department of Justice (1983a). *Prisoners and alcohol,* NCJ-86223. Washington, DC: Bureau of Justice Statistics Bulletin.

U.S. Department of Justice (1983b). *Prisoners and drugs,* NCJ-87575. Washington, DC: Bureau of Justice Statistics Bulletin.

U.S. Department of Justice (1983c). *Career patterns in crime,* NCJ-88672. Washington, DC: Bureau of Justice Statistics Bulletin.

U.S. Department of Justice (1987). *Recidivism among young parolees,* NCJ-104916. Washington, DC: Bureau of Justice Statistics Bulletin.

U.S. Department of Justice (1989). *Drugs of abuse* (Drug Enforcement Administration). Washington, DC: U.S. Government Printing Office.

Wesson, D. R., Havassy, B. E., & Smith, D. E. (1986). Theories of relapse and recovery and their implications for drug abuse prevention. In F. Tims & C. Leukefeld (Eds.), *Relapse and recovery.* National Institute on Drug Abuse Research Monograph No. 72. (U.S. Department of Health and Human Service, Public Health Service, Alcohol, Drug Abuse and Mental Health Administration, National Institute on Drug Abuse, DHHS Publication No. [ADM] 86-1473.) Rockville, MD: National Institute on Drug Abuse.

Wexler, H. K., & Williams, R. (1986). The Stay'n Out therapeutic community: Prison treatment of substance abusers. *Journal of Psychedelic Drugs 18,* 221-230.

Widom, C. S. (1989a). Child abuse, neglect, and violent criminal behavior. *Criminology, 27,* 251-271.

Widom, C. S. (1989b). The cycle of violence. *Science, 244,* 160-166.

Wish, E. D., O'Neil, J., Crawford, J. A., & Baldau, V. (1992). Lost opportunity to combat AIDS: Drug users in the criminal justice system. In T. Mieczkowski (Ed.), *Drugs, crime, and social policy.* Boston: Allyn and Bacon.

Zarek, D., Hawkins, J. D., & Rogers, P. D. (1987). Risk factors for adolescent substance abuse: Implications for pediatric practice. *Pediatric Clinics of South America, 31,* 481-493.

Chapter 7

TASC—THE NEXT 20 YEARS
Extending, Refining,
and Assessing the Model

JAMES SWARTZ

Over 20 years ago, in August 1972, the first Treatment Alternative to Street Crimes program (TASC) began operations in Wilmington, Delaware. Though the subsequent ride has been somewhat bumpy, with changes in funding and federal support and the growing pains of childhood and adolescence that any new program experiences while gaining definition and structure, it appears that TASC programs have now reached maturity and have become vital and lasting links between the criminal justice and treatment systems.

From its beginnings in Delaware, TASC has grown to currently include about 125 programs operating in over 20 states. There is also now a National Consortium of TASC Programs (NCTP) for coordinating and guiding TASC program related activities. That TASC has been so successful and lasting is not only a measure of the solidity and foresight of the original conceptualization. It is also a tribute to the energy and resourcefulness of the many people who have believed in the TASC model and who have often struggled to gain funding, support, and a home for their individual programs within contexts that have, at times, been expressly hostile to their efforts. As a result of their perseverance, however, and the continued critical support and guidance of federal agencies such as the National Institute of Justice (NIJ), the Bureau of Justice Assistance (BJA), and the National Association of State Alcohol and Substance Abuse Directors (NASADAD) among others, TASC has evolved into a well-defined and widely accepted model.

The basic functions of TASC include but are not limited to identifying and assessing addicted criminal justice offenders, referring them to an appropriate substance abuse treatment program, and monitoring and reporting on client progress while they are in treatment. In addition to these services, some TASC programs also directly incorporate substance abuse treatment, although this is not a critical element of the standard TASC model. The ultimate goal of TASC is to reduce and, if possible, extirpate the commission of crimes by addressing and ameliorating drug addiction, which has been conclusively shown to drive and intensify criminal behavior (e.g., Inciardi, 1986; 1992; McGlothlin, 1985; Nurco, Ball, Shaffer, & Hanlon, 1985; Speckart & Anglin, 1986b). It is this focus on the connection between the criminal aspects of addiction and the addictions of criminals that has distinguished the TASC model from more traditional criminal justice sanctions programs (e.g., probation), which do not typically address drug addiction in any formalized fashion.

This chapter does not focus on what TASC presently is however. The TASC model has become widely known and articulated and there are many readily available and excellent descriptions and histories of TASC programs, the 10 critical elements that define the TASC model, and guides for staff training and operating a urinalysis monitoring program within the context of TASC (Cook & Weinman, 1988; also, see Inciardi & McBride, 1991, pp. 34 and 35, for a fuller description and listing of these materials). Instead, the main emphasis of this chapter is on the growth and adaptation of the TASC model to the changing natures of drug use and crime and to the perceived demands of the future. Now that TASC has reached maturity and achieved a broad level of acceptance, it seems like a good time to examine what issues may be next and to consider how the model can be extended, refined, and assessed to facilitate its continued adaptability, growth, and vitality over the next 20 years. Although this chapter has been written with an audience of TASC administrators and interested parties in mind, many of the thoughts and comments expressed are also applicable to a more general audience of those involved with providing substance abuse treatment services to criminal offenders.

Specifically, three broad areas are discussed in as many sections of this chapter: First, how the TASC model can be extended beyond that of a *bridge* between the two divergent but complementary systems of criminal justice and substance abuse treatment to that of a *network* that identifies the multiple needs of criminal justice clients and manages the linkage of clients with multiple services originating from multiple systems. Second, a consideration of how TASC can work at getting better at what it does.

Though most of us who presently work in TASC programs believe they are effective and meaningful (with data to support this: e.g., Hubbard, Collins, Rachal, & Cavanaugh, 1988; Leukefeld & Tims, 1990), we also know that there is still room for improvement in terms of both functioning (e.g., identification of client needs, client-treatment matching) and outcomes (e.g., treatment retention, the level of the reductions achieved for criminal behavior and drug use). This section suggests several possible ways to improve these areas.

Finally, we (TASCers) can expect to be held more and more accountable with respect to the effect that TASC programs have. It is obvious that in times of fiscal restraint every dollar counts and that all social service agencies, including TASC, will be called on to demonstrate their utility and economy in empirically defensible ways. Though there have been several evaluations of TASC in the past and are several ongoing evaluations in the present, there will almost certainly be a call for more at all levels from the national to the local. And because the drugs-crime scene has changed so much since the 1970s or even early 1980s, it is no longer sufficient to cite research studies such as the Drug Abuse Reporting Program (DARP) and the Treatment Outcome Prospective Study (TOPS) as justifications for the efficacy of TASC programs. Because so much is at stake —indeed in some cases, the continued funding and existence of the program —TASC program administrators will need to do their part to make sure that any evaluations conducted provide fair assessments of their programs' impact and are not merely the products of the most convenient or politically expedient methods or simply the results of poor evaluation research methodology. Such slipshod work can often distort or even fail to address the full impact that TASC has with disastrous consequences, undoing with one stroke the laborious efforts of many years work. The third section suggests some basic rules of thumb and pragmatic outcome criteria that, in the author's opinion, provide the bases for a fair evaluation of the effectiveness of TASC programs.

EXTENDING THE MODEL: REACHING OUT

Since its inception, the TASC model has been metaphorically referred to as a bridge because it connects the criminal justice and the substance abuse treatment systems. This concept made a great deal of sense in the 1970s and early 1980s when addiction was seen as a rather uncomplicated and relatively unitary phenomenon that was related to crime in a direct fashion. The proposed resolution to the problem was concomitantly also straightforward and simple: target, treat, and reduce the addiction and the criminal behavior will also be lessened. Since then, however, the relationship between drugs and crime has been studied intensively and found to be more complicated than originally thought (e.g., Goldstein, 1985; Speckart & Anglin, 1986a). The multiple deficits/problems that we now know addicts frequently have had not been systematically identified and measured. Thus, without trying to sound whimsical or nostalgic about subjects that qualify for neither sentiment, the criminality associated with drug addiction, the nature of addiction itself, and the relationship between the two seemed much less complicated then.

The population of main concern to the criminal justice and research communities in the 1970s was narcotics addicts, primarily those who abused heroin. Cocaine had yet to gain a foothold (among other than the wealthy and upper middle class) and, in any case, was not considered to be an addictive drug. Though other drugs, including licit ones, may have been more widely used and abused, such as alcohol for instance, it was felt that the heroin addict was responsible for committing the most and the most serious crimes. In response, one of the driving ideas behind the creation of TASC was to identify and place these heroin addicts in substance abuse treatment, monitor their progress and, if successful, reduce their criminal behavior. To a certain extent then, the TASC bridge, in addition to representing the link between the criminal justice and treatment systems, metaphorically and functionally also represented these straightforward conceptualizations of the problem and of the population to be served.

Over the past 20 years, however, much has changed. It appears now that if the heroin addict as a "pure" type ever existed, this is no longer the case and that polydrug use is more the norm than the exception (O'Brian & Wiebel, 1992). Many addicts who come to the attention of the criminal justice system not only have intense and long-standing addictions to heroin but also opportunistically use any other drug available on the street (Shaffer, Nurco, Ball, & Kinlock, 1985). Additionally, heroin has been supplanted by cocaine as the drug of most concern to law enforcement officials and treatment agencies (although heroin addiction has not gone away or lessened in prevalence). At first thought to be a nonaddictive, relatively harmless drug, cocaine has indeed proven to be very addictive, particularly when smoked as crack or freebase. Cocaine has also reached a much wider market than heroin ever has and cocaine use, abuse, and addiction are currently exceedingly common among arrestees, creating an immensely large additional pool of problematic and crime-prone drug users. For example, in Chicago alone, based on data from the Drug Use Forecasting project (DUF), it has been estimated that in 1988 approximately 87,000 arrestees had been using cocaine within 48 hours of their arrest compared to about 27,000 opiate users (see Wish, 1991, for an explanation of the derivation of these figures). Cocaine users are at least as criminally prone as heroin users (Johnson, Lipton & Wish, 1987) and the trade and distribution of cocaine has left an unprecedented wave of violence and lethality in its wake (McBride & Swartz, 1990).

Moreover, a great deal of research has been done that has not only studied more carefully the nature of the link between drugs and crime but has also examined the character of drug addiction in its own right. Research in the latter area, particularly the work of McLellan and his associates in Philadelphia, has shown that drug addiction typically occurs as only one part of an entire constellation of problems and deficits (DeLeon, 1991; McLellan, Luborsky, Woody, O'Brien, & Kron, 1981; Rounsaville, Tierney, Crits-Cristoph, Weissman, & Kleber, 1982). Many addicts are undereducated, have psychological and medical problems, have poor social skills, and lack both the skills and training for employment. The profile of multiple deficits and problems is especially true of addicts who come to the attention of the criminal justice system who, in addition to the above, by definition, have legal difficulties. They typically are also the most socially deviant users, lacking ties to conventional systems of social support and structure. And because many addicts seen by the criminal justice system are also IV drug users or exchange sex for drugs, the advent of AIDS and the potential risk of its spread within these communities has added an ominous and troublesome dimension to a situation that needed none.

In some instances, the multiple problems of addicts are the direct result of years of repeated drug use and abuse—for instance, medical problems. In others, the problems and deficits precede and instigate or exacerbate the addiction such as poor education and a lack of vocational skills. But regardless of the exact relationship, the implication is that treatment of the addicted criminal justice offender will have a higher degree of success if all of the problem areas are addressed, not simply the addiction. It makes little sense, for example, to work with addicts to achieve and maintain abstinence and then return them undereducated or still lacking in vocational skills to the highly stressful conditions of being jobless and without much community support. The probability of a treatment "success," however that may be defined (see below), is greatly diminished under such circumstances.

Some treatment programs have the resources and staffing to explicitly include a multifaceted approach to deal with the ancillary problems of addicts (cf. DeLeon, 1991). Many programs, however, do not and instead must concentrate their efforts on relieving the addiction—no small task in and of itself. Nor is it specifically within the purview of treatment programs to provide linkage services to other community-based service agencies when warranted. In some cases, linkage services consist solely of providing the client with the name and phone number of a referral with no follow-up support or help in making the contact. In contrast, the TASC model *embodies* the concept of linking clients to needed services. Thus, with relatively little modification, the TASC model can be extended to become not only a bridge between the criminal justice system and drug treatment but also a network between clients and a variety of service agencies, all specialized in one area or another where addicts require additional help. Figure 7.1 shows the modified TASC model of a TASC Area Network (TAN), contrasted to the more traditional TASC bridge. It is important to note that this modified version of the TASC model, though slightly more complex than the original, remains true to the original intent of TASC, which is the successful rehabilitation (habilitation) of the addicted criminal justice offender.

Conceptualized as a network, TASC programs would be responsible for identifying the multiple treatment needs of criminal justice clients and then making and monitoring the appropriate referrals not only to drug treatment but also to a variety of other necessary services such as GED classes, vocational training, AIDS education and prevention, and medical and psychological care. Because these problems have been recognized for some years now, many TASC programs may already be providing this additional network of referrals and linkages, albeit on an informal basis. The advantage of formalizing the approach is that the experiences, successes, and failures of TASC programs in implementing the expanded model can be shared in the public forum and through this type of dialogue be improved and refined over time. For instance, we probably need to know more about how to time and coordinate such a net of service referrals with drug treatment in order to achieve optimum results. Process (and outcome) evaluations of TASC would then routinely include determinations of how well *all* of the client needs were being managed as part of the estimation of the functioning and success of TASC programs.

Several final points in this area. Within TASC itself, there is a press for service diversification. One such impetus is the pervasive existence of pretreatment waiting periods. Over the past 5 to 7 years, increases in the

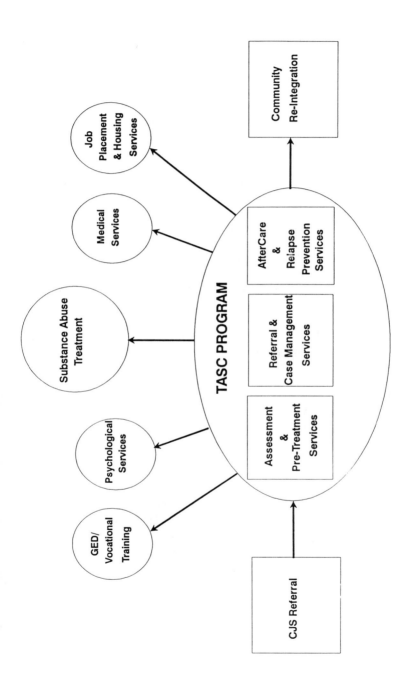

Figure 7.1. A Revised TASC Program Model: The TASC Area Network (TAN) of Multiple Referrals and Diversified Internal Services

133

number of arrests and prosecutions of drug users spurred by the war on drugs, and increased illicit drug use, primarily attributable to cocaine, has created a correspondingly larger number of TASC referrals and subsequently a greater demand for treatment. However, treatment capacity has not kept pace with the demand. The result is that at many TASC sites there are treatment waiting lists of varying size and duration. In Illinois, for instance, some clients can wait for residential treatment for as long as 6 months. This time period, although problematic (some clients abscond or get rearrested because they simply cannot manage their addictions for this long a period of time), can also be used to provide additional services that enhance the client's likelihood of remaining until treatment becomes available and of staying in treatment once it has begun. For example, in Chicago, TASC clients are routinely screened through urine testing and regular contacts with their case counselors and must attend treatment readiness groups during the pretreatment waiting period. These groups provide basic information about the causes and consequences of addiction and about HIV/AIDS risk and prevention. Also, during the pretreatment waiting period, an attempt is made to educate and prepare clients for the demands and rigors of treatment and to confront the denial so commonly seen in addicts that constitutes a primary obstacle to successful engagement in treatment. In other words, although waiting periods are an unavoidable problem in an era of continuing treatment shortages, the time need not be unproductive.

Another area ripe for expansion and diversification of TASC services is that of treatment aftercare (continuing care). The first few months after completion of treatment constitute a particularly critical period with respect to relapse or sustained abstinence. For many addicts the transition back to the community is simply too abrupt or difficult and the social cues too prominent and pervasive with the result that they quickly fall into their old behavioral patterns, including drug use. Better results might be achieved if the transition were less abrupt and navigated with continued assistance. TASC programs are in a good position to extend the monitoring of clients into the transition period and to either provide a re-referral into treatment, if that is needed, or assist the client in other ways with reintegrating back into community life.

REFINING THE MODEL: HONING IN

Despite our best efforts, and many individual success stories, some TASC clients do quickly drop out of treatment, and even among those who remain longer, some will ultimately relapse, resume using drugs, commit new crimes, and eventually get rearrested. There are probably multiple reasons for this but it is fair to say that even under the best of circumstances, addiction is a chronic problem with many, as yet poorly understood facets. Addicts who are fortunate enough to have been well educated, have steady incomes, and good social support and thus do not need to turn to crime to support their addictions, often experience similar difficulties with relapse. The fact that many TASC clients more often than not have additional burdens and problems to overcome makes relapse even more understandable in their circumstances. Moreover, there is as yet no perfect therapy regimen for treating addiction. Client-treatment matching is still a rather primitive art and the client and treatment attributes that make one type of treatment better for some and not for others is not well understood. Therefore, despite recent gains and advances, treatment still needs to be improved and modified so that retention rates and program impact are maximized. With respect to TASC programs in particular, identification, referral, and case management practices represent additional aspects that can be targeted for improvement.

One of the best ways TASC programs can help themselves is to implement self-monitoring as a regular part of their program functions. The purposes of a routine self-monitoring component would be to better understand the reasons underlying client failures and then to apply this understanding to the revision and refinement of the TASC model to achieve higher success rates. These efforts can range from the informal, such as regular staff meetings to discuss and understand both the successful and unsuccessful cases, to participation in formal outcome evaluation research studies. For example, on the informal side, the monitoring of case outcomes may reveal that one treatment facility has a much higher dropout rate than others or that certain types of clients do better at one facility versus another. The political and diplomatic issues of these types of situations aside, such simple analyses could effect an immediate change in referral patterns that would boost success rates.

On the more formal side, consider the data shown in Figure 7.2, which are based on a sample of about 100 Chicago TASC clients placed in treatment during 1989.[1] The majority of Chicago TASC clients who are incarcerated during their trials (about 50% of the total referral pool) remain incarcerated after sentencing until a treatment bed in a residential facility becomes available. This additional wait in jail is necessitated by the shortage of residential treatment beds mentioned above. The other half of Chicago TASC referrals also must wait for treatment but they do so while in the community. This is because they have either been able to post bond or the judge considered them a good risk and has granted them a recognizance bond. As the top panel in Figure 7.2 shows, when the jailed clients finally do enter treatment, they drop out at a much faster rate than the bonded clients. By 6 months, 60% of the incarcerated clients have dropped out of treatment compared to only about 50% of the clients who enter residential treatment directly from the community. From this first pass at the data then, we know that our jailed clients are more difficult to keep in treatment though the reasons why are not yet clear. Obviously, we want to do better at keeping the incarcerates in treatment, but first we must understand exactly why it is that they drop out sooner in order to adjust either our own (TASC's) or treatment's approach.

There are several places to begin looking for answers. First, it could be that the types of clients who are kept incarcerated are different from the bonded clients—and, indeed, this is the case. Compared to the group of TASC clients who wait in the community, the incarcerates tend to have a higher number of prior convictions and to have a higher proportion of heroin and cocaine users. Both of these factors suggest that the incarcerates are a more entrenched group of addicts, more impulsive, and more recalcitrant to intervention. When these additional factors are added to the analyses, as in the second (drug use) and third (conviction history) panels, it becomes clear that they do have a bearing on treatment retention but in slightly different ways. More intense drug use (e.g., heroin and cocaine addiction) affects treatment retention regardless of pretreatment incarceration status; those with more intense use drop out earlier. In contrast, the number of prior convictions is only a factor for the incarcerated group and is not predictive of treatment retention for the bonded clients.

Now that the group of TASC clients at risk for early treatment dropout and some of the risk factors have been identified, the next step is to further investigate so that specific steps can be taken to improve the situation. We could, if we so desired, carry these analyses to another level and cross all three variables—incarceration status, drug use, and conviction history—to further clarify the relationships. In addition, based on the results of the analyses, we might want to conduct discussions with TASC and/or treatment staff about specific cases in order to get a more detailed, clinical perspective. In some of the actual discussions that were held between TASC research and clinical staff, for instance, the clinical staff pointed out that the jailed clients receive little or no pretreatment preparation and as a result experience an abrupt shift from the jail to the treatment environment. They suggested that more pretreatment support and/or referral to an

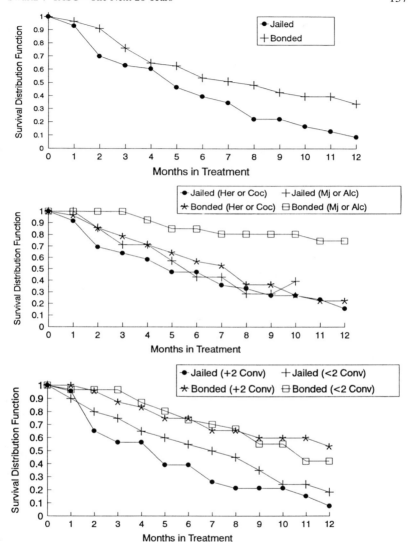

Figure 7.2. The Relationship Among Incarceration Status, Drug Use, Conviction History, and Treatment Retention for Chicago TASC Clients

available in-jail treatment program would better prepare these clients for community-based treatment and subsequently increase their retention time. Some of these changes have already been implemented by Illinois TASC in its programming and we are now waiting for the first cohort of clients to pass through the program to see if there has been a corresponding improvement.

In addition to closely monitoring client characteristics and the type and level of TASC services, TASC programs are in the somewhat unique though delicate position of being able to monitor differences in treatment programs. There is a growing literature making the case that there is a wide variability in the type, quantity, and quality of treatment services offered by programs, even among those operating within the same treatment modality (e.g., Anglin & Fisher, 1987; Inciardi, 1988; Siddall & Conway, 1988). And, more important, this variability has been found to exert a large effect over retention and success rates. For instance, returning to the previous example, it may be that a majority of the incarcerated clients have been referred to a program that is not well-suited to the needs or profiles of relatively entrenched criminal justice clients and that a change in this referral practice is in order. As another example, Anglin (1988) has suggested that the flexibility of the treatment programs and probation officers was an important positive influence on the outcomes of referrals to the California Civil Addict Program (CAP), so that perhaps jailed clients may do better if referred to programs that are more flexible in implementing their treatment protocols.

Regardless of where the changes are needed, however, the main point is that in looking at data in this way, TASC programs can systematically discover and target (i.e., hone in on) an area for improving service provision and outcomes. Once changes are implemented, they can then generate the raw data for the next cycle of analyses and refinements. Moreover, along with directly influencing service provision, such analyses can also indirectly influence and benefit program direction. Perhaps to no one's surprise who has worked in this area for very long, one implication of the results just discussed is that the group of addicts who most need treatment (e.g., those with two or more prior convictions and heroin or cocaine addictions) are also the most difficult to treat. Thus, indirectly, an important corollary issue has been raised: In a time when treatment resources are scarce, should these resources be targeted for those who will make the most of the opportunity or for those who most need the opportunity? As the above results show, these two groups are not always the same. This is a difficult question to answer but one that is worth analyzing and debating with the resolution providing further grounds for programmatic enhancement.

An implicit and essential part of being able to self-monitor a program in the fashion just described is the routine collection of accurate and meaningful client and service data. Further, for the purpose of analysis, these data must be automated. In the past, surveys of TASC programs such as the Tyon study (1988) were limited by the fact that many TASC agencies did not have fully automated client data bases from which data could be abstracted and summarized. Even for those who did have automated systems, the data were often incomplete or coded idiosyncratically. Thus, historically, many TASC programs would simply have been unable to conduct the kind of self-monitoring and evaluation necessary for improving their own programs, let alone participate in a national survey. Fortunately, sensing this lack, BJA recently funded the development of a public domain TASC client data base system called TASC-MIS™. Developed by SEARCH (The National Consortium of Justice Information and Statistics), this system is relatively inexpensive and easy to use and provides TASC programs with the capacity to automate their critical functions and capture the kind of information needed for program self-monitoring and evaluation. For TASC programs in need of these capabilities, the TASC-MIS™ software developed by SEARCH represents an excellent opportunity.[2]

ASSESSING THE MODEL: DEFENDING YOUR LIFE

In a particularly memorable scene from the first Dirty Harry movie, Harry is asked to go to the State's Attorney's office following his (Harry's) use of rather unorthodox means to capture a particularly heinous criminal. Instead of being congratulated for ridding the city of a terrible menace who has systematically raped and murdered a series of young women, Harry is called on the carpet by the State's Attorney and told the case will not be prosecuted because of a slew of technical violations. During his harangue, the State's Attorney repeatedly emphasizes that the rights of the rapist-murderer had been violated during the investigation and arrest. Looking back with a sneer, Clint Eastwood, the actor who played the title character, disdainfully replies, "Well I'm all broken up about that man's rights."

Though Harry is a fictional character, the attitude expressed in that scene has been very real and seemingly pervasive over the past 12 years. The implicit notion is that the criminal justice system has become too lenient, too caught up in irrelevant procedural technicalities, and biased toward the rights of criminals as opposed to the rights of victims. Moreover, this perceived leniency is viewed as drastically compromising community safety. This attitude was crystallized in and exploited by the now infamous Willy Horton commercial used to great success by the Bush campaign in the 1988 presidential election. The direct consequence of these perceptions has been a "get tough" on crime movement that has been manifested, in part, as determinant and longer sentences of offenders at both the state and federal levels. In particular, crimes directly related to drug use and distribution have been the targets of these latest statutory efforts at controlling crime.

A debate on the merits of this approach or the validity of the perceptions on which it is based is outside the scope of this chapter. However, the implications for TASC programs have been and remain significant. From the perspective of the get-tough viewpoint, drug abuse treatment for criminal justice offenders is often seen as being coddling, nonpunitive, and a threat to community safety because the majority of treatment is conducted outside of prisons and jails. Thus, viewed in such a skeptical light, treatment programs and agencies such as TASC that are involved in the delivery of treatment to criminal justice offenders have been called on to show greater accountability and to demonstrate empirically their efficacy. Though past research has, in fact, shown that treatment in conjunction with criminal justice sanctions is effective (e.g., Anglin, 1988; Collins & Allison, 1983; Hubbard et al., 1988; Leukefeld & Tims, 1990), outcome evaluations justifying this approach are still being demanded. And, irrespective of some of the motivations for demanding such evaluations, the changes in patterns of drug use discussed above would seem to dictate that a comprehensive reevaluation of the efficacy of drug treatment for the criminal justice offender, inclusive of TASC programs, is warranted. Some such studies are already under way and it is very likely there will be more to come.

Fair enough. It is reasonable to require that publicly-funded programs provide data on how well those dollars have been spent and in the specific case of the community-based treatment of criminal justice offenders, that they show that community safety is not compromised. However, with so much at stake in the results (e.g., the continued existence of the program), it is imperative that any evaluation study of TASC and drug abuse treatment programs be designed and conducted with the utmost care. In my experience, though, this has not always been the case and some researchers who undertake such work either ignore or do not seem to fully appreciate the issues specific to providing services to the criminal justice client and to measuring their impact. Therefore, because there is a strong possibility that many TASC programs will be evaluated in the near future, it is important that TASC administrators have at least a rudimentary appreciation of some of these issues so that their programs do not become unwitting participants in poorly designed studies that are likely to yield invalid and negative results. In the interest of brevity, only two of the most salient issues will be discussed here: subject comparability and outcome measures.[3]

In comparison to other criminal justice clients, TASC clients represent some of the most difficult and entrenched addict-criminals (Inciardi & McBride, 1991). In programs where this is the case, it is imperative that an appropriately matched comparison group of equally difficult cases is used and not just one that is conveniently identifiable and readily available (e.g., probationers who were not referred to TASC). In the instances where a group is selected on the basis of expediency because they *appear* to come from the same population as TASC clients, there is a high possibility of a systematic bias attributable to the TASC referral process. For example, it could be that those probationers with milder addictions or with a shorter and less serious criminal justice history are not referred to TASC. The result of using this group as a control would almost certainly bias the outcome against TASC and increase the chances of finding no differences between the two groups or of finding results where TASC appeared to have a negative impact. Therefore, an evaluation of TASC clients should only use a group matched on age, ethnicity, gender, addiction status, and criminal history (e.g., number of prior arrests and/or convictions, not simply top arrest charge). Of course it is more difficult to work through matching clients in this manner, but it allows for a far more valid and fair evaluation than is the case when these client variables are not taken into account.

The second, and perhaps the most important of all the issues, has to do with which measures are chosen to represent program outcome. Almost invariably, and despite an overwhelming amount of data to the contrary, rearrest rate is used as the sole measure of TASC (or treatment) program efficacy. It should be stated in no uncertain terms, the use of simple rearrest rates as the sole index of the effect of TASC programs is a poor idea. Given the stubborn persistence of the use and support for using *only* rearrest rates as outcomes, however, the preceding sentence bears repeating and highlighting: *Rearrest rate as the sole index of program effect is a poor idea.* Even in conjunction with other measures, rearrest rates in and of themselves may not prove to be especially enlightening.

There are some good reasons why: First, rearrest represents only a small fraction of the criminal activity of an individual. Some studies have shown that this fraction is less than 1% of the total criminal activity of a street addict (Inciardi, 1986; Nurco et al., 1985). Thus, assessing program impact by using rearrest rates (or any other single point measure such as violation of probation) as the sole indicator of criminal activity is restricting the measurement to what amounts to a tiny portion of an individual's behavior. Most researchers know that using a scale with a very narrow range greatly decreases the chances of finding significant results simply because there is no room for change. And this is precisely the same problem with using such a crude measure as rearrest. The chances of finding an effect or impact on a variable that has such a relatively low rate of occurrence is small with the prospect that the results will show no or only small differences between TASC clients and a control group of non-TASC clients. Second, as Nurco et al. (1985) have pointed out, rearrest is not so much an indicator of criminal activity as it is a measure of involvement with the criminal justice system and/or how aggressive and active that system is. Rearrest rates are just as dependent on how many police are available, how often they patrol the communities, and how aggressive their arrest policies are as they are on the criminal activity of an individual. Further, because drug abuse and crime *are* complicated behaviors, we should not expect that accurately measuring them is a simple task that can be accomplished with a single measure.

Given these serious problems, why does the overreliance on rearrest rates persist? One reason may be that rearrest data are generally easy to collect and do not require that interviewers be hired and trained to administer long and sometimes complex questionnaires. Another reason is that rearrest *seems* like an *objective* measure, sanctioned with the imprimatur of the criminal justice system itself. After all, rearrest data are contained on the *official* records (i.e., rap sheets), recorded for perpetuity and often existing on computer files, adding further to the aura of objectivity and officialness. Rearrest information is also a very familiar concept, one that is easily understood by all parties involved from program administrators to policymakers to the general public—no fancy explanations or statistical manipulations required. With the current heavy concern on jail and prison crowding, administrators and politicians look specifically to rearrest statistics to determine if a program will help reduce the constant flood of new arrestees and prisoners. Additionally, the alternative, relying on the self-report of the addict, by comparison, seems to be fraught with the potential for all kinds of misrepresentation and exaggeration and is much more difficult to collect. Why should anyone believe the criminal-addict when there is *official* data available?

In fact, arrest records are neither more objective nor more valid than the self-report of subjects given the appropriate circumstances and conduct of the study (e.g., Nurco et al., 1985; Hser, Anglin, & Chou, in press). When subjects have been interviewed under the appropriate circumstances (e.g., the establishment of a good rapport with the researcher, assured confidentiality, and a nonthreatening setting) they admit to committing many *more* crimes than are on the arrest records, not fewer, which would be the expected direction of misrepresentation. Also, the arrest records can themselves be fraught with omissions and inaccuracies due to clerical errors, a poor records-keeping system, or other such factors.

A simple example will clarify these issues further: TASC client A, after going through the program for about a year, drops out of treatment. During the following year, he commits crimes but far fewer than before entering TASC. He also uses drugs but again, only about half as much as he did before entering the program. After 14 months, he is rearrested during one of his relapse periods. Probation client B is also a drug addict but is not referred to treatment. He continues using drugs and committing crimes at the same rates as before his probation because nothing has been done to address his addiction. After 7 months he is again rearrested. Using rearrest as the sole indicator of program outcome, both clients appear the same and one would conclude that the TASC program had no effect. As can be seen quite readily though, this is not the case and the TASC program had a very significant effect, virtually doubling the length of time before rearrest and substantially reducing the addictive and criminal behaviors of the client even though he did drop out of treatment.

Drug addiction is a chronic, recurring problem characterized most commonly by multiple periods of relapse and remission over any number of years before a lasting abstinence is achieved, if ever. Against this backdrop, it would be much more accurate and realistic to construe the effects of TASC programs as bringing about significant *reductions in the intensity* of the addictive and criminal behaviors. The all-or-nothing measure of rearrested versus not rearrested does not allow for such comparisons, however. The impact of TASC and treatment programs should, therefore, be measured in light of the realities of this kind of a scenario wherein successful outcomes are not all-or-nothing propositions but lie along a continuum of relative effects. Below is a non-exhaustive list of some proposed outcome measures with brief operational definitions that, as a group, would better reflect the total effect of TASC programs than do rearrest rates alone:

1. *Treatment retention:* The length of time a client has remained in a treatment program. TASC clients probably remain in treatment longer and hence get a bigger treatment "dose."

2. *The intensity or rate of criminal behavior:* This can be defined as either the actual number of crimes committed over a given time period, the percentage of time involved in committing crimes, or the number of "crime-days" per year as defined by Nurco et al. (1985). On average, TASC clients should be significantly lower on any of these measures compared to their baseline rates.

3. *The intensity or rate of drug use:* This can also be defined in a number of ways, such as the length of time until relapse occurs, the number of relapses within a given time period, or the actual number and quantity of drugs used and the frequency of use. TASC clients should have shorter and fewer periods of relapse and use drugs less frequently during these periods. Correspondingly, periods of abstinence should be longer.

4. *The length of time before rearrest:* The time between arrests will be longer for those TASC clients who are arrested again (i.e., they will survive in the community longer because they are committing fewer crimes). And yes, rearrest rates are also expected to be lower for TASC clients, though because of the low rate of occurrence, the difference in rearrest rates should not be expected to be as dramatic as the actual reduction in rate of criminal behavior.

5. *Employability:* Higher proportions of TASC clients will be employed and will sustain their employment for longer periods of time.

6. *AIDS risk behaviors:* TASC clients will have lower rates of injection drug use and engage less frequently in other risky practices (e.g., unprotected sex, needle sharing, the exchange of sex for drugs) than comparable non-TASC clients. In addition, the rate of sero-conversion (i.e., the proportion changing from HIV negative to HIV positive over a given time period) should be lower for TASC clients.

There may also be a deeper issue here that goes back to the current political climate and the subsequent pressure to demonstrate unrealistically glowing results. In most cases, the findings from evaluations of

TASC or treatment programs will be used either to defend the continued funding and existence of the program if they are positive or to recommend that the money be spent elsewhere, such as for more jail space and police, if they are negative or even if they are only mediocre. Success rates of at least 50% or higher—whereby success is defined as completion of treatment, full employment, abstinence, and no rearrest—are thus expected. Realistically though, this high a rate of success with the hard-core heroin and cocaine addicts that many TASC programs often work with is not likely even under the best of circumstances. No amount of deliberate obfuscation or data manipulation can or should alter that fact. In the current climate of public opinion, where treatment of addicted criminal offenders is viewed with skepticism and being seen as soft on crime is politically disastrous, defending any such program that achieves less than even 100% positive results can be a frustrating and harrowing experience. Moreover, the subtleties of some concepts such as reductions in rates of behaviors and time until rearrest can get easily lost or twisted around in the crucible of public discourse where ideology rather than data often drives the discussion.[4] Because of these and other similar concerns, many TASC administrators probably shy away from being evaluated at all for fear that the results, even expressly positive ones, will, in effect, curtail or eliminate their operations.

We should not let this happen, however, and none of the above means that outcome studies should be avoided. Well-conducted evaluation research provides much valuable information that can serve as the basis for retaining and improving model programs and eliminating poor ones. Nor does it mean trying to live up to unrealistically high expectations given the population that is being served and the difficult problems that are being addressed; measuring a program against impossibly high standards makes failure a virtual certainty. It does mean that being honest and realistic about program outcomes has its price and that education of both the public and the politicians on what the likely courses of drug addiction and crime are and how treatment does and does not effect them should be a continuing priority. It also means being unapologetic about results that, although less than ideal, are both significant and defensible especially in comparison to more traditional types of sanctions such as simple incarceration. In the long run, undergoing careful and well-designed outcome studies can only improve and be beneficial to TASC programs, to the clients they serve, and to the public who is safer because TASC exists and continues to evolve.

NOTES

1. Figure 7.2 consists of three separate survival analyses of client data. For the purposes of this chapter, it is not important to understand the technical points of this type of analysis. Generally speaking, each line shows a survival curve that represents the proportion of clients remaining in treatment at any given time. The higher curves represent better treatment retention (i.e., more clients remaining in treatment past a certain point), whereas the lower curves indicate faster treatment dropout rates. For a detailed discussion of the use and interpretation of survival analysis with drug treatment data, the reader is referred to Anglin & Fisher (1987); Hser, Anglin, & Liu (1991); and Fisher & Anglin (1987).

2. Further information on TASC-MIS^{TM} software may be obtained by writing to SEARCH at 7311 Greenhaven Drive, Suite 145, Sacramento , CA 95831, or by calling (916) 392-2550.

3. For a more detailed discussion of some of the other issues involved in assessing the outcomes of drug treatment programs, the reader is referred to Wells, Hawkins, & Catalano (1988a, 1988b).

4. In a recent meeting where the author was presenting data that showed treatment reduced but did not completely extinguish criminal behavior, some members of the audience fixated solely on the fact that the treated group was still committing crimes and should be locked up regardless of the rate of their behavior. They completely missed the larger point that even though some of these subjects were, in fact, rearrested and locked up for periods of time (they were not in the community committing crimes with some sort of guardian angel telling the police not to arrest them because they had been in treatment), they were committing fewer crimes and these events occurred less often than for the untreated group. The lesson in all this, if there was one, seemed to be that even with the data on your side, community-based treatment can be a tough sell in the current climate.

REFERENCES

Anglin, M. D. (1988). The efficacy of civil commitment in treating narcotic addiction. In C. G. Leukefeld & F. M. Tims (Eds.), *Compulsory treatment of substance abuse: Research and practice* (DHHS Publication No. ADM 88-1578, pp. 8-34). Washington, DC: U.S. Government Printing Office.

Anglin, M. D., & Fisher, D. G. (1987). Survival analysis in drug program evaluation: Part II. Partitioning treatment effects. *The International Journal of the Addictions, 22*(4), 377-387.

Collins, J. J., & Allison, M. A. (1983). Legal coercion and retention in drug abuse treatment. *Hospital and Community Psychiatry, 34*(12), 1145-1149.

Cook, L. F., & Weinman, B. A. (1988). Treatment alternatives to street crime. In C. G. Leukefeld & F. M. Tims (Eds.), *Compulsory treatment of substance abuse: Research and practice* (DHHS Publication No. ADM 88-1578, pp. 99-105). Washington, DC: U.S. Government Printing Office.

DeLeon, G. (1991). The therapeutic community and behavioral science. *The International Journal of the Addictions, 25*(12A), 1537-1557.

Fisher, D. G., & Anglin, M. D. (1987). Survival analysis in drug program evaluation: Part I. Overall program effectiveness. *The International Journal of the Addictions, 22*(2), 115-134.

Goldstein, P. J. (1985, Fall). The drugs/violence nexus: A tripartite conceptual framework. *Journal of Drug Issues,* pp. 493-505.

Hser, Y., Anglin, M. D., & Chou, C. (in press). Reliability of retrospective self-report by narcotics addicts. *Psychological Assessment: A Journal of Consulting and Clinical Psychology.*

Hser, Y., Anglin, M. D., & Liu, Y. (1991). A survival analysis of gender and ethnic differences in responsiveness to methadone maintenance treatment. *The International Journal of the Addictions, 25*(11A), 1295-1315.

Hubbard, R. L., Collins, J. J., Rachal, J. V., & Cavanaugh, E. R. (1988). The criminal justice client in drug abuse treatment. In C. G. Leukefeld & F. M. Tims (Eds.), *Compulsory treatment of substance abuse: Research and practice* (DHHS Publication No. ADM 88-1578, pp. 57-80). Washington, DC: U.S. Government Printing Office.

Inciardi, J. A. (1986). *The war on drugs: Heroin, cocaine, crime, and public policy.* Mountain View, CA.: Mayfield.

Inciardi, J. A. (1988). Some considerations on the clinical efficacy of compulsory treatment: Reviewing the New York Experience. In C. G. Leukefeld & F. M. Tims (Eds.), *Compulsory treatment of substance abuse: Research and practice* (DHHS Publication No. ADM 88-1578, pp. 126-138). Washington, DC: U.S. Government Printing Office.

Inciardi, J. A. (1992). *The war on drugs II: The continuing epic of heroin, cocaine, crack, crime, AIDS, and public policy.* Mountain View, CA.: Mayfield.

Inciardi, J. A., & McBride, D. C. (1991). *Treatment alternatives to street crime: History, experiences, and issues* (DHHS Publication No. ADM 91-1749). Washington, DC: U.S. Government Printing Office.

Johnson, B. D., Lipton, D. S., & Wish, E. D. (1987). *Facts about the criminality of heroin and cocaine abusers and some new alternatives to incarceration.* New York: Narcotic and Drug Research, Inc.

Leukefeld, C. G., & Tims, F. M. (1990). Compulsory treatment for drug abuse. *The International Journal of the Addictions, 25*(6), 621-640.

McBride, D. C., & Swartz, J. A. (1990). Drugs and violence in the age of crack cocaine. In R. A. Weisheit (Ed.), *Drugs, crime and the criminal justice system* (pp. 141-170). Cincinnati, OH.: Anderson Publishing.

McGlothlin, W. H. (1985). Distinguishing effects from concomitants of drug use: The case of crime. In L. Robins (Ed.), *Studying drug abuse* (pp. 153-172). New Brunswick, NJ: Rutgers University Press.

McLellan, A. T., Luborsky, L., Woody, G. E., O'Brien, C. P., & Kron, R. (1981). Are the "addiction-related" problems of substance abusers really related? *The Journal of Nervous and Mental Disease, 169*(4), 232-239.

Nurco, D. N., Ball, J. C., Shaffer, J. W., & Hanlon, T. F. (1985). The criminality of narcotics addicts. *Journal of Nervous and Mental Disease, 173,* 94-102.

O'Brian, M. U., & Wiebel, W. (1992). Chicago: Patterns and trends in substance abuse for Chicago. In *Epidemiological trends in drug abuse: Proceedings community epidemiology work group, December 1991* (DHHS Publication No. ADM 92-1918, pp. 77-90). Washington, DC: U.S. Government Printing Office.

Rounsaville, B. J., Tierney, T., Crits-Cristoph, K., Weissman, M. M., & Kleber, H. D. (1982). Predictors of outcome in treatment of opiate addicts: Evidence for the multidimensional nature of addicts' problems. *Comprehensive Psychiatry, 23*(5), 462-478.

Shaffer, J. W., Nurco, D. N., Ball, J. C., & Kinlock, T. W. (1985). The frequency of nonnarcotic drug use and its relationship to criminal activity among narcotic addicts. *Comprehensive Psychiatry, 26*(6), 558-566.

Siddall, J. W., & Conway, G. L. (1988). Interactional variables associated with retention and success in residential drug treatment. *The International Journal of the Addictions, 23*(12), 1241-1254.

Speckart, G., & Anglin, M. D. (1986a). Narcotics use and crime: A causal modeling approach. *Journal of Quantitative Criminology, 2*, 3-28.

Speckart, G., & Anglin, M. D. (1986b). Narcotics use and crime: An overview of recent research advances. *Contemporary Drug Problems,* 741-769.

Tyon, L. P. (1988). *Final report: Baseline management and assessment data project* (unpublished). Portland, OR: National Consortium of TASC Programs and the Bureau of Justice Assistance.

Wells, E. A., Hawkins, J. D., & Catalano, R. F., Jr. (1988a). Choosing drug use measures for treatment outcome studies. I. The influence of measurement approach on treatment results. *The International Journal of the Addictions, 23*(8), 851-873.

Wells, E. A., Hawkins, J. D., & Catalano, R. F., Jr. (1988b). Choosing drug use measures for treatment outcome studies. II. Timing baseline and follow-up measurement. *The International Journal of the Addictions, 23*(8), 875-885.

Wish, E. D. (1991). U.S. drug policy in the 1990s: Insights from new data from arrestees. *The International Journal of the Addictions, 25*(3A), 377-409.

Chapter 8

THE ASSESSMENT AND REFERRAL OF CRIMINAL JUSTICE CLIENTS
Examining the Focused Offender Disposition Program

JAMES A. INCIARDI

DUANE C. MCBRIDE

BETH A. WEINMAN

The expanding number of drug using arrestees and the magnitude and increasing volume of drug cases in local courts have overwhelmed judicial systems throughout the United States in recent years (Inciardi, 1993). In response, during the second half of the 1980s numerous urban jurisdictions established specialized drug courts to expedite the processing of drug offenders. In addition, many communities expanded or established treatment services for all types of drug-involved arrestees, probationers, inmates, and parolees (Leukefeld & Tims, 1992). At the federal level, Congress passed the Anti-Drug Abuse Act in 1986, a piece of comprehensive legislation that, among other things, targeted areas for identifying and meeting the needs of the drug-involved offender population.

A lead agency in the federal effort was the Bureau of Justice Assistance (BJA). Previously, BJA had been investigating drug testing technologies, primarily urinalysis testing, with pretrial arrestees. Studies of arrestees in Washington, DC and New York City had found that persons who tested positive by urinalysis at arrest for one or more "hard" drugs (usually heroin, cocaine, or PCP) had a greater number of *re*arrests than did arrestees with a negative test result (see Wish, 1990). Importantly, these and related studies emphasized that extremely high proportions of arrestees were drug-involved and that urinalysis appeared to be an effective technology for identifying the drug-using arrestee population (Toborg & Kirby, 1984; Wish, Cuadrado, & Martorana, 1986).

The expanded use of urinalysis in the District of Columbia and elsewhere to test and monitor all pretrial arrestees found that urine surveillance reduced the rate of pretrial misconduct, including rearrest (Carver, 1986; Holden, Wakefield, & Shapiro, 1990; Wish, 1990). These studies produced a groundswell of support for drug testing technology. Throughout the mid-1980s, urinalysis technology became increasingly reliable and easy to use. Policymakers began looking to urine testing as an answer to many of the problems society was experiencing with drug abuse. One use of the technology that became appealing to some was to replace drug treatment with urine monitoring. It was argued that while "habilitation" or "rehabilitation" might not be the end result, the arrestee or offender who had to submit to a regular course of drug testing in combination with criminal justice supervision was less likely to re-offend. At the same time, judges were finding that their calendars and courtrooms were facing increasing numbers of drug-using offenders. Alternative sentences to drug treatment or drug testing were often considered, but the judiciary was also struggling with questions of sorting and referral. How were judges to best determine the most appropriate course of treatment for the individual arrestee or offender appearing before them? Even if urinalysis was an effective tool for identifying drug-using offenders, the issue of how to use information derived from urinalysis in criminal justice decision making was yet to be unraveled.

THE FOCUSED OFFENDER DISPOSITION PROGRAM

The issues associated with the appropriate use of urinalysis testing and treatment for drug-involved arrestees resulted in the funding of the Focused Offender Disposition Program (FOD). BJA approached the National Association of State Alcohol and Drug Abuse Directors (NASADAD) to realize two goals:

1. Develop and test the reliability and utility of an assessment instrument that would sort drug-using offenders in a way that would enable the courts to make appropriate referrals for drug treatment, drug testing, or perhaps other human services.

2. Develop a program methodology that would also demonstrate if there existed a drug-abusing offender population that would benefit from a course of drug testing only.

The basic purpose of the Focused Offender Disposition Program was to develop an initial classification system that would provide courts with reasonable criteria for deciding on the broad type of treatment needed by any given drug offender. Classification systems have long been a part of court and prison systems. They emerged first as a means for sorting offenders by level of risk to the community for purposes of bail and probation and as a mechanism for determining the level of security and custody in correctional institutions. With the application of mental health and social service models to the criminal justice and prison classification systems, there have been attempts to develop procedures that would reasonably inform the courts, presentence investigation and probation officials, and prison reception and classification bureaus of the health and other service needs of accused, convicted, and/or sentenced offenders. The large proportion of drug-using offenders coming before the courts today has focused classification approaches on the problems of drug dependence and treatment.

The need for clear, effective, and easily administered classification systems is fairly obvious. Court and treatment personnel are typically overwhelmed with large numbers of cases. Moreover, they are faced with making fairly rapid decisions about treatment need and suitability, as well as the appropriate *type* of treatment for a given client. A cursory review of local attempts to deal with this problem reflects a wide variety of approaches (Inciardi, McBride, Weinman, & Dembo, 1992). Typically, strategies are either highly complex or unsystematic and inordinately subjective, resulting in a general lack of suitable models that can objectively ascertain, at an initial level, the treatment needs of drug-involved offenders. As such, the existence of a reliable and easily understood and administered client sorting instrument is considered vital to courts and treatment programs.

DEVELOPING THE DEMONSTRATION PROGRAM

To develop the Focused Offender Disposition Program demonstration, NASADAD had to review the research and practice in many related areas that the effort would span. A five-step plan was established:

1. A review of the literature in pertinent areas was initiated and divided into five subject areas: treatment research; treatment approaches; treatment effectiveness; treatment/patient matching; and, urinalysis testing.

2. A survey was conducted with a sample of 35 judges from 35 separate jurisdictions to determine how the judiciary was currently handling cases involving the drug-involved offender population.

3. A review of clinical and diagnostic drug-offender assessment instruments was conducted.

4. A work group was established to review each of the initial steps in the development of the demonstration program and to develop a drug-offender sorting instrument.

5. The work group was called on to develop and outline the methodology and operations of the demonstration program.

In 1988, NASADAD solicited proposals to test the classification instrument and research plan that was under construction. Fifteen sites submitted proposals, and the final participants were Phoenix (Arizona), Birmingham (Alabama), and Chicago (Illinois). At all three sites, the local Treatment Alternatives to Street Crime (TASC) program was the successful applicant organization. It was not surprising to either BJA or NASADAD representatives that TASC programs had been selected by the proposal review team. TASC already represented an established bridge between the two separate institutions that would be involved in the Focused Offender Disposition Program: the criminal justice system and the drug treatment community (see Swartz, Chapter 7 of this book).

THE OFFENDER PROFILE INDEX (OPI)

As noted above, a major goal of the Focused Offender Disposition Program was to develop and test a broad classification scheme. Rather than a complex clinical assessment that yielded a specific treatment plan, the intent was to structure a broad "sorting" instrument that would suggest such treatment/intervention alternatives as outpatient versus residential, long-term versus short-term, or urine surveillance only. In developing the instrument, NASADAD worked within specific theoretical and practical frameworks. The social control perspective (Hirschi, 1969) and the "stakes in conformity" perspective found in studies of prediction in criminology and substance-abuse treatment outcome (see Elliott, Huizinga, & Ageton, 1985; Farrington & Tarling, 1985; Gibbons, 1965; Inciardi & Babst, 1971; Maisto & Caddy 1981; Maisto & Cooper, 1980; Maisto & McCollam, 1980;

Toby, 1957) were chosen as the guiding framework for developing the instrument, because they could be operationalized with information used in criminal justice settings by judges and probation departments to determine community risk and service needs.

Essentially, the social control and stakes in conformity perspectives argue that an individual's commitment to conforming behavior (and conversely, his or her freedom to be deviant) relates primarily to one's involvement in and commitment to conventional activities and relationships. Thus, if a person has a job, is self-supporting, has conventional friends, has finished at least high school, has no previous arrests, and was arrested for only a minor offense (such as marijuana possession), it would appear that the individual has a high stake in conformity and a high probability of success on probation (with urine monitoring). However, a high school dropout with drug-using friends, who is unemployed and uses crack-cocaine daily, may well require intensive treatment services to successfully intervene in a drugs/crime life-style. Because the stakes in conformity array is based on such highly practical information as employment, education, criminal record, previous treatment, and living arrangements—items routinely used by the criminal justice system—it was felt that it would more likely be accepted by the courts.

NASADAD utilized its work group, an expert panel of clinicians and researchers in the fields of drug abuse and criminology, to operationalize stakes in conformity into specific content areas and to develop specific measurement questions. The content areas included family support, education, school, employment, home/residential stability, criminal justice involvement, psychological functioning, and drug treatment history.

Each content area was measured by three to five specific questions. The answers were summed and the resultant scores were divided into high, medium, and low categories. Low scores were considered low stakes in conformity and high scores were considered high stakes in conformity. In addition to these stake areas, the Offender Profile Index also contained a Drug Severity Index, scored on the basis of types of drugs used and frequency of recent use. The use of injection drugs, for example, resulted in a low drug severity score and thus the need for more intensive services.[1] The infrequent use of marijuana, however, resulted in a higher drug severity score and thus the recommendation for less intensive intervention. Decisions about categorical cutting points were made by members of the NASADAD expert panel and were based on their experiences with drug-using criminal justice populations. The summed scores yielded by the OPI recommended alternative treatment options—long-term residential, short-term residential, outpatient (during the project, the OPI was modified to provide for regular and intensive outpatient treatment), and urine monitoring only.

In addition to the scores generated by the OPI, there were two other areas of inquiry—six questions measuring readiness for treatment and a brief HIV/AIDS risk assessment. These additional data elements were not incorporated into the OPI scoring or treatment recommendations but were analyzed to display the prevalence of HIV/AIDS risk in these drug-using offender populations and to indicate if readiness for treatment was related to treatment retention and success.

As a final note here, it should be emphasized that because the cutting points for scoring the OPI were based solely on experiential data, it was necessary that the instrument be treated as a "living document." That is, it was subject to change as quantitative and process data were collected at the sites. It was important that no questions were raised by the courts, or the community at large, about the safety of the community with such an experimental design. When questions did occur regarding cutting points or the appropriateness of OPI recommendations, the project staff decided that any uncertainty would be answered with a response that was in the best interests of community safety.

PROJECT METHODS

The Offender Profile Index was designed for drug-using offender populations at any stage of the criminal justice process. However, in all three sites, the overwhelming majority of project clients were probationers. As illustrated in Figure 8.1, the design called for a quasi-random assignment of cases to assessment by either the OPI or the local TASC assessment instrument, with a further alternative assignment to "treatment as assessed" or "urine monitoring only."[2] Although this was not a pure random design, it was more manageable by local sites and easier to monitor for compliance. Comparisons of the social demographic characteristics between the four study groups in Phoenix and Birmingham indicated that at entry into the project there were basically no significant differences between groups. In Chicago, a true random assignment was instituted.

Project management was conducted by TASC staff at each site with monitoring provided by NASADAD personnel and consultants. Baseline

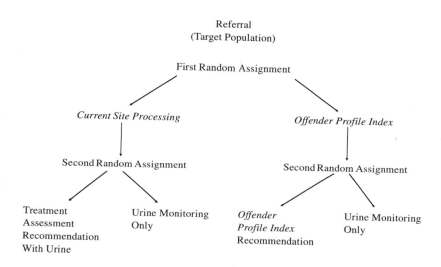

Figure 8.1. Random Assignment Design for OPI Development

data collection including the OPI, Readiness for Treatment, or the local assessment was accomplished through face-to-face interviews conducted by trained local site staff. A training manual and instruction in the use of the OPI was provided by NASADAD staff and consultants. Treatment progress and termination data were prepared by participating treatment facilities and forwarded to the TASC program on forms developed by NASADAD. All data collection instruments were then sent to NASADAD for processing and analysis in an SPSS-PC system. In addition to these data, process evaluation data were obtained by interviewing samples of clients, treatment staff, judges, and probation officers. The process evaluation interviews focused on two specific areas:

1. The day-to-day mechanics of how the project operated at each site.
2. Subjective experiential views of the project and the OPI, with a specific focus on the goal of the project to improve initial classification of drug-using offenders.

FINDINGS

In Birmingham, a total of 602 subjects received the Offender Profile Index; in Phoenix, there were 423; and in Chicago, the number was 397. In all sites, the target was 400. Because each study site was characterized by major differences—nature of the drug problem, types of drug-using criminal justice populations being served, types of clients being referred, missions and perspectives of probation departments and the judiciary, criminal justice workloads, and drug treatment systems and the availability of services—each was analyzed separately.

The study population consisted primarily of male, African Americans between the ages of 22 and 39 who had attained fewer than 11 years of education. The only major difference in sociodemographic characteristics by site was the higher proportion of Caucasians in Phoenix. For the majority of the cases in Phoenix and Chicago, the primary charge at arrest was either possession, manufacture, or distribution of illegal drugs. In Chicago, this was likely because of the fact that most of the cases came from the county's newly established drug court.

Overall, the OPI interview data suggested that the Focused Offender Disposition Program had been successful in these ways:

1. Reaching its target numbers of drug-using offenders.
2. Identifying drug-using offenders with minimal treatment experience and in need of services.
3. Assessing drug-using offenders and referring them to substance-abuse treatment services.[3]

In contrast, the project had difficulty in reaching or identifying injection or crack-using offenders. At all study sites, the project experienced what might be called "creaming" and "slippage." *Creaming* refers to the tendency of many judges to limit project referrals to only the less drug-involved clients. *Slippage* refers to loss of project clients between assessment and actual treatment entry.

With respect to creaming, the data indicated a narrower than expected range of drug use patterns and stakes in conformity. Process evaluation interviews with judges and probation officials indicated that because this was a new and experimental program, there was some hesitancy in sending "hard" drug users with many previous arrests and other low stakes in conformity to it. Although it appeared that the TASC sites involved in the project made significant efforts to identify and reach these types of users, they had only limited success in doing so. Regardless, the limited numbers of what might be called "heavy drug users" resulted in limited referrals to services other than urine monitoring.

With regard to the slippage problem, many clients were lost between assessment and treatment entry. Phoenix, for example, experienced major problems in maintaining the cooperation of the probation department in requiring clients to report for treatment services. When clients failed to report to treatment, no sanctions were applied by the courts. Birmingham, however, assessed a number of clients who, for a variety of reasons, were never placed on probation as anticipated. Thus, they were not at liberty to receive services. And in Chicago, treatment programs experienced significant reductions in funding, resulting in rapidly expanding waiting lists. The majority of clients in Chicago who were referred to treatment waited at least 4 months before entry. Given the time frame of the project, this meant that about 80% of the Chicago clients never entered treatment. Going beyond these site-specific problems, all sites experienced difficulties associated with the size and complexity of the criminal justice and treatment systems that made it difficult to track individual clients.

In addition to the creaming and slippage problems, the design allowed the sites, on the basis of clinical and other judgments, to override the assignment to "urine monitoring only" for up to 25% of all cases. And finally, a number of clients did not actually receive the services that would be implied by their study group assignment. For example, it was found in numerous instances that a "urine only" assignment was often a misnomer. That is, when many "urine only" clients reported for urine collection, TASC case managers had significant therapeutic contacts with them. Given these problems and circumstances, the differences in the various study groups were minimal. And for all of these reasons, less than one-fourth of all project clients entered treatment within the framework of the project design.

Going further, empirically assessing project impact was also problematic. For example, the study design called for assignment to one of four study groups:

1. OPI assessment and treatment as assessed.
2. OPI assessment and assignment to urine monitoring only.
3. Assessment with the local instrument and treatment as assessed.
4. Local instrument assessment and assignment to urine monitoring only.

Overall, comparisons between the study groups in terms of length of stay in treatment, drugs in urine, and treatment completion did not reflect statistically significant differences between the OPI or local assessment or between these latter groups and the clients assigned to urine only. This lack of differences likely resulted primarily from the problems of creaming and slippage. The limited variance and the small numbers receiving treatment made it impossible to systematically address the basic project research questions. Moreover, the data could not be used to address the issue of treatment effectiveness. However, the data did indicate that those in all study groups who remained in treatment reduced their drug use, as evidenced by increased proportions of clean urines.

SYSTEM REACTIONS TO THE OFFENDER PROFILE INDEX

As part of the overall strategy to develop, implement, and test the appropriateness of the Focused Offender Disposition Program in general and the usefulness of the Offender Profile Index in particular, an important aspect of the project was "process evaluation." In general terms, *process evaluation* consists of a comprehensive description of how programs are conceptualized, planned, implemented, and modified. Such evaluations attempt to assess the quality and purpose of program activities relative to the desired results (see Scarpitti, Inciardi, & Pottieger, in press). The specific purposes of the FOD process evaluation related to three issues:

1. The need for a detailed program description in order to fully understand how the project was proceeding and if what was planned was actually occurring.
2. The need to know what factors/events/variables emerged that either resulted in a change of program design, *forced* a change in program design, or facilitated program implementation.
3. The need to assess the utility of the OPI for criminal justice practitioners.

To accomplish these ends, extensive face-to-face interviews were conducted by NASADAD staff and consultants with virtually everyone associated with the project—judges, probation officers, TASC administrators and case managers, and treatment program representatives. As for the utility of the Offender Profile Index, the vast majority of the reviews were quite positive. Judges favored the OPI because its quantitative scoring mechanism provided an objective numerical assessment of treatment need on which probation and diversion decisions could be made. It also supplied judges with information that was typically unavailable to them at sentencing. Probation officers favored the OPI because it provided them with a comprehensive overview of a client's drug severity, as well as measurements of conformity domains that were easily verifiable from probation records and field visits. Officials at TASC sites, including several who were not part of the project but nevertheless had access to the instrument, preferred the OPI to their local assessment instrument because it yielded the same treatment referral recommendations in a less time consuming and more efficient manner. In fact, the Birmingham TASC site modified its local assessment instrument by incorporating much of the OPI.

By contrast, there were several TASC case managers who disliked the OPI for two reasons: (1) its numerical scoring precluded the use of clinical skills and insights in making treatment decisions, and (2) it failed to provide enough client data to construct a comprehensive treatment plan. These objections, however, were the result of a misunderstanding of the purpose of the OPI. It was never intended as a comprehensive appraisal of mental health and social functioning for treatment planning. Rather, it was designed as a broad sorting instrument for general needs assessment only.

As the project endured and the OPI became available to court and correctional practitioners across the country, it was generally viewed as an easily scored assessment instrument that provided general guidelines for treatment need. In 1992, furthermore, the State of Delaware adopted the OPI as the needs assessment tool for systemwide treatment planning. A copy of the Offender Profile Index and instructions for its use appear as an appendix to this chapter.

DISCUSSION

The Focused Offender Disposition Program found that there was a significant need for drug treatment services in the probationer populations in the three cities targeted. Process interviews also documented that the Offender Profile Index was viewed positively by judges, probation officers, the majority of the TASC people interviewed, as well as criminal justice managers because it utilized what they considered commonsense information that provided reasonable and objective criteria for defensible decision making. The OPI is continuing to receive acceptance by agencies attempting to utilize an initial assessment instrument to classify types of service needs.

By contrast, empirical data collected during the course of the project found that there were few significant differences between the study groups on such basic variables as length of stay in treatment, drugs found in urines, and reasons for termination. As such, the data did not provide *statistical* evidence for the ability of the OPI to improve treatment needs assessment over what the local systems were already doing. Moreover, the data could not be used to argue the relative effectiveness of "urine monitoring only" versus conventional treatment. However, the authors' observations and process evaluation interviews suggested some explanations for the lack of differences between the study groups, particularly in the areas of "system conditions" and "study group distinctions."

System Conditions. As many in the drug field have often experienced, field research faces many difficulties. The Focused Offender Disposition Program was no exception. For example, although the design called for random assignment, some adjustments were necessary in order to get the cooperation of judges and probation departments. Specifically, for clients randomized to urine only whom a judge, probation officer, or TASC case manager/assessor viewed as a risk to the community and/or in great need of treatment, procedures had to be established that would permit the shifting of those clients to more intensive intervention. It was anticipated that this situation would be unusual, yet process evaluation interviews found the practice to be quite common. Understandably, in criminal justice and treatment systems that consider the needs and safety of offender/clients and public the major priorities, research protocols *must often be set aside.* At the same time, probation officers or judges frequently removed a client's participation in the project as a condition of his or her probation. This reduced the number of cases available for process and outcome analyses.

In addition, it is important to recognize that field research occurs in a shifting and rapidly changing social environment. Numbers of cases and role incumbents that appear stable at the beginning of a project are not necessarily so later on. Budget changes in a local jurisdiction have considerable effects on the availability of treatment slots and the length of waiting lists. All of these issues impacted the Focused Offender Disposition Program. To cite but one example, and as already noted, budget reductions for publicly funded drug treatment occurred in Chicago after the initiation of the study. By the end of the project, clients were waiting for up to 6 months for treatment entry.

Study Group Distinctions. A number of factors caused a blur in the distinctions between study groups. As noted above, to insure judicial cooperation it was necessary to allow the movement of many "urine only" clients into treatment programs. In addition, some TASC case managers who did not agree with the OPI referral determination often directed clients to an alternative level of intervention. These managers also admitted to urging clients who had been assessed or randomized to "urine only" to specifically request treatment, thus separating them from the research randomization loop. Moreover, it was learned that many clients who were randomized to "urine only" actually sought treatment on their own. Thus, very quickly the boundaries between study groups began to smear.

Although many of the difficulties in this project were the inevitable results of the idiosyncracies of field research and the tensions between treatment and research, some steps can be recommended that might reduce the problems in future studies.

1. Research protocols should be administered by research rather than clinical personnel. The potential for role confusion is considerable among clinical case managers required to use an objective, nonclinical instrument. The use of research interviewers does increase costs, but it also increases the probability of maintaining the study design.

2. It is time that researchers accept the fact that random experimental designs are not always possible in treatment research. Political and clinical systems are unwilling to accept the rigid requirements of a random assignment. Moreover, randomization has also been found to actually change the structure, process, and integrity of the treatment being evaluated (see Inciardi, Isenberg, Lockwood, Martin, & Scarpitti, 1992).

3. Agreements among all parts of each system involved in the research need to be explicitly developed and acknowledged prior to implementation. In addition, all staff who have responsibility for making the project work should participate in the agreement and subsequent training.

Finally, evaluating field research projects such as the Focused Offender Disposition Program is especially difficult when there are few reliable measures that apply to the basic thrust of the program. Even if the various study groups had not been contaminated through slippage and creaming in the judicial sector, through manipulations of the randomization either by design or by the clinical judgments of case managers, or through the long waiting lists caused by a lack of treatment program beds, what would be the appropriate measures of success? Length of stay in treatment? Abstinence versus relapse? Revocation of probation? Recidivism? Although these variables are generally used for treatment evaluations, because the project had no control over treatment program service delivery or efficacy, it was difficult to determine exactly what these variables were addressing, and for several reasons. *First*, client outcome was dependent on many variables, including the clinical efficacy of the drug treatment programs to which clients were referred. Few, if any, of the programs have ever been systematically studied and evaluated. *Second*, a systematic field follow-up of project clients was not built into the funding of the Focused Offender Disposition Program. As such, before and after assessments of drug severity and stakes in conformity remained unknown. *Third*, revocation of probation and recidivism are related to so many intangible factors in the criminal justice system and the greater environment that their significance as independent measures of outcome is suspect. Revocation is often a political decision, based on the availability of jail and prison space, differential patterns of law enforcement, community standards, and alternative orientations of parole and probation officers (see Dembo, 1970; Inciardi & McBride, 1977; Stephens, 1971; Takagi, 1969).

What was more tangible, however, was the experience with the Offender Profile Index. Although the data analysis was unable to document the utility of the OPI, the process evaluation interviews did indicate a high level of support. Judges and probation officers commented that the instrument provided a reasonable, objective, easy to understand initial classification approach based on indicators that were commonly thought to relate to problems and service needs. The experiential utility of the OPI was further illustrated by its adoption by TASC sites and by the State of Delaware for a systemwide needs assessment survey.

NOTES

1. It is important to note that the *greater the drug use*, the *lower the severity score*; and conversely, the *lesser the drug use*, the *higher the drug severity score*. Low scores for high drug use are used in the Drug Severity Index to maintain consistency with the scoring patterns in the rest of the OPI.

2. The quasi-random design involved a systematic *every other* assignment to "treatment as assessed" or "urine monitoring only."

3. For a thorough examination of these data, see McBride and Inciardi (1993) and McBride, Inciardi, and Weinman (1992).

REFERENCES

Carver, J. A. (1986, September/October). Drugs and crime: Controlling use and reducing risk through testing. *NIJ Reports*. U.S. Department of Justice, National Institute of Justice.

Dembo, R. (1970). *Personality orientations of parole officers.* Unpublished doctoral dissertation, New York University.

Elliott, D. S., Huizinga, D., & Ageton, S. S. (1985). *Explaining delinquency and drug use.* Beverly Hills, CA: Sage.

Farrington, D. P., & Tarling, R. (1985). *Prediction in criminology.* Albany, NY: State University of New York Press.

Gibbons, D. C. (1965). *Changing the lawbreaker: The treatment of delinquents and criminals.* Englewood Cliffs, NJ: Prentice-Hall.

Hirschi, T. (1969). *Causes of delinquency.* Berkeley, CA: University of California Press.

Holden, G. A., Wakefield, P., & Shapiro, S. J. (1990, February). *Treatment options for drug-dependent offenders: A review of the literature for state and local decision makers.* Washington, DC: U.S. Department of Justice, Office of Justice Programs, Bureau of Justice Assistance.

Inciardi, J. A. (1993). *Criminal justice.* Fort Worth, TX: Harcourt Brace Jovanovich.

Inciardi, J. A., & Babst, D. V. (1971). Predicting the post-release adjustment of institutionalized narcotics addicts. *Bulletin on Narcotics, 23*, 33-39.

Inciardi, J. A., Isenberg, H., Lockwood, D., Martin, S. S., & Scarpitti, F. R. (1992, February 4-5). *Assertive community treatment with a parolee population: An extension of case management.* Paper presented at the National Institute on Drug Abuse Technical Review Meeting on Case Management, Rockville, MD.

Inciardi, J. A., & McBride, D. C. (1977). The parole prediction myth. *International Journal of Criminology and Penology, 5*, 235-244.

Inciardi, J. A., McBride, D. C., Weinman, B. A., & Dembo, R. (1992). *Drug offender assessment instruments.* Washington, DC: Bureau of Justice Assistance.

Leukefeld, C. G., & Tims, F. M. (1992). *Drug abuse treatment in prisons and jails.* Rockville, MD: National Institute on Drug Abuse.

Maisto, S. A., & Caddy, G. R. (1981). Self-control and addictive behavior: Present status and prospects. *International Journal of the Addictions, 16*, 109-133.

Maisto, S. A., & Cooper, A. M. (1980). A historical perspective on alcohol and drug treatment outcome research. In L. C. Sobell & E. Ward (Eds.), *Evaluating alcohol and drug abuse treatment effectiveness: Recent advances* (pp. 1-14). New York: Pergamon Press.

Maisto, S. A., & McCollam, J. B. (1980). The use of multiple measures of life health to assess alcohol treatment outcome: A review and critique. In L. C. Sobell & E. Ward (Eds.), *Evaluating alcohol and drug abuse treatment effectiveness: Recent advances* (pp. 15-76). New York: Pergamon Press.

McBride, Duane C., & Inciardi, James A. (1993). The Focused Offender Disposition Program: Philosophy, procedures, and preliminary findings. *Journal of Drug Issues, 23*, 143-161.

McBride, Duane C., Inciardi, James A., & Weinman, Beth A. (1992). *The drug testing technology/Focused Offender Disposition Program.* Washington, DC: National Association of State Alcohol and Drug Abuse Directors.

Scarpitti, F. R., Inciardi, J. A., & Pottieger, A. E. (in press). Process evaluation techniques for corrections-based drug treatment programs. *Journal of Offender Rehabilitation.*

Stephens, R. C. (1971). *Relapse among narcotic addicts: An empirical test of labeling theory.* Unpublished doctoral dissertation, University of Wisconsin.

Takagi, P. (1969). The effect of parole agents' judgements on recidivism rates. *Psychiatry, 32,* 192-199.

Toborg, M. A., & Kirby, M. P. (1984, October). Drug use and pretrial crime in the District of Columbia. *Research in Brief,* U.S. Department of Justice, pp. 1-4.

Toby, J. (1957). Social disorganization and stake in conformity: Complementary behaviors in the predatory behavior of hoodlums. *Journal of Criminal Law, Criminology, and Police Science, 46,* 12-17.

Wish, E. D. (1990). Drug testing and the identification of drug abusing criminals. In J. A. Inciardi (Ed.), *Handbook of drug control in the United States* (pp. 229-244). Westport, CT: Greenwood Press.

Wish, E. D., Cuadrado, M., & Martorana, J. A. (1986). Estimates of drug use in intensive supervision probationers: Results from a pilot study. *Federal Probation, 50,* 10-13.

OFFENDER PROFILE INDEX
Instrument and Instructions

USING THE OFFENDER PROFILE INDEX

The Offender Profile Index is *not* a clinically oriented instrument designed to yield a comprehensive substance-abuse treatment plan. Rather, it is a broad "sorting" or classification instrument appropriate for determining which *type* of drug-abuse treatment intervention to use—long-term residential, short-term residential, intensive outpatient, regular outpatient, or urine monitoring only. Diagnoses and assessments for comprehensive treatment planning are best accomplished at the particular program to which the client is directed.

The administering of the Offender Profile Index involves a face-to-face interview that can be completed in about 30 minutes. It can be administered by any trained professional with basic interviewing skills. The assessment is essentially self-scoring, and a numerical score corresponds with a specific referral recommendation. A complete copy of the instrument appears at the end of this document and has been printed in a manner designed for easy reproduction.

As noted earlier, the Offender Profile Index and its associated service recommendations are based on "stakes in conformity." In this behalf, research findings have indicated that individuals with *high* stakes in conformity (as measured by educational attainment, employment history, living arrangements, and arrest history) are less likely to commit crimes than persons with low stakes in conformity. Data further indicate that persons with high stakes who do commit crimes are less likely to be recidivists than persons with low stakes, and therefore require less supervision and fewer services.

The specific background data and stake in conformity indices that are included in the Offender Profile Index are the following:

1. Sociodemographic and Offense Characteristics
2. Drug Severity Index
3. Family/Support Sub-Index
4. Educational Stake Sub-Index
5. School Stake Sub-Index
6. Work Stake Sub-Index
7. Home Stake Sub-Index
8. Criminal Justice History Sub-Index
9. Psychological Stake Sub-Index
10. Treatment Stake Sub-Index
11. HIV Risk Behaviors Sub-Index

Each of the indices and their scoring are discussed in the pages that follow.

General Instructions

The OPI is basically self-explanatory. The interview should be conducted in as private an environment as possible to help ensure accurate answers. The interviewer should explain the basic purpose of the OPI to the subject, focusing on the need to determine the type and level of services required and the need for client cooperation. Answers to the specific questions are indicated by circling the appropriate response or writing it in. Make sure ALL applicable items are answered and are legible.

Cover Page: Several items are to be entered on the cover page. The first is the client identification number. Since different institutions use different types of identifiers, an ID number arbitrarily consisting of 6 digits has been included here. This can be modified as necessary. The cover page also asks the interviewer to note whether or not verification of the client's criminal justice history has been conducted. This is done to help ensure accuracy in client self-report.

Finally, the cover page asks the results of a preliminary urinalysis test, to be taken before the client is interviewed. This urinalysis is another attempt to ensure client accuracy in self-report. Having the pre-OPI urinalysis report available at the time of the interview allows the interviewer to fully probe the extent of a client's drug use history.

Background Questions

The first series of questions in Part I of the OPI focuses on basic background and sociodemographic characteristics.

Jurisdiction: This item specifies the jurisdiction or court where the case is being handled.

Sociodemographic Characteristics: The next few items include a variety of client identifiers—name, social security number, date of birth, age, sex, and ethnicity. These items provide basic information that will assist in describing the populations served.

Offenses: These refer to charges in the client's current case. If the client has more than four criminal charges, list only the four primary ones. Since exact terminology for offenses tends to vary from one jurisdiction to the next, these items are left for the interviewer to fill in.

Client Cooperation: This item asks about a client's general state of cooperation. *Uncooperative* clients are those who refuse to answer the questions posed during the interview process. A client is also deemed uncooperative if he or she refuses the intervention strategy recommended. However, *denial* of drug use should not be automatically considered as uncooperative behavior. If the client has a "possession" charge, or exhibits "track marks" or the burns and sores about the mouth typical of chronic crack smokers, but denies drug use, perhaps urinalysis or a restatement of the purpose of the interview is in order. *Mentally disoriented* clients are those who exhibit extreme confusion, or bizarre behaviors that prohibit the conducting of a meaningful interview. Individual clients deemed uncooperative or mentally disoriented should be referred for psychiatric assessment, or returned to court for an alternate disposition.

Signature and Date of Interview: A signature is recommended for the sake of identifying who conducted the interview should some question rise at a later date. Signatures must be legible. The date of the interview should include month, day, and year.

Drug Severity Index

The Drug Severity Index forms Part II of the OPI. This index was developed after reviewing the many attempts to scale drug-use patterns described in the research literature. It examines types of drugs used and frequency of use to assign an index score. Drug severity should be based on a client's last 90 days on the street, whether that be prior to arrest or while on probation. Descriptive information on age of first use and first continued use, although not scored, is useful for better understanding the characteristics of the overall target population.

At first glance the drug severity index might appear quite complex since there are drugs, drug groups, frequency codes, and severity codes. Some explanation plus a little practice with the instrument will demystify it all rather quickly.

First, there are 17 drugs grouped into four major categories. Category A includes alcohol and marijuana. Category B includes inhalants, hallucinogens, and sedative pills. Category C includes stimulant pills, non-intravenous (IV) cocaine, ampheta-mines and ice, crack, oral opiates, and basuco (coca paste). Category D includes all forms of IV drug use, speedballing, and the use of street methadone. Categories A through D reflect a progression of involvement in drug abuse.

Second, there are four drug frequency codes, all of which are self-evident.

Third, there are seven possible drug severity scores, ranked from 6 to 0. Code 6 indicates minimal drug use, and hence low drug severity. At the other end, code 0 indicates the intravenous (IV) use of heroin, and thus extremely high drug severity. More specifically:

6 = code 0 in A through D
or
code 1 in A and B

A client receives a drug severity score of 6 if he or she does not use any of the drugs listed (a frequency code of 0) or uses any of the drugs in categories A or B less than once a week (a frequency code of 1). These individuals are considered light or non-users.

5 = code 2 in A
or
code 0 or 1 in B

A client receives a drug severity score of 5 if he or she uses alcohol or marijuana (category A) no more than once a week (a frequency code of 2), and uses any of the drugs in category B less than once a week or not at all (frequency code of 0 or 1). These individuals are considered moderate to heavy alcohol and/or marijuana users.

4 = code 3 in A
or
code 2 or 3 in only one drug in B

A client receives a drug severity score of 4 if he or she uses alcohol or marijuana daily (frequency code of 3 in category A), or uses no more than one drug in category B once a week or more (a frequency code of 2 or 3). These individuals are considered heavy alcohol and/or marijuana users, who may also use one other drug fairly regularly.

3 = code 2 or 3 in two or more drugs in B
or
code 1 in C

A client receives a drug severity score of 3 if he or she uses two or more drugs in category B at least weekly (frequency code of 2 or 3). A person may also receive a drug severity score of 3 if he or she uses any drug in category C less than once per week. These individuals are considered moderate to heavy polydrug abusers.

2 = code 2 or 3 in C

A client receives a drug severity score of 2 if he or she uses speed, crank, or some other form of stimulant pills, snorts cocaine, and/or smokes crack, ice, or basuco (category C) once a week or more (a frequency code of 2 or 3). These individuals are considered regular amphetamine or cocaine users, but do *not* use their drugs intravenously.

1 = code 1 in D

A client receives a drug severity score of 1 if he or she uses any drugs intravenously or illegal methadone (category D) less than once a week (a frequency code of 1). These individuals are considered *light* IV drug users.

0 = codes 2 or 3 in D

A client receives a drug severity score of 0 if he or she uses illegal methadone at least weekly or takes other drugs intravenously at least weekly (a frequency code of 2 or 3 in category D). These individuals are considered heavy IV users.

As noted earlier, although the drug severity index may appear confusing at first, its logic becomes readily apparent after it is administered a few times. Moreover, with most clients there are scoring shortcuts. For example, if the client's drug use is limited to alcohol or marijuana, then the drug severity score is either a 5 or a 6. If the client is an IV drug user, then the severity score is automatically a 0 or 1. Likewise, there are other patterns that will emerge after repeated use of the instrument. Enter the appropriate drug severity score in the space provided at the lower right corner of the page at the end of the Index.

Family/Support Stake Sub-Index

Part III of the OPI begins the stake in conformity sub-indices. The purpose of the Family/Support Stake Sub-Index is to document the stability of the client's human relationships as well as the crime or substance-use problems of those with whom he or she is close. This sub-index is based on four specific items: living arrangements; *stability* of living arrangements; proportion of friends who have been incarcerated 30 days or more; and the proportion of friends who *have* received or *are* receiving alcohol or other drug treatment.

Living Arrangements: Question 1 asks the client to indicate with whom he or she is currently living. A score of 2 is recorded in the space provided to the right of the question if the client is living with a spouse, sex partner, or family. A score of 1 is recorded if the client is living alone or with friends; and a score of 0 is noted if he or she lives on the street or in some type of institution.

Stability of Living Arrangements: Question 2 asks about the length of time the client has been in his or her current living pattern. If it has been 1 year or more, a score of 2 is recorded; if it has been 6-12 months, a score of 1 is recorded; and if it has been less then 6 months, a score of 0 should be recorded.

Questions 3 and 4 focus on whether the client's spouse, sex partner, or whomever else he or she is living with has been treated for an alcohol or drug problem or has gone through detoxification. "Detox" is mentioned separately here since many street drug users don't consider it to be "treatment." Whether or not the client's spouse, sex partner, or whomever else he or she is living with has been incarcerated for 30 days or longer is also asked.

Question 5 asks the client about the number of his or her close friends, *prior* to his or her arrest. "Close friends" has not been operationally defined here because it is a subjective designation that will likely vary from one individual to the next. For one client it may be a crime partner or "running" partner. For another it may be a drinking or bowling friend. For still others it may include people in whom they can confide. In any case, most people consider "close" friends to be persons with whom they have considerable contact, identify with, look up to, or in some other way have a significant relationship. (It should be noted here that the answers to Questions 3, 4, and 5 are not used to score the Family/Support Stake Sub-Index. For analytical purposes, however, the information is important.)

Proportion of Friends Incarcerated 30 Days or More: Question 6 focuses on how many of the client's close friends (the friends numbered in Question 5) have served time in jail or prison. If half or more have been incarcerated for 30 days or longer, then a score of 0 is recorded; if it is none or almost none, then a score of 2 is recorded.

Proportion of Friends Receiving Treatment: Question 7 focuses on the number of close friends who have been treated (including detox) for substance abuse. If half or more have been treated, a score of 0 should be recorded in the space provided; if it is less than half, a 1 should be recorded; and if it is none or almost none, then a score of 2 should be recorded.

Computing the Family/Support Sub-Index Score. As is indicated on the OPI, the Family/Support Sub-Index score is computed by totaling the scores in Questions 1, 2, 6, and 7. If that figure totals 6 to 8, circle the 2 in the Family/Support score line (the last line on the page). This score indicates that the client has a high degree of stable nondeviant relationships, and thus a *high* family/support stake in conformity. If the summed score is 4 or 5, circle the 1 on the last line. This indicates a *moderate* stake. If the summed score is 3 or less, circle the 0. This indicates that the client has *minimal or no* stable relationships with non-drug users or noncriminals.

Educational Stake Sub-Index

The purpose of the Educational Stake Sub-Index is to document the educational attainment of the client. Those who have higher educational levels are assumed to have higher stakes in conventional behavior.

The four questions in this sub-index simply ask for the total number of years of normal education (Question 1). If the client has less than 12 years of schooling (i.e., less than the completion of high school), questions 2 and 3 determine if he or she has a GED or has had any vocational or technical training. Question 4 asks for the specific vocational/technical courses completed.

In filling out this section, one needs first to record the number of grades completed in the space provided to the right of Question 1. If this number is 12 or more, proceed directly to the scoring. If it is less than 12, ask questions 2, 3, and 4. Record the answers to 2 and 3 by circling the appropriate item. The answer to Question 4 should be entered clearly and concisely in the space provided.

Computing the Educational Stake Sub-Index Score. A score of 2 is circled if the client has completed 12 or more years of education; *or* has earned a GED ("yes" in Question 2); *or* has completed 9 or more years, plus vocational or technical training ("yes" in Question 3). These individuals are seen as having a *high* educational stake. A score of 1 is circled if the client has completed 9-11 years of education but has not earned a GED, *and* has not had any vocational or technical training. These individuals are seen as having a *moderate* educational stake.

A score of 0 is circled if the client has completed 8 years of education or less. These individuals are seen as having a *low* educational stake.

School Stake Sub-Index

Because of the relatively young age of many offenders, it is possible that some might still be attending high school or a vocational training program at the time of processing rather than having full or part-time employment. Thus, it is important to determine if they have a current school stake. The fact that someone makes the effort to attend classes suggests some level of stake in conformity.

Question 1 asks if the client is currently attending school. If the answer is "no," item 2 on this page instructs you to circle 0 in the school stake score at the bottom of the page and proceed to the next sub-index (Work). If the answer is "yes," ask Question 3. Question 3 attempts to determine if the client is currently a full- or part-time student. If he or she is full-time, circle 2 in the School Stake Score. If he or she is part-time, then circle 1.

The enrollment verification is obtained by recording the specific name of the school, as well as its address and school telephone number. No less than a 10% random sample of cases should be verified. Please note at the bottom of the page if the information was verified and whether it was accurate.

Work Stake Sub-Index

The Work Stake Sub-Index is intended to document the client's current or recent employment activity. Question 1 asks how many weeks the client worked during the past year either outside the home or as a homemaker with responsibilities for others. In the space provided below and to the right of Question 1, assign a weight of 2 for 35 weeks or more; a weight of 1 for 20-34 weeks; and a weight of 0 for less than 20 weeks.

Question 2 asks if the client is currently employed. Circle the appropriate answer. If "yes," ask Question 3; if "no," ask Question 4.

Question 3 asks the client to indicate how many hours he or she typically works outside the home or as a homemaker. In the space provided below and to the right of Question 3, assign a weight of 2 if the client works 35 hours or more a week; a weight of 1 if the client works 14-34 hours a week, and a weight of 0 if the client works less than 15 hours a week.

Question 4 is asked of those who are not currently employed, focusing on their most recent job—inside or outside the home. Assign a weight of 2 in the space provided below and to the right of Question 4 for those who worked 35 hours or more per week; a weight of 1 for those who worked 15-34 hours per week; and a weight of 0 for those who worked less than 15 hours per week at their last job.

Space is provided to record the client's current or last employer, address, telephone number, and supervisor's name. For a homemaker, the pre-sentence investigation report (if available) can be used to verify client information. No less than 10% of the clients should have their employment verified. Since a recent pay stub serves as adequate verification, *all* clients should be asked if they can provide one. At the bottom of the page indicate if there was verification and if the information was accurate.

Computing the Work Stake Sub-Index Score. The Work Stake Sub-index is scored by summing the weights derived from the answers in Questions 1, and 3 *or* 4. At the bottom of the page, circle 2 when the sum of scores is equal to 4; circle 1 when the sum of scores is 2 or 3; and circle 0 for those with 0 or 1. Those with a score of 2 are considered to have a *high* work stake; those with a 1 have a *moderate* work stake; and those with a 0 are considered to have a *low* work stake.

Home Stake Sub-Index

The purpose of this sub-index is to document the type and stability of the client's residence during the past year. Question 1 asks for the client's current residence and telephone number. Please record the information clearly. *This should be verified for all clients.* A recent bill or postmarked letter with the client's name and address will suffice, and it should be the responsibility of the client to get this type of document to the interviewer.

Questions 2 and 3 solicit the length of time at the residence in Question 1. If the client has lived at the current address at least 12 months, proceed to question 5. Question 5 asks if the client contributed to the payment of his or her lodging—whether it be rent or mortgage. Check the appropriate space indicating if the client contributes "all," "some," or "none" of the rent or mortgage money.

Space is provided for verification. As noted above, the most recent residence of *all* clients' residences should be verified. In addition, the date of the residence check, the name of the checker, and the results of the check must be indicated in the space provided.

Computing the Home Stake Sub-Index Score. The Home Stake Sub-index score is computed on the basis of three items: contributions to rent or mortgage, number of residences, and validity of residence information.

A score of 2 is circled if the client pays *all* of the rent or mortgage (Question 5), has had less than four residences in the last 12 months (Questions 3 & 4), and the residence has been verified as correct. *All three* of these conditions must be met! A score of 2 is considered to indicate a *high* home stake.

A score of 1 is circled if the client made *some* contribution to his or her housing costs (Question 5), had less than 6 residences in the last 12 months (Question 4), and provided correct residence information. *All three* of these conditions must be met! A score of 1 is considered to indicate a *moderate* home stake.

A score of 0 is circled if the client made *no* contribution to his or her housing costs (Question 5), *or* had 6 or more residences in the last year (Question 4), *or* if the residence information was found to be false. As such, if *any* of these three conditions are met the score becomes 0 and is considered to indicate a *low* home stake.

Should a client or a member of his or her household be unable to provide residence verification information, the score becomes 0. Different residence information yielded by the verification process should be recorded.

Criminal Justice History Sub-Index

The Criminal Justice History Sub-Index is designed to indicate the extent of client involvement with the criminal justice system. The questions are very straightforward. Question 1 asks the client to indicate the total number of arrests he or she has had in the last 5 years. Question 2 asks for the total number of

convictions in the last 5 years. Question 3 asks for the total time served in detention, jail, or prison (in months) during the past 5 years. The client's self-report
should be comparable to the criminal justice verification of arrests done by the
interviewer.

Computing the Criminal Justice History Sub-Index Score. A score of 2 is circled
for the Criminal Justice History Sub-Index if the client has had 2 arrests or less
and/or no more than 45 days of incarceration. A score of 2 is considered to indicate
a relatively *high* stake in noncriminal behavior.

A score of 1 is circled if the client has had 3-10 arrests *and/or* 46 days to 6 months
of incarceration in the last 5 years. A score of 1 is considered to indicate a *moderate*
stake in noncriminal behavior.

A score of 0 is circled if the client has had 11 or more arrests *and/or* has been
incarcerated for more than 6 months in the last 5 years—reflecting a *low* stake in
noncriminal behavior.

In scoring this sub-index, time incarcerated should weigh more heavily than
the number of arrests, since time incarcerated usually indicates the severity of
crimes committed.

Psychological Stake Sub-Index

The general focus of the various sub-indices thus far has been on objective
behaviors and verifiable facts. However, it is also important to include one
sub-index that focuses on emotional health. This is not a psychiatric diagnostic
tool but rather a simple attempt to give a rough indicator of emotional functioning.

Question 1 asks the respondent to indicate if he or she has ever acted out of
control—even when not on drugs. A score of 2 is recorded on the line to the right
and below question 1 if the client indicates there have been no such "out of
control" episodes. A score of 1 is recorded if there was one such episode, and a
score of 0 if there were two or more episodes.

Question 2 asks if the client ever attempted or seriously considered suicide. A
score of 2 is recorded in the space to the right and below question 2 if the client
answered "no" to both parts of Question 2. A score of 1 is recorded if the client
considered suicide but *never* attempted it. A score of 0 is recorded if the client
attempted suicide.

Question 3 asks about treatment for nervous or mental problems. A score of 2
is recorded in the space to the right and below Question 3 if the client has never
been treated for nervous or mental problems. A score of 1 is recorded if the client
has been treated once, and a score of 0 is recorded if the client has been treated
more than once.

Computing the Psychological Stake Sub-Index Score. First, sum the scores recorded for Questions 1, 2, and 3. This is the *total composite score* for this sub-index

and should be recorded in the space provided. A Psychological Stake Sub-Index Score of 0 is circled if the total composite score is 0 or 1. This score is considered to indicate potentially severe psychological problems. A score of 1 is circled if the total composite score is 2, 3, or 4. This score is considered to indicate a moderate level of psychological problems. A score of 2 (for a total composite score of 5 or 6) is considered indicative of a high degree of stable emotional functioning.

Treatment Stake Sub-Index

This brief sub-index consists of only one question: "How many months have you spent in treatment during the past 5 years?" Circle 2 if the client has been in treatment 12 months or more in the last 5 years, and circle 0 if the client has been in treatment for less than 12 months.

Although the logic of this scoring may appear a bit peculiar at first, it is based on the research finding that individuals who have spent 12 months or more in drug-abuse treatment are more likely to have positive treatment outcomes than those who have not. A treatment stake score of 2 is considered to indicate a high stake in successful treatment outcome. A score of 0 is considered to indicate a low stake in successful treatment outcome.

HIV Risk Behaviors Sub-Index

This section of the OPI is designed to provide information on the AIDS-related risk behaviors of the client population. *The information obtained is not used in computing the final OPI score.* Rather, it represents a step in documenting the distribution of risk behaviors of those coming to the attention of the local criminal justice system. The questions are straightforward and self-explanatory, and they require that the appropriate answer be circled in each instance. *Five* specific risk behaviors are focused on:

1. The number of sex partners
2. The use of condoms
3. Anal penetration
4. The sharing of needles
5. The cleaning of needles

There are separate questions for males, females, and IV drug users. Questions 1 and 2 are for everyone. Questions 3 through 6 are for males only; Questions 7 and 8 are for females only; and Questions 9 through 13 are for IV drug users of both sexes. At the bottom of the last page of the index, the interviewer is asked to indicate if the client is at high risk for HIV infection. A client is considered to be at high risk for HIV infection if he or she did any of the following:

1. Had unprotected sex with multiple partners during the past year
2. Had any sexual contacts with IV drug users
3. Shared drug paraphernalia with IV drug users and did not properly clean them before use
4. Engaged in sex involving anal penetration

Profile Summary

Part IV of the OPI involves the actual computation of the total score and the determination of recommended services. The drug use severity score and the stake in conformity scores for each of the 8 sub-indices can be obtained from the bottoms of the appropriate pages in the instrument. Sum the 8 sub-index scores and record as indicated adjacent to the line labeled Total Stake in Conformity Score.

The higher stake in conformity scores combined with less serious and less frequent drug use results in a recommendation of less intensive services. At the other end of the continuum, low stake in conformity scores and/or IV drug use result in a recommendation of long-term, residential treatment.

Services Recommended

1. *Long-Term Residential Treatment*: Long-term residential treatment is recommended for any client who uses illegal methadone or any drugs intravenously—heroin, other narcotics, cocaine, or amphetamines.

Intravenous (IV) drug use has been found to be the culmination of a drug-using career. Given the many psychological, behavioral, and physical consequences associated with IV drug use, the intense supervision and services of long-term residential care are required.

2. *Short-Term Residential Treatment*: Short-term residential treatment is recommended for any client with a drug use severity score of 2, and a stake in conformity of less than 12. These individuals use non-IV stimulants or oral opiates on a weekly basis and require the services and supervision provided within the context of short-term residential care.

3. *Intensive Outpatient Treatment*: Intensive outpatient treatment is recommended in two situations:
   (1) The first involves persons with a drug use severity score of 3 and a stake in conformity score of less than 12. Although this person may be using several drugs regularly, he or she may not yet need the more rigid monitoring of a short-term facility; thus, he or she is placed in the most stringent of the nonresidential categories.

(2) The second involves persons with a drug use severity score of 2 and a high stake in conformity (12 or higher). These persons are somehow able to maintain a job and stable living arrangements, while using non-IV cocaine, crack, amphetamines, or oral opiates on a weekly basis. Therefore, these individuals require some level of intensive attention but do not require residential treatment.

4. *Outpatient Treatment*: Outpatient treatment is recommended in two situations:
   (1) The first involves persons with a drug use severity score of 4 and a total stake in conformity of less than 12. These individuals are daily users of alcohol and/or marijuana who also use one Category B drug and have low to moderate stakes in conformity. Because drug use has apparently progressed beyond experimental or social, recreational levels combined with less than optimal stakes in conformity, it is believed that the additional supervision and services of outpatient treatment are required.
   (2) The second involves the client with a more serious drug problem, for example, a drug use severity of 3. Clients in this group are polydrug users. Even with a high stake in conformity score (12 or better), outpatient treatment is recommended for these typically nonrecreational users.

5. *Urine Only*: Urine monitoring only is recommended in two situations:
   (1) The first includes clients with a drug severity score of 5 or 6. Individuals with this drug severity score only use alcohol *and/or* marijuana, or use other drugs (including sedatives, inhalants, and hallucinogens) less than once a week. Since they are non-users of other drugs, they qualify for urine only *regardless of their stake in conformity score.*
   (2) The second includes clients who have a total stake in conformity score of 12 or more (and thus a high stake) and have a drug severity score of 4 (daily users of alcohol and/or marijuana plus one drug in category B). Because of their minimal illegal drug use and/or their relatively high stakes in conformity, they are considered the best candidates for a urine monitoring program.

The Need for AIDS Education/Intervention

If the conclusion was reached that the client is at high risk for HIV infection, then "yes" should be circled at the end of the instrument, and HIV/AIDS prevention/intervention services should be provided. At a minimum, AIDS prevention literature should be made available to all clients.

OFFENDER PROFILE INDEX

CASE #__ __ __ __ __ __

CRIMINAL JUSTICE VERIFICATION

Arrests Verified: _____

Date of Verification: _____

Not Verified: _____

URINALYSIS RESULTS (PRELIMINARY):

Negative for All Drugs: _____

Positive for:

Cocaine	_____
Opiates	_____
Amphetamines	_____
THC	_____
Benzodiazepines	_____
Barbiturates	_____
Phencyclidine	_____

Date of Test: _____

Confirmed: Yes ____   No____

PART I: Background Information

Jurisdiction: _____

Client's Name: _____
                      Last   First   Middle

Social Security Number: ___ - __ - ____

Date of Birth: ____/ __ / __
               Month/Day/Year

Age: _____

Please circle appropriate responses:

Sex: 1. Male   2. Female

Ethnicity:

1. White	6. Asian or Pacific Islander
2. Black American	7. Hispanic/Mexican
3. Black/Haitian	8. Hispanic/Cuban
4. Black/Other Caribbean	9. Hispanic/Puerto Rican
5. Native American	10. Hispanic/Other

Type of Client:
1. Pre-Sentencing
2. Sentencing
3. Post-Sentencing

Offenses:

1._____	3._____
2. _____	4._____

UNCOOPERATIVE/DISORIENTED CLIENTS: If client refuses to cooperate or appears too disoriented to provide the information requested, the interview should be terminated and the appropriate indicator circled.

Client was:
1. Mentally disoriented
2. Uncooperative
3. Cooperative, continue interview

_____   _____
Interviewer's Signature   Date of Interview

PART II: Drug Use Severity Index

Illegal Drugs and/or Nonmedical Use of Prescription Drugs	Age of 1st Use	Age of 1st Continued Use	CODING FREQUENCY: 3 = daily 2 = 1/wk or more 1 = less than 1/wk

A.

1. ALCOHOL ____ ____ ____
2. MARIJUANA, kif, hashish, etc. ____ ____ ____

B.

3. INHALANTS, glue, solvents, etc. ____ ____ ____
4. HALLUCINOGENS lsd, pcp, etc. ____ ____ ____
5. PILLS, downers, prescribed sedatives, tranquilizers ____ ____ ____

C.

6. PILLS, uppers, speed, crank ____ ____ ____
7. AMPHETAMINES, ice, crystals ____ ____ ____
8. OPIATES, pills, Dilaudid, codeine, and T's and Blues ____ ____ ____
9. COCAINE, non-IV, inhalation, snorting ____ ____ ____
10. CRACK, freebase ____ ____ ____
11. BASUCO, coca paste ____ ____ ____

D.

12. HEROIN (IV)	_____	_____	_____
13. COCAINE (IV)	_____	_____	_____
14. SPEED (IV)	_____	_____	_____
15. OTHER (IV) NARCOTICS			
16. COCAINE/HEROIN (IV) speedball	_____	_____	_____
17. ILLEGAL METHADONE	_____	_____	_____

SCORING:

6 = 0 in A - D *or* 1 in A
5 = 2 in A *or* 1 in B
4 = 3 in A *or* 2 or 3 in only *one* drug in B
3 = 2 or 3 in *two* or more drugs in B *or* 1 in C
2 = 2 or 3 in C
1 = 1 in D
0 = 2 or 3 in D

DRUG USE SEVERITY SCORE _____

PART III: Stake in Conformity Index

A. Family/Support Stake Sub-Index

    1. With whom are your currently living?   _____
        a. spouse/sex partner   = 2
        b. parents/family   = 2
        c. alone/friends   = 1
        d. street/institution   = 0

    2. If (a) or (b) above, how long have you been living in that   _____
        arrangement?
        1 year or longer   = 2
        6 to 12 months   = 1
        less than 6 months   = 0

    3. Has your spouse/sex partner or any of the people with   _____
        whom you are currently living EVER been incarcerated
        for 30 days or longer? (1) Yes (2) No

    4. Has your spouse/sex partner or any of the people with   _____
        whom you are living ever been treated for a drug or
        alcohol problem or gone through detox?   (1) Yes (2) No

    5. How many *close* friends do or did you have prior to your
        arrest? _____ (not scored)

    6. How many of these friends have EVER been incarcerated   _____
        for 30 days or longer?
        half or more   = 0
        less than half   = 1
        none or almost none   = 2

    7. How many of these friends have ever been treated   _____
        for a drug or alcohol problem, or have gone through detox?
        half or more   = 0
        less than half   = 1
        none or almost none   = 2

TOTAL COMPOSITE SCORE for questions 1, 2, 6, 7 above: _____

    Family/Support Stake Sub-Index Scoring
        Assign a weight of 0 for a composite score of 0 - 3
        Assign a weight of 1 for a composite score of 4 - 5
        Assign a weight of 2 for a composite score of 6 or greater

FAMILY/SUPPORT STAKE SCORE (circle the appropriate score): 0   1   2

B. Educational Stake Sub-Index
1. What is the highest grade in school that you completed?   _____
        (If 12 years or more, proceed to scoring below)
2. If less than 12, did you receive a GED? (2) Yes (1) No
        (If client received GED, proceed to scoring below)
3. Have you attended any vocational/technical courses? (2) Yes (1) No
        (If no, proceed to scoring below)
4. If yes, what courses or training programs did you complete?

_____

_____

Educational Stake Sub-Index Scoring
    Assign a weight of 2 for: 12 or more years of schooling, or GED, *or* 9 or
    more years + completed skills training
    Assign a weight of 1 for: 9 - 11 years without completed skills training
    Assign a weight of 0 for: 8 years or less

EDUCATIONAL STAKE SCORE (circle the appropriate score): 0   1   2

C.   School Stake Sub-Index

    1. Are you currently attending school? (2) Yes (1) No

    2. If **NO**, score 0 below and go to Work Stake Sub-Index

    3. If **YES**, is schooling full- or part-time?

        If full-time, score 2 below

        If part-time, score 1 below

Interviewer: Obtain enrollment verification information below:

      (1) Not Verified   (2) Inaccurate   (3) Accurate

Enrollment Verification Information

    Name of School: _____

    Address: _____

         _____

    Telephone Number: _____

SCHOOL STAKE SCORE (circle the appropriate score): 0   1   2

D. Work Stake Sub-Index

1. How many weeks have you worked outside the home and/or as a homemaker (with responsibility for others) during the past 12 months?

    Assign a weight of 2 for 35 weeks or more
    Assign a weight of 1 for 20-34 weeks
    Assign a weight of 0 for less than 20 weeks

2. Are you currently employed outside the home and/or as a homemaker (with responsibility for others)? (2) Yes (1) No

3. If **YES**, how many hours a week do you typically work?

    Assign a weight of 2 for 35 or more hours/week
    Assign a weight of 1 for 15-34 hours/week
    Assign a weight of 0 for less than 15 hours/week

4. If **NO**, how many hours a week did you work on your last job?

    Assign a weight of 2 for 35 hours or more/week
    Assign a weight of 1 for 15-34 hours/week
    Assign a weight of 0 for less than 15 hours/week

INTERVIEWER: Obtain employment verification information below

Employment Verification Number

Name of Employer: _____

Address: _____

_____

Telephone Number: _____

Supervisor's Name: _____

    (1) Not Verified   (2) Inaccurate   (3) Accurate

Work Stake Sub-Index Scoring

    Sum of Scores (from questions 1 *and* 3 or 4) =

    Assign a weight of 2 for a composite score of 4
    Assign a weight of 1 for a composite score of 2-3
    Assign a weight of 0 for a composite score of 0-1

WORK STAKE SCORE (circle the appropriate score): 0 1 2

E.   Home Stake Sub-Index

1. What is your most recent residence:

_____
Street

_____
City   State   Zip Code

Telephone: _____

2. Dates you resided there: From _____ to _____
3. Number of months at that residence: _____
   (If 12 months or more, proceed to question #5)
4. How many residences have you had during the past 12 months? _____
5. During the past 12 months, how much were you contributing to the
   rent or mortgage of the place(s) where you were living?
         (1) none   (2) some   (3) all

VERIFICATION

_____ place of last residence verified as correct
_____ dates of last residence verified as correct
_____ place of last residence verified as incorrect
_____ dates of last residence verified as incorrect
_____ residence not verified

Date of residence check: _____

Name of checker: _____

Home Stake Sub-Index Scoring

Assign a weight of 0 if the client: made no contribution to the rent or mortgage
      during the past 12 months or had 6 or more residences, or if most recent
      residence was false.

Assign a weight of 1 if the client: made some contribution to the rent or
      mortgage during the past 12 months or had 4-5 residences, *and* most
      recent residence was verified as correct.

Assign a weight of 2 if the client: made the total contribution to the rent or
      mortgage, *and* had less than 4 residences, *and* the residence was verified
      as correct.

HOME STAKE SCORE (circle the appropriate score): 0   1   2

F. Criminal Justice History Sub-Index
   1. Total arrests in last 5 years:
   2. Total convictions in last 5 years: _____
   3. Total time served (months) in last 5 years: _____
                                                      _____

Criminal Justice History Scoring

   Assign a weight of 2 if client had no more than 2 arrests and/or 45 days
        incarcerated in the last 5 years

   Assign a weight of 1 if client had 3 to 10 arrests and/or 6 months incarcerated
        in the last 5 years

   Assign a weight of 0 if client had 11 or more arrests and/or more than 6 months
        incarcerated in the last 5 years

NOTE: In scoring, time incarcerated should weigh more heavily than number
of arrests.

CRIMINAL JUSTICE STAKE SCORE (circle the appropriate score): 0   1   2

G. Psychological Stake Sub-Index

    1. Have you ever felt if you had acted out of control, or have others told you that you had acted out of control, at any time when you were NOT under the influence of alcohol or drugs? (1) Yes   (2) No

        If **YES**, how many times in the last year?   _____

            Score 2 if none

            Score 1 if only 1 time

            Score 0 if 2 or more times   _____

    2. Have you ever attempted suicide? (1) Yes   (2) No

        If **NO**, have you ever seriously considered suicide?

        (1) Yes   (2) No

        Score 2 if no to both questions

        Score 1 if yes to considered

        Score O if yes to attempted   _____

    3. Have you ever been treated for nervous or mental problems?

        (1) Yes   (2) No

        If **YES**, how many times did you receive treatment?   _____

        Score 2 if never treated

        Score 1 if treated once

        Score 0 if treated 2 or more times   _____

TOTAL COMPOSITE SCORE FOR QUESTIONS 1-3 ABOVE: _____

Psychological Stake Sub-Index Scoring

        Assign a weight of 2 for a composite score of 5-6

        Assign a weight of 1 for a composite score of 2-4

        Assign a weight of 0 for a composite score of 0-1

PSYCHOLOGICAL STAKE SCORE (circle appropriate score): 0   1   2

H.   Treatment Stake Sub-Index

1. How many months have you spent in drug-abuse treatment   _____
   during the past 5 years?

   Assign a weight of 2 for 12 months or more
   Assign a weight of 0 for less than 12 months

TREATMENT STAKE SCORE (circle the appropriate score): 0   1   2

I. HIV Risk Behaviors Sub-Index

1. How many sex partners have you had in the last year?   _____
2. What proportion of the time were condoms used?   _____
    1. None
    2. About a quarter
    3. About half
    4. About three-quarters
    5. Almost all

FOR MALES ONLY

3. What proportion of your sex partners were prostitutes?   _____
    1. Almost all
    2. About three-quarters
    3. About half
    4. About a quarter
    5. None
4. What proportion of these sex partners were IV drug users?   _____
    1. Almost all
    2. About three-quarters
    3. About half
    4. About a quarter
    5. None
5. What proportion of these sex partners were males?   _____
    1. Almost all
    2. About three-quarters
    3. About half
    4. About a quarter
    5. None
6. *If any were males,* what proportion of the time did sexual   _____
    contact involve anal penetration?
    1. Almost all
    2. About three-quarters
    3. About half
    4. About a quarter
    5. None

FOR FEMALES ONLY

7. What proportion of your sexual partners were IV drug users?   _____
    1. Almost all
    2. About three-quarters
    3. About half

    4. About a quarter

    5. None

8. What proportion of the time did sexual intercourse involve   _____
   anal penetration?

    1. Almost all

    2. About three-quarters

    3. About half

    4. About a quarter

    5. None

For IV Drug Users Only (Ask Both Males and Females)

9. When you had your own works, how often did you share   _____
   them with others?

    1. More than half the time

    2. About half the time

    3. About a quarter of the time

    4. Almost never

10. After sharing your works, how often did you clean them   _____
    before using them yourself?

    1. Almost never

    2. About a quarter of the time

    3. About half the time

    4. More than half the time

    5. Never shared

11. What do you usually use to clean your works?   _____

    1. Never clean them

    2. Other (specify) _____

    3. Water

    4. Alcohol

    5. Bleach

12. When you did not have your own works, how often did you   _____
    clean the works you borrowed?

    1. Almost never

    2. About a quarter of the time

    3. About half the time

    4. More than half the time

13. On these occasions, how did you clean these works?   _____

    1. Never clean them

    2. Other (specify) _____

    3. Water

    4. Alcohol

    5. Bleach

INTERVIEWER: Is client at high risk for HIV infection? Yes____ No____

PART IV: Profile Summary

   1. Drug Use Severity Score   _____

   2. Stake in Conformity
        A. Family/Support Stake Score   _____
        B. Educational Stake Score   _____
        C. School Stake Score   _____
        D. Work Stake Score   _____
        E. Home Stake Score   _____
        F. Criminal Justice Stake Score   _____
        G. Psychological Stake Score   _____
        H. Treatment Stake Score   _____

TOTAL STAKE IN CONFORMITY SCORE   _____

Profiles (circle one)

1. Long-Term Residential Treatment

   0 or 1 drug severity

2. Short-Term Residential Treatment

   2 in drug severity *plus* conformity stake of less than 12

3. Intensive Outpatient Treatment (must have contact with client in a therapeutic session of at least 1 hour's duration, 3 times/week or more)

   (a) 3 in drug severity plus conformity stake of less than 12
   OR
   (b) 2 in drug severity plus conformity stake of at least 12

4. Outpatient Treatment (must have contact with client in a therapeutic session of at least 1 hour's duration, no less than 1 time/week

   (a) 4 in drug severity plus conformity stake of less than 12
   OR
   (b) 3 in drug severity plus conformity stake of at least 12

5. Urine Only

   (a) 5 or 6 drug severity
   OR
   (b) 4 drug severity plus conformity stake of at least 12

Is AIDS prevention/intervention indicated?   Yes _____ No _____

In completing the interview it has been determined that the client experiences overriding mental health problems and is not suitable for drug intervention.

                                        (Circle)   Yes   No

Chapter 9

INMATE DRUG TREATMENT PROGRAMMING IN THE FEDERAL BUREAU OF PRISONS

BETH A. WEINMAN
DOROTHY LOCKWOOD

Drug abuse treatment began at the federal level in the United States with the Public Health Service (USPHS) "narcotics farms," one at Lexington, Kentucky, in 1935 and the other at Fort Worth, Texas, in 1938. These facilities were later termed Clinical Research Centers and were designed primarily for federal prisoners, although voluntary patients were admitted. Shortly after implementation, these programs experienced poor outcomes. For instance, many voluntary patients failed to remain, transition programs to the community did not exist, and relapse rates were high (Leukefeld, 1989).

Partially in response to these program failures, Congress enacted the Narcotic Addict Rehabilitation Act (NARA PL 89-793) in 1966 as a federal civil commitment program. NARA established court-ordered treatment, initially at Lexington and Fort Worth, as an alternative to incarceration. The law required screening to determine the benefits of treatment for addicts. Screening inmates prior to admission into the program ensured that clients appropriate for treatment entered the programs. In addition, NARA required addicts to participate in a maximum of 6 months inpatient treatment and a period of aftercare, strengthening program retention (Lindblad & Besteman, 1986).

AUTHORS' NOTE: This chapter was co-written by a government employee as part of official duties; therefore, the material is in the public domain and may be copied or reproduced without permission.

These initial efforts underscore the complexity of providing drug treatment in correctional settings. Balancing the priorities of incarceration and the goals of treatment is a challenge, exacerbated by changing political concerns and federal funding levels. Nonetheless, the Federal Bureau of Prisons continues to fulfill the responsibility of providing drug treatment to the many inmates with significant drug abuse problems. Among the federal programs, diverse approaches have emerged, contributing to the development of effective drug abuse treatment in correctional settings (Hayes & Schimmel, 1993).

THE BUREAU'S CURRENT DRUG ABUSE PROGRAM INITIATIVES

Even amid the acceptance of a "nothing works" philosophy during the 1970s (Martinson, 1970), the Bureau continued to provide drug abuse treatment. The "war on drugs" during the 1980s created a surge in drug abuse treatment funding and programs as well as an increase in the numbers of inmates in need of drug abuse treatment. At that time, the Bureau underwent a substantial increase in its population with close to 50% of all inmates serving time for drug-related offenses (Murray, 1992). At this juncture, it was necessary for the Bureau to review its treatment policies and restructure its drug treatment programming. New efforts were based on a growing body of research on what does work in drug abuse treatment, on the Bureau's experience in drug treatment, and on the increasing number of inmates with varying treatment needs.

Through several work group sessions, the Bureau of Prisons designed a four-tier treatment strategy to respond to the increased and varied need of its drug-dependent population. As part of this strategy, the Bureau also adopted a specific treatment philosophy and treatment curriculum to guide the development and implementation of new programs. The programs comprising this four-tier system cover the spectrum from education to transitional services, including drug education, nonresidential drug abuse treatment, unit-based residential treatment, and transitional services. Recognizing that drug abuse results from many different causes and circumstances, several treatment approaches are employed within this treatment framework, including rational emotive therapy, rational behavioral therapy, criminal thinking confrontation, interpersonal and communication skills building, relapse prevention, wellness training, traditional group and individual counseling paradigms, pre-release services, and transitional readiness training.

In cooperation with the National Institute on Drug Abuse, the Bureau of Prisons is also conducting an outcome evaluation of this effort. The purpose of this evaluation is to provide information on the effectiveness of drug treatment for the inmate population as well as provide a greater understanding of causes of drug addiction among the prison population (Pelissier & McCarthy, 1992).

The psychology services department in each Bureau correctional institution administers the federal drug abuse treatment programs. Both psychologists and other professional staff with experience in drug treatment provide the treatment services. A standard intake and assessment procedure has been developed where all inmates entering the Bureau of Prisons are informed of the available treatment options as part of admissions and orientation. After orientation, the staff of psychology services screens each inmate to determine if a substance abuse problem exits. Simultaneously, unit management staff review inmates' files looking for any of three significant criteria that would constitute a need for drug abuse treatment: (1) the judge recommended the inmate participate in a drug abuse treatment program; (2) the inmate's instant offense was related to drug abuse; and (3) the inmate has been re-incarcerated because of a violation of supervision that is related to drug abuse. Based on the results of these assessments, inmates are referred to the appropriate drug treatment program. Participation in any program is voluntary. Each program is described below.

DRUG ABUSE EDUCATION

All inmates meeting any of the criteria discussed above are required to participate in the Bureau's 40-hour drug abuse education program. Inmates assessed in need of drug abuse education who fail to enter or to complete the program are restricted to the lowest inmate job pay grade throughout incarceration. This educational program is designed to address the most basic aspect of drug abuse. It is intended to prepare drug-involved offenders for more intense treatment. For a small segment of the drug-abusing offender population, drug abuse education may be the only services needed.

The Bureau's drug abuse education program focuses on the physiological effects of drug abuse, addresses the high-risk behaviors for HIV, hepatitis, tuberculosis, and other diseases related to drug use and drug-using behaviors, and discusses the benefits of drug treatment and behavior change. Through a group process, the education program begins to break through the denial associated with addiction in hopes of motivating inmates to continue treatment in a Bureau residential drug treatment program.

NONRESIDENTIAL DRUG ABUSE TREATMENT

For those inmates either unwilling to enter residential treatment or unable to enter residential treatment because of inadequate time remaining on their sentences, nonresidential drug abuse treatment is available through psychology services in every institution. Nonresidential treatment provides services analogous to outpatient treatment in the community. Nonresidential treatment also provides inmates with drug abuse treatment and support services while they are awaiting intake into a residential treatment program. While participating in nonresidential treatment, inmates live in the general prison population and receive treatment from the psychology services department. They work with a psychologist on a regular basis to complete comprehensive assessments and to develop individualized treatment plans. Similar to community-based outpatient treatment, inmates sign a treatment agreement and consent forms, allowing transfer of information. Therefore, when inmates move to another institution or are released from prison with stipulations for continued treatment, assessments and treatment plans are transferred to other treatment providers.

RESIDENTIAL DRUG ABUSE TREATMENT

Thirty of the Bureaus of Prisons institutions offer residential drug abuse treatment programs. These programs are unit-based where inmates from all institutional security levels reside together. The programs are structured, following a disciplined course of treatment. The Bureau has designed two types of residential treatment programs. Twenty-seven of the 30 programs are based on the "comprehensive" model, a 9-month program that provides 500 hours of treatment and has a staff-to-inmate ratio of 1:24. The other three programs are "pilot" programs at FMC Lexington, Kentucky; FMC Butner, North Carolina; and FCI Tallahassee, Florida. These programs are 12-month programs that provide 1,000 hours of treatment with a 1:12 staff ratio. These two models are being compared, examining the client outcome differences based on intensity of treatment and resource allocation. However, the fundamental components of both programs are the same and are described below.

Orientation and Assessment

On entry, inmates participate in orientation, which acclimates them to the treatment program philosophy, structure, rules, and regulations. Both residential treatment programs are founded on group processes. During orientation, the group process is discussed with a focus on the role and expectations of clients and counselors. The importance of maintaining confidentiality and of participating in group therapies are emphasized. In addition, the role of the counselor is discussed during orientation. Because the counselors in these prison based programs are also correctional staff, often the correctional and treatment roles are perceived as conflicting and the group process can be stifled. During orientation, inmates come to understand that although counselors will not ignore violations of Bureau policies, they do ensure confidentiality of issues discussed in group and are responsible for facilitating group therapies (Hayes & Schimmel, 1993).

Concurrently, a full battery of assessment is conducted on each inmate. The assessments emanate from both a theoretical and an empirical framework. Theoretically, criminologists have argued that the best assessment approaches are based on criminological theory focusing on the etiology of crime and emphasize personality factors, peer group involvement, and stakes in conformity. However, empirically based assessments focus on the correlation between offender characteristics and desired outcomes. Referred to as a multifactor approach, empirically based assessments employ data collected in routine criminal justice processing to determine risk and appropriate security (McBride, 1991). Information from these assessments are combined to provide effective treatment for the individual inmates as well as to predict risk patterns of each inmate, which are then addressed and managed through treatment.

Treatment Components

Treatment therapy and counseling are conducted in a group format for at least 4 hours a day. Inmates are required to attend both group and individual sessions, to complete all assignments, and to actively participate in the various therapies offered. Group and individual counseling are conducted throughout the program and are tailored for the individual needs and responses to treatment of each inmate. The techniques and content of counseling sessions are also correlated with the various treatment modules administered throughout the program. Each of these modules is described below.

The *criminal thinking confrontation* module is based on the work of Samuel Yochelson and Stanton Samenow and aims to teach inmates to identify thinking errors (Yochelson & Samenow, 1986). The philosophy of this model is that drug-abusing behavior is closely tied to criminal thinking and entrenches the individual into self-defeating habits, including deception and manipulation. According to Yochelson and Samenow, such habits and behaviors must be addressed through confrontation. The fundamental aspect of this module is to learn to confront thinking errors, and confrontation of negative attitudes and behaviors is used throughout the entire treatment regime as a means to effect behavior and thinking changes.

The *rational emotive therapy/rational behavioral therapy (RET/RBT)* module is founded on the teachings of Maxie Mautsby, Jr. (1975) and Albert Ellis (1975). Within this module, inmates learn methods to record and report thoughts and feelings. Through this process, they learn how perceptions of reality occur and, as a result, they develop more accurate perceptions of reality. They also learn how to assess troublesome situations as well as how to correct thinking errors. The goal of this module is to enable inmates to recognize and handle uncomfortable feelings generated from change as well as to change unrealistic thinking (Hayes & Schimmel, 1993).

Social skill deficits are addressed in a module designed to build *interpersonal and communication skills*. In the course of this module, inmates learn, among other things, listening skills, various communication styles, and how to manage anger. Marital and family relationships, including parenting issues, long-term guilt, shame, and fear are also discussed. Specific issues raised within this module are addressed in individual counseling sessions so that the needs of each inmate can be met in a more focused setting.

The *wellness* module emphasizes the need for a healthy, pro-social life-style. Individual assessments are conducted to aid inmates in developing a personalized wellness plan. Other institutional staff, such as medical staff, chaplains, wellness coordinators, and food service personnel, are encouraged to contribute to and support the inmates' wellness plans.

Fifty hours of treatment are dedicated to the *relapse prevention* module. Based on Marlatt and Gordon's (1985) work, inmates learn to identify events and situations that lead to relapse. The risk of relapse is reduced partially by recognizing these events and situations. In addition, inmates begin to address stimuli that trigger relapse by applying what they learned in the cognitive skills module and the criminal confrontation module. Through role-play, inmates learn how to deal with potential relapse situations. Group feedback further aids inmates in developing appropriate responses to such situations, strengthening their relapse prevention plans.

The final module is the *pre-release and transitional living readiness* component. This module aims to prepare inmates for reintegration to the community. By reviewing what has been taught throughout the program, this module focuses on using these skills in the community. For instance, conflict often arises in transitioning to the community due to inmates' unrealistic expectations of friends and family members. Inmates are taught to avoid such conflicts by rethinking their expectations and developing more realistic perceptions of what they deserve on release. Finally, concrete living skills, such as applying and interviewing for a job, looking for an apartment, opening a bank account, and budgeting finances, are taught. Also, issues concerning interacting with probation officers and living in a Bureau of Prisons contract community corrections center are discussed.

Transitional Services

Aftercare or transitional drug treatment services are essential to any drug treatment effort. Therefore, the Bureaus of Prisons had dedicated considerable resources to this component. Inmates are released either to a Bureau of Prisons contract community corrections center or directly to the supervision of the U.S. Probation Office. On release, a treatment summary and treatment recommendations are sent to the appropriate supervising authority to ensure additional treatment and support are provided during transition to the community. This coordination, coupled with community supervision, encourages inmates to continue a drug-free existence. Treatment services in the community are provided by community-based drug treatment programs under contract with the Bureau of Prisons or U.S. Probation. While in the custody of the Bureau, inmates are required to continue the treatment program defined by the Bureau staff in collaboration with the treatment staff. They also must submit to regular urinalysis testing and follow other program requirements, such as finding employment. Failure to participate in treatment and fulfill these requirements may result in return to prison.

CRITICAL ELEMENTS OF DRUG ABUSE TREATMENT IN CORRECTIONS

Implementation of any treatment effort in corrections is difficult. The problems are exacerbated in the case of implementing drug abuse treatment programs in correctional settings. Philosophical conflicts occur between correctional staff and drug treatment staff. Correctional staff prioritize custody and security; whereas, treatment staff emphasize autonomy, privileges, and rewards. Frequently, the need for program autonomy conflicts with institutional security. In addition, the federal prison system's mandatory sentencing reform, which eliminated parole, reduced the incentives for inmates to voluntarily participate in treatment. To avoid the common pitfalls of administering drug abuse treatment programs in correctional settings, the Bureau of Prisons established critical program elements to guide this effort. They are based on experiences of federal, state, and local programs as well as research findings on successful drug treatment implementation in corrections (Carter, 1991; Gerstein & Harwood, 1990; Leukefeld & Tims, 1992). Performance indicators are tasks that must be completed in order to develop the critical elements. Performance indicators are designed to assist in the coordination between correctional staff and treatment staff.

Critical elements are divided into two groups. Organizational elements define the coordination between correctional staff and treatment staff and must be in place before program operations begin. Operational elements guide program implementation and must be established to achieve successful program operations. Ten critical elements and their corresponding performance indicators are outlined below. These elements were essential in the development and implementation of the Bureau of Prison's drug abuse treatment programming. They are intended as a guide for other correctional authorities initiating drug abuse treatment efforts.

Organizational Elements

Element 1: Program Advisory Panel

Purpose: To coordinate efforts of participating organizations and to create ownership of the treatment program by key participants.

Performance Indicators:

1. Advisory panel members should include the warden, correctional administrator(s), correctional officer(s), psychology and education services staff, and treatment administrators and staff. Requests to serve on the advisory panel outlining each member's responsibility should be sent with letters of acceptance or refusal filed. Advisory panel responsibilities include the following:

- Development and documentation of the program's mission and philosophy
- Development of a program implementation plan addressing implementation time frame, treatment approaches, duration of treatment, incentives and sanctions for clients, eligibility criteria, staff training, and start-up.

2. Advisory panel meetings shall be documented and minutes distributed to each member. Significant agreements, policies, and procedures should be documented and disseminated under separate cover.

3. A regular meeting schedule should be set. At a minimum, a meeting of the advisory panel should be held no less than every 2 months through program development and implementation. At a minimum, a meeting of the advisory panel should be held no less than every quarter throughout the remainder of program operation.

Element 2: Broad-Based Support From Correction Authorities

Purpose: To establish and maintain ongoing communication and formal agreements within the correctional institution and to assure effective support for a credible treatment program.

Performance Indicators:

1. Six months prior to program implementation, meetings should be held with administrative correctional personnel and other appropriate correctional and treatment staff to detail and document the following:

- Description of treatment services to inmates
- Eligibility criteria for entry into the treatment program
- Inmate screening procedures, delineating who is responsible for administration
- Inmate referral mechanisms, specifying who is responsible for making referrals
- Inmate discipline policies and procedures
- Incentives and sanctions policies, specifying who is responsible for administration
- Drug testing policies, specifying who is responsible for administering the test, reporting results, enforcing sanctions, and maintaining records
- Success/failure criteria
- Information exchange between treatment and correctional staff
- Staff orientation
- Inmate orientation
- Data requirements
- Lines of authority and communication
- A regular meeting schedule to discuss problems, successes, and revisions

2. Letters detailing each of the above agreements should be developed and disseminated, with annual review of agreements.

Element 3: Philosophy and Design of a Comprehensive Treatment Strategy

Purpose: To provide correction administrators, staff, and inmates with a standard structure and philosophy of treatment to guide program implementation.

Performance Indicators:

1. A structured unit-based treatment program, segregated from the general prison population with a decentralized administration should be selected.

2. Specific treatment approaches should be selected and fully described. Treatment components should incorporate a number of approaches and include the following:

- Program orientation
- Assessment
- Drug education
- Self-help programs
- Traditional group and individual counseling
- Cognitive behavior therapies
- Therapeutic community ideologies
- Culturally sensitive programming
- Program aspects directed to special populations
- Aftercare planning

3. The treatment component duration, timing, and success criteria, including impact of successful completion on release status, should be documented and disseminated.

Element 4: Treatment Program Management Coordinated With the Correctional System, But Also Autonomous

Purpose: To ensure treatment program integrity and organizational capability to carry out the program mission as well as to meet the agreed on expectations of both the corrections and treatment systems.

Performance Indicators:

1. An organizational chart, displaying the treatment program as an autonomous unit within the larger correctional organization, should be filed with the correctional institution and the treatment program.

2. Written agreements distinguishing between the roles of the treatment staff and the correctional officer during routine operations should be developed and periodically reviewed. Both treatment and correctional staff should be familiar with these agreements and aware that roles will change during emergency operations.

3. Agreements outlining the treatment program administrator's responsibility should also be developed and reviewed periodically. These agreements should address the following:

- Program management
- Program budget
- Lines of authority and communication
- Data requirements
- Record keeping
- Inmate security issues

Element 5: Policies and Procedures for Staff Recruitment and Training

Purpose: To ensure that all drug abuse treatment staff satisfactorily understand the philosophy, mission, and intention of providing drug abuse treatment in a correctional setting, including established policies and procedures.

Performance Standards:

1. Thorough applicant screening procedures should be developed, satisfying both correctional and treatment concerns.

2. Policies for hiring ex-addicts and ex-offenders should be developed and agreed on by both correctional and treatment administrators.

3. A training plan for the treatment staff that includes job-related goals for enhanced treatment efficacy and coordinated training with other institutional staff should be developed and reviewed annually.

4. Personnel records should document that each staff member has received an updated written description of the treatment program, detailed job descriptions, job performance evaluations, and appropriate operational guidelines.

Element 6: Data Collection and Program Evaluation

Purpose: To provide timely, accurate, and necessary information to treatment administrators and other staff for managing and developing program services, determining operational effectiveness, providing appropriate information to correctional administrators and funding sources, and meeting public information needs.

Performance Indicators:

1. Standardized reports should be developed and routinely produced and disseminated.

2. Standardized data collection forms with well-documented procedures should be developed to record information such as the following:

- Number of inmates referred, screened, and accepted
- Inmate demographics and socioeconomic characteristics prior to incarceration, such as age, race, sex, education, and employment status
- Other related inmate characteristics, such as instant offense, drug-dependent status, primary drug of abuse, drug testing results, reason for treatment participation, and number of incident reports while in the treatment program and while in the general prison population
- Number of inmates in each phase of treatment
- Information on releasees, including aftercare plans for graduates and reason for dismissal for discharged inmates
- Number, type, and attendance of specific treatment therapies conducted
- Expenditures by budget line-item category

3. Data analysis should be conducted routinely to determine program effectiveness, program problems, and problem resolution. Findings from analyses should be used for public information, program management, and program evaluation.

4. Dissemination of data and analyses should be recorded.

Operational Elements

Element 7: Inmate Eligibility Criteria

Purpose: To set clear standards for inclusion and exclusion of inmates from the prison-based treatment program.

Performance Indicators:

1. Inmate eligibility criteria must be formally established and include the following:

- Current and/or previous drug involvement, as documented by self-report, drug testing results, medical reports, and/or reports from other agencies
- Sufficient incarceration time remaining on the inmates' sentences to complete the treatment program
- Informed voluntary consent, evidenced by a signed agreement to participate in treatment and comply with the treatment and corrections requirements

2. Written agreements from each cooperating corrections department supporting the established inmate eligibility criteria should be made.

Element 8: Inmate Referral, Screening, and Assessment

Purpose: To provide a standardized process for inmates to enter treatment, to ensure correctional and treatment staff efforts are coordinated, to ensure all inmate eligibility criteria are met, and to ensure standardized data are collected.

Performance Standards:

1. Documented procedures for systematic inmate identification and referral from corrections personnel to treatment program unit staff should be developed.

2. Documented policies and procedures to access each inmate's prior social history and classification information should be developed.

3. Standardized screening forms incorporating relevant data collected at other points in the criminal justice system should be developed and systematically used. These forms should include the following:

- Drug involvement
- Correctional classification information
- Previous assessment summaries
- Agreements from inmates to participate in treatment that confirm the inmates' understanding of the treatment programs rules, regulations, and expectations.

4. Standardized diagnostic and clinical tools used to assess the treatment needs, to establish the treatment plans, and to match inmates with the appropriate levels of treatment should be developed.

Element 9: Program Incentives and Sanctions

Purpose: To ensure effective and credible treatment of all inmates as well as to motivate participation and to respond to inappropriate behavior.

Performance Standards:

1. Treatment success and failure should be clearly defined, specifying criteria for each.

2. Quality-control measures for client progress documentation should be delineated and observed with routine supervisory review.

3. Procedures for assessing client progress should be developed and should include the following:

- Notification to appropriate corrections staff of each inmate's acceptance into the treatment program
- Specified intervals for treatment reports, data entry, and team reviews
- Specified procedures for notification of unit staff on an inmate's failure in treatment

Element 10: Transitional Services Component

Purpose: To ensure the continuation of treatment on each inmate's release from the institution.

Performance Standards:

1. Agreements and procedures of referral to community supervision and community-based treatment, with community supervising authorities, such as probation and community treatment providers, should be developed. Referral information should include the following:

- Release forms that allow for the transfer of information from the institution to the community
- Treatment summary and recommendations from the institutional treatment program

2. Agreements and protocols between the community supervision staff and the community-based treatment providers are encouraged.

REFERENCES

Carter, D. (Ed.). (1991, June). *Intervening with substance-abusing offenders: A framework for action.* Washington, DC: National Institute of Corrections.

Ellis, A. (1975). *A new guide to rational living.* N. Hollywood, CA: Wilshire.

Gerstein, D. R., & Harwood, H. J. (Eds.). (1990). *Treatment drug problems, Volume 1: A study of the evolution, effectiveness, and financing of public and private drug treatment systems.* Washington, DC: National Academy Press.

Hayes, T., & Schimmel, D. (1993). Residential drug abuse treatment in the Federal Bureau of Prisons. *Journal of Drug Issues, 23*(1), 61-73.

Leukefeld, C. G. (1989, August). *Opportunities for enhancing drug abuse treatment with criminal justice authority.* Paper presented at the National Institute on Drug Abuse Technical Review on Improving Drug Abuse Treatment, Rockville, MD.

Leukefeld, C. G., & Tims, F. M. (Eds.). (1992). *Drug abuse treatment in prisons and jails,* NIDA Publication No. 118. Rockville, MD: NIDA.

Lindblad, R. A., & Besteman, K. J. (1986, May). *A national civil commitment program for treatment of drug addiction.* Paper presented at the National Institute on Drug Abuse Technical Review on Civil Commitment, Rockville, MD.

Maddux, J. F. (1978). History of the hospital treatment programs, 1934-1974. In W. R. Martin & H. Isbell (Eds), *Drug addiction and the public health services.* Washington, DC: U.S. Government Printing Office.

Marlatt, A., & Gordon, J. (Eds.). (1985). *Relapse prevention: Maintenance strategies in the treatment of addictive behaviors.* New York: Guilford Press.

Martinson, R. (1970). What works? Questions and answers about prison reform. *Public Interest, 35,* 22-54.

Maultsby, M. (1975). *Help yourself to happiness through rational self-counseling.* New York: Institute for Rational Emotive Therapy.

McBride, D. C. (1991). *Drug assessment strategies.* Paper presented at the National TASC Conferences on Establishing Linkages, Key West, FL.

Murray, D. (1992). Drug abuse treatment programs in the Federal Bureau of Prisons: Initiatives for the 1990's. In C. Leukefeld & F. M. Tims (Eds.), *Drug abuse treatment in prisons and jails.* NIDA Publication No. 118. Rockville, MD: NIDA.

Pelissier, B., & McCarthy, D. (1992). Evaluation of the Federal Bureau of Prisons drug treatment programs. In C. Leukefeld & F. M. Tims (Eds.), *Drug abuse treatment in prisons and jails,* NIDA Publication No. 118. Rockville, MD: NIDA.

Yochelson, S., & Samenow, S. (1986). *The criminal personality, Volume III: The drug user.* Northvale, NJ: Jason Aronson.

Chapter 10

FROM REFORM TO RECOVERY
Advances in Prison Drug Treatment

HARRY K. WEXLER
DOUGLAS S. LIPTON

INTRODUCTION

Projects REFORM and RECOVERY were major federally funded technical assistance projects that have provided guidance and support for much of the expansions in prison substance abuse programs across the nation. The story of how projects REFORM and RECOVERY evolved includes many of the advances in prison drug treatment from 1987 through 1992. During these 6 years the states that have participated in REFORM and RECOVERY have led a "paradigmatic shift" in the direction of corrections in the United States—a movement away from the model emphasizing "security and control" and toward a model emphasizing "habilitation and treatment."

The movement toward a corrections-treatment perspective has been based on a growing body of research demonstrating the effectiveness of prison-based therapeutic communities in significantly reducing recidivism rates. This chapter will review the need for offender substance abuse treatment; summarize the growing body of research on the effectiveness of offender drug treatment; describe the recent correctional history that

AUTHORS' NOTE: The work reported in this paper has been contributed to by our colleagues at NDRI, Bruce Johnson, Greg Falkin, John Blackmore, Judy Ryder, Susan Crimmins, the REFORM and RECOVERY technical assistant consultants, and personnel from the participating states. A special acknowledgment is deserved by Mr. Nick Demos, who served as project officer for both the REFORM and RECOVERY projects.

209

has set the stage for this important change in corrections; describe principles and guidelines (generated by Projects REFORM and RECOVERY) for the planning and implementation of effective prison substance abuse treatment programs; and discuss the recommendations proposed by several groups (practitioners, researchers, policymakers) for the next steps needed to support and expand effective prison substance abuse treatment. (See Falkin, Wexler, & Lipton, 1992, for an excellent overview of drug treatment in state prisons.)

NEED FOR OFFENDER DRUG TREATMENT

Research during the last decade demonstrates a considerable need to expand and improve treatment for drug-involved offenders. First, there is abundant evidence that crime rates are higher among drug-dependent offenders than non-using offenders. Second, a substantial proportion of offenders are dependent on drugs; the vast majority have used drugs to some degree; and most drug-using offenders have significant life-style problems associated with substance abuse. Third, evaluation research during the decade of the 1980s has shown that (some forms of) drug treatment can be effective in significantly reducing recidivism as well as reducing drug use and other associated life-style problems. Fourth, despite the considerable need for effective treatment interventions, existing programs tend to be overburdened, and most drug-involved offenders either receive very limited treatment or none at all.

The Drug Use Forecasting (DUF) system of the National Institute of Justice periodically assesses drug use among persons arrested in 22 cities. Of those cities now participating in DUF, significant levels of cocaine and other drug use continues to be evident among arrestees regardless of charge. In the last several years, there has been no evidence of an increase in heroin use in male arrestees; opiates have been found in fewer than 20% of tested males (except New York, where the heroin positive rate has ranged between 17% and 29%) (Lipton, 1991). In contrast, cocaine levels have been consistently high in most cities. The highest rates of cocaine use—above 70%—have been found in Miami, Los Angeles, New York, and Philadelphia.

Overall, the U.S. prison population has grown about 55% over the past 8 years largely fueled by the major influx of drug-using offenders. These offenders are responsible for a relatively large amount of crime, and among them, the most predatory are the heroin-using "violent predators."

When compared to non-drug using offenders, severe drug users committed 15 times as many robberies, 20 times as many burglaries, and 10 times as many thefts (Chaiken & Chaiken, 1983). Studies in Baltimore (Ball, 1986; Ball, Rosen, Flueck, & Nurco, 1981) and New York (Johnson et al., 1985) demonstrate that active drug use accelerates the users' crime rate by a factor of 4 to 6, and that crime content is at least as violent, or more so, than that of non-drug using counterparts. The subjects of these studies were heroin users. Initial impressions from crack-crime studies indicate crack-related crime is as high or higher than heroin-related crime and is certainly more violent (Brownstein & Goldstein, 1990; Johnson, Williams, Dei, & Sanabria, 1990).

Similar rates of drug use have been found in studies of probationers and prisoners. Over half the probationers in a 1986 urinalysis study of the intensive supervision program in Brooklyn, New York, tested positive for drugs other than marijuana (including marijuana, two-thirds tested positive) (Wish, Brady, & Cuadrado, 1986). The vast majority of the nation's prisoners (over 80%) are recidivists; about three-quarters previously used drugs (Innes, 1988). Many of these prisoners have severe substance abuse problems. Indeed, about one-third of the inmates previously used a major drug (heroin, methadone, cocaine, LSD, PCP) on a regular basis; over half reported using drugs during the month prior to committing the crime for which they were incarcerated (Innes, 1988). Slightly more than half were under the influence of alcohol and/or drugs at the time of the offense for which they were incarcerated.

Drug-dependent offenders are responsible for a substantial, indeed disproportionate, amount of crime in comparison to non-users (Chaiken, 1986; Inciardi, 1979; Johnson et al., 1985). Studies of serious substance abusers, in particular offenders who use heroin and cocaine, show that they have extremely high crime rates (Ball, 1986; Ball et al., 1981; Chaiken & Chaiken, 1983; Collins, Hubbard, & Rachal, 1985; Johnson et al., 1985; McGlothin, Anglin, & Wilson, 1977). As the extent of abuse increases, the frequency and severity of their crimes escalate (Chaiken, 1986; Chaiken & Chaiken, 1982; Collins et al., 1985; Johnson et al., 1985; Speckart & Anglin, 1986). Furthermore, many of these drug users are also involved in drug dealing, an enterprise that also has its attendant effect on other forms of crime, especially crimes of violence (Chaiken & Chaiken, 1982; Goldstein, 1981, 1985; Johnson et al., 1985).

Empirical studies of the association between drug use and crime provide an appreciation of the enormous impact drug abuse has on crime. Indeed, the extensive research on the relationship between drug abuse and crime provides convincing evidence that *a relatively few severe sub-stance abusers are responsible for an extraordinary proportion of crime* (Gropper, 1985; based on the work of Ball, Shaffer, & Nurco, 1983; Johnson et al., 1985; and Inciardi, 1979). Drug-dependent offenders generally lead life-styles manifested by hedonistic, self-destructive, and antisocial be-haviors; they also have problems related to poor interpersonal skills, a lack of job skills, dependency on others, and frequent conflict with crim-inal justice authorities (Collins et al., 1985; Wexler, Lipton, & Johnson, 1988). Offenders involved in the regular use of hard drugs or polydrug abuse are typically at high risk for recidivating after release from the criminal justice system (Chaiken & Chaiken, 1982; Innes, 1988; Wexler, Lipton, & Johnson, 1988).

Although a large proportion of the nation's offenders lead life-styles associated with problems of drug abuse, only a small percentage receive treatment while in the criminal justice system. The National Criminal Justice Association survey of treatment options for drug-dependent of-fenders confirms that treatment services are often less available for offenders than for other drug-dependent clients. Furthermore, virtually all the state drug treatment and criminal justice agencies that responded to the survey (there were 147 respondents) claimed that "there is too little funding for treatment services generally . . . [and] that there are not enough drug treatment facilities or appropriate placements for drug-dependent clients" (National Criminal Justice Association, 1990, p. 2).

EFFECTIVENESS OF OFFENDER
SUBSTANCE ABUSE TREATMENT

In the fields of substance abuse and corrections, there has been a pervasive belief that prison-based rehabilitation is ineffective. As a result, the dominant sentiment has been that treatment efforts should be reserved for the inmate once released into the community (see Wexler and Williams, 1986, for a discussion of the impediments to treatment effectiveness). However, there is evidence that prison-based drug treatment is an effec-tive means of controlling recidivism and that intensive programs such as therapeutic communities are well suited for serious drug abusers while they are incarcerated.

The results of a 5-year study of the "Stay'n Out" prison therapeutic community (TC) indicate that this program is effective in reducing recidi-vism rates (Wexler, Falkin, & Lipton, 1988, 1990). Among the most important results of this study was the finding that the percentage of TC males rearrested (27%) was significantly lower than for the no-treatment control (41%) and comparison treatment groups (35% for the milieu group, 40% for the counseling group). Similarly, the percentage of TC females rearrested (18%) was significantly lower than the no-treatment control group (24%) and counseling group (30%). More to the point, the research found a strong relationship between time in program and treatment outcomes. For male inmates who participated in Stay'n Out, the percentage of those who had no parole violations during community supervision rose from 50% for those who remained less than 3 months to almost 80% for parolees who were in the program between 9 and 12 months while in prison. Similar findings were obtained for the females, although the percentages of those discharged positively from parole were higher than for their male counterparts (79% for females in treatment less than 3 months, 92% for the 9 to 12 month group).

The efficacy of the therapeutic community as a suitable modality for the treatment of inmates is further substantiated by Field (1989) in his study of the Cornerstone Program. The study compared measures of recidivism for four groups of Cornerstone participants: (1) program graduates; (2) clients who spent over 6 months in the program; (3) clients who spent between 2 and 6 months in treatment; and (4) clients who were in treatment for less than 2 months. The results indicate that 63% of the graduates were rearrested; however, less than half of the graduates were arrested and convicted for a new offense and only about 25% were arrested, convicted, and reincarcerated. These results compare quite favorably to the three groups that did not graduate. For example, 79% of the nongraduates who were in treatment for over 6 months were rearrested, 72% of them were convicted, and 63% were reincarcerated. Rearrests occurred for 92% of the clients who dropped out in less than 2 months during the 3-year follow-up, 89% were convicted of a new offense, and 85% were reincarcerated. These findings are consistent with those of the Stay'n Out program, which showed that increased time in program is associated with more positive treatment outcomes.

Furthermore, a series of studies conducted over the past two decades has demonstrated the effectiveness of community-based therapeutic community approaches (DeLeon, 1985; Tims, 1981). Practically all of the studies reveal that both the immediate and the long-term outcome status of the clients followed are significantly improved over pretreatment status. Drug use and criminality decline while employment and social adjustment improve after treatment (Barr & Antes, 1981; Brook & Whitehead, 1980;

DeLeon, 1984; DeLeon, Wexler, & Jainchill, 1982; Holland, 1982). The magnitudes of these positive outcomes generally increase with time in program. Findings regarding the effectiveness of community-based treatment for the criminal justice client suggest that treatment can be an effective alternative to incarceration for many criminally active drug abusers (Hubbard, Marsden, & Rachal, 1989).

Although the number of studies of effective treatment programs is limited, a growing body of research points to some important conditions for successful correctional rehabilitation (Lipton, 1983; Wexler, 1986; Wexler, Lipton, & Johnson, 1988). Among the most important conditions are (1) an isolated treatment unit, (2) motivated participants, (3) a committed and competent staff, (4) adequate treatment duration, (5) an array of treatment options, (6) cooperative and supportive relationships with correctional staff and administration, and (7) continuity of care that extends into the community. The guidelines above for successful correctional treatment, however, are merely suggestive because few studies have linked the nature of treatment that clients receive to treatment outcomes (Hubbard et al., 1989).

RECENT HISTORY OF PRISON
SUBSTANCE ABUSE TREATMENT

Until recently, the idea of rehabilitating prisoners was considered largely futile. Prison treatment was seen as an ill-fated "liberal" attempt to help irredeemable offenders. "Just deserts," a retributive philosophy based on control and infliction of punishment, had replaced rehabilitation in the armamentarium of correctional administrators. The popular phrase "nothing works," typically invoked during discussions of prison rehabilitation, was supported by an extensive review of the outcomes of 30 years of rehabilitation efforts for criminal offenders produced by Lipton, Martinson, and Wilks (1975). Their overall conclusion was that "the field of corrections has not as yet found satisfactory ways to reduce recidivism by significant amounts" (p. 627).

Thus, largely out of frustration, the "liberal" ideal of rehabilitation was put away as a primary goal of corrections and the "just deserts" philosophy of punishment and deterrence replaced it. This was accompanied by the increasing utilization of determinant sentencing by many states, which increased prison populations and extended the time inmates spent in prison. To some correctional administrators, however, it seemed inhumane and short-sighted to simply warehouse convicted felons and ignore the difficult challenge of rehabilitation. Some rehabilitative programming did continue in a few states in the decade between 1975 and 1985 and some of it was successful. In the 1980s, extraordinary increases in prison populations and associated rises in costs confronted correctional policymakers with the need to deal with overcrowding and rising budgets. It became imperative to find ways to keep offenders from returning and avoid spending more and ever more to build more and larger jails and institutions.

One source of the increasing numbers of individuals requiring incarceration was the increase in serious drug involvement among offenders. Also, the public concern in 1986 regarding the spread of "crack" created a demand for action. At this time, several important research findings were receiving national attention—the culmination of a decade of research that clearly showed the powerful drug-crime relationship, and the Stay 'n Out prison therapeutic community outcome evaluation results showing significant decreases in recidivism. All these factors set the stage for several federal laws that appropriated millions of dollars for drug enforcement, prevention, education, and treatment. In particular, interest in correctional rehabilitation for drug abusing offenders was reflected in the Anti-Drug Abuse Act of 1986, which included millions of dollars for substance abuse treatment of which a substantial amount was intended for correctional drug treatment.

PROJECT REFORM

At this same time, the researchers at National Development and Research Institutes, Inc. (NDRI: formerly Narcotic and Drug Research, Inc.) had been reexamining correctional rehabilitation and drug abuse treatment in prisons across the country (Wexler & Lipton, 1987; Wexler, Lipton et al., 1988). A set of guiding principles emerged for effective rehabilitation with drug-abusing offenders and with offenders generally. These findings and principles were shared with the staff of the Bureau of Justice Assistance (BJA) who were charged with guiding the administration of the expenditures for correctional drug treatment. BJA's strategy included funding an array of technical assistance projects to guide the implementation of this part of the law. One of these projects was Project REFORM (Comprehensive State Department of Corrections Treatment Strategy for Drug Abuse project). NDRI was chosen as the National Program Coordinator and asked to assist a total of 11 states in developing comprehensive statewide treatment strategies for drug treatment of prison inmates.

During the 5 years of Project REFORM operations (1987-1991), the 11 participating state departments of correction (Alabama, California, Connecticut, Delaware, Florida, Hawaii, New Jersey, New Mexico, New York, Oregon, Washington) developed state plans and implemented many substance abuse initiatives. Detailed descriptions of the project and its results are available (Lipton & Wexler, 1988; Wexler, Blackmore, & Lipton, 1991).

Each state's REFORM involvement was divided into two phases, planning and implementation. During the planning phase correctional officials focused on developing comprehensive state plans for the initiation or enhancement of substance abuse treatment services systemwide. On completion of these plans, each state was eligible to apply to BJA for implementation funds. These funds were used to implement some (but not all) of the interventions included in the state plans. NDRI provided technical assistance in submitting these grant proposals, developing the state plans and implementation of programs.

Funds were used primarily for the development of correction-based treatment programs, staff training interventions, and program evaluation strategies. A variety of local training initiatives were provided by NDRI staff and consultants.

In all, 16 new correction-based residential programs were implemented in these states. Assistance was also provided regarding implementation of 27 new prison-based outpatient programs in the participating states. Substance abuse educational courses/programs (provided in multiple prison facilities) were implemented in 2 states. Drug/alcohol abuse resource information centers (i.e., central locations in correctional facilities where books, pamphlets, videos, etc. on substance abuse issues are made available to inmates and staff) were established in 7 states. On an individual program basis, REFORM generated, synergized, or catalyzed the following:

- 39 assessment and referral programs implemented and 33 expanded or improved
- 36 drug education programs implemented and 82 expanded or improved
- 44 drug resource centers implemented and 27 expanded or improved
- 20 in-prison 12-step programs implemented and 62 expanded or improved
- 11 urine monitoring programs implemented and 4 expanded or improved
- 74 pre-release counseling and/or referral programs implemented and 54 expanded or improved

- 39 post-release treatment programs with parole or work release implemented and 10 expanded or improved
- 77 isolated unit (milieu) treatment programs initiated and/or improved, including: 16 brief (≤6 weeks) programs, 19 short-term (6-12 weeks), 34 intermediate (5-9 months), and 8 long-term (9-15 months) treatment programs

Other REFORM-related accomplishments included (1) the increased use of urinalysis in correctional facilities; (2) the development of formal, systemwide incentives for offenders regarding treatment involvement; (3) development of a variety of innovative strategies aimed at enhancing "continuity of care"—that is, extending treatment and services from the prison to the community to which offenders return; (4) development of substance abuse program computerized management information systems for the processing of participant substance abuse and program information; and (5) a positive shift in attitude among many senior correctional administrators and legislators toward the potential for using prison-based treatment to produce profound change among serious drug-using offenders.

Project REFORM held national training workshops twice a year for participant states, provided on-site technical assistance, published a newsletter, developed and maintained a clearinghouse, and actively disseminated prison drug treatment information to professional groups. When the BJA funding of REFORM was completed, the Center for Substance Abuse Treatment (CSAT; then known as the Office for Treatment Improvement) established project RECOVERY (Technical Assistance and Training Services to Demonstration Prison Drug Treatment Programs) to continue these technical assistance activities for 18 months (1991-1992). Although most of the original 11 REFORM states remained involved in RECOVERY, an additional 7 who received CSAT treatment grants were added (Colorado, Georgia, Michigan, North Carolina, North Dakota, Pennsylvania, Virginia). Texas and Ohio, who were not recipients of CSAT treatment grants, also participated in RECOVERY activities. A handbook, based largely on the planning and implementation of correctional substance abuse programs in these states, was produced (Wexler et al., 1992).

SUCCESSFUL CORRECTIONAL INTERVENTION

Participants in Projects REFORM and RECOVERY believed that a primary goal for corrections is the reduction of recidivism, that is, to intervene in the lives of offenders so that they do not return to prior patterns of criminal behavior. Both projects were guided by general principles of successful correctional intervention developed on the basis of clinical experience in the field of drug abuse treatment in corrections and a review of the existing drug abuse research and treatment literature. These principles are articulated on three levels: state, institutional, and individual. Flowing from these principles are planning and implementation guidelines based on experience working with the participating states.

State-Level Principles

1. *Alignment:* Align all relevant state agencies at the outset toward goals of project including achieving reduced recidivism (i.e., return to prior forms of conduct).
2. *Endorsement:* Obtain governor's imprimatur and endorsement. Have liaison assigned by governor to oversee continuing coordination among departments.
3. *Advisory Board:* Have governor appoint an advisory board including key legislators, key committee chairs, and key community constituencies (including community-based drug abuse treatment programs) as well as representatives from key state agencies including the single state substance abuse agency.
4. *Agreement:* Obtain agreements and commitments from the various criminal justice agencies necessary for cooperation in the main mission of the program, including parole.
5. *Attention:* Set in motion attention by the media and for ongoing public and political support from key individuals and/or organizations such as foundations interested in correctional improvement.
6. *Evaluation:* Establish statewide correctional program evaluation system to permit program operators to document success and thereby sustain themselves. Set in motion evaluation of program implementation, process, outcome, and cost-effectiveness.

Institutional-Level Principles

1. *Diagnosis:* Establish an assessment/diagnostic process and assign clients to a treatment regimen matched to their needs.
2. *Sequencing:* Within the framework of the expected release date, sequence treatment plan components appropriate for each offender and initiate treatment to provide sufficient time to match the prisoner's stay with program completion.

3. *Management:* Assign a case manager to manage the treatment plan components throughout custody and community supervision.

4. *Communication:* Regularly hold case conferences to bring together treatment and custody personnel involved in each case for updating progress and addressing any related issues.

5. *Isolation:* Separate program participants from the general population as soon as possible to avoid the pervasive influence of the insidious inmate subculture. Create an isolated living unit to neutralize the influence of the prison code.

6. *Environment:* Create an environment that is safer and cleaner than the general population area. Make staying in the program more desirable than leaving.

7. *Contact:* Reduce the contact between program participants and the general population to a minimum. Successful programs are designed so that participants relate primarily to the staff and each other rather than to general population inmates.

8. *Rules:* Establish clear, unambiguous rules and consequences for breaking such rules. Successful programs are guided by a few clearly stated, cardinal principles (such as no drugs or violence to others), the violation of which leads to immediate dismissal from the program.

   Require lesser rule-breaking to be dealt with immediately, and consistently value, recognize, and reward compliance with rules.

9. *Contracts:* Establish clear behavioral contingencies. Successful programs are based on mutual agreement or contracts between inmates and staff that guide the relationship of inmates and staff among themselves and with each other.

10. *Rewards and Sanctions:* Promulgate a system of positive and negative reinforcements for inmates and staff alike to foster achieving desirable behaviors and deter undesirable ones. Program time contracts, involving early release for satisfactory program completion, are potent motivators, with the added benefit of reducing correctional costs by shortening time served. Similarly, lower security contracts, holding out the prospect of transfer to a less secure facility, work release assignment, and halfway house or camp for satisfactory completion of components of program also hold promise for motivating clients and reducing security costs.

11. *Role Models:* Employ ex-offender/ex-addict staff to serve as counselors wherever possible. Former addict-inmates who have graduated from treatment programs and have demonstrated work histories and clean criminal and drug use records (for 3 years) can be of extraordinary value as role models as well as counselors in prison-based treatment programs.

12. *Teams:* Recovered ex-addicts work best in teams alongside specially trained and motivated correction officer counselors.

13. Integrity and Flexibility: The program leadership has to stay committed to the program's vision despite changing fiscal and administrative support and political realities.

14. *Autonomy and Adaptability:* The program has to stay relatively free of institutional restrictions and general population incursions that will compromise its goals, without alienating security staff or correctional managers.

15. *Openness:* The program must encourage access by all interested parties and develop outside funding sources and influential supporters.

16. *Duration:* Retain participants long enough to have maximum impact (e.g., 9-12 months prior to release for a therapeutic community). Retaining clients in treatment beyond 12 months may produce diminishing returns.

17. *Continuity:* Establish continuity of intervention, from outset of custody to termination of custody: Whenever possible, sustain the significant program elements, including contingency contracts, in follow-up treatment and aftercare programs in the community.

18. *Reentry:* Incorporate into the program a planned reentry phase, with escorted referral to community-based treatment programs or halfway houses. Initiate joint reentry planning with parole and/or other community supervision staff at least 3 months prior to an inmate's release date.

19. *Surveillance:* Conduct frequent (at least 3 times a week) urine surveillance with a sensitive and reliable apparatus such as the enzyme multiplied immunoassay test (EMIT). Less sensitive detection systems (such as thin layer chromatography), even when administered by experienced personnel, can fail to detect cocaine in two-thirds of the positive urines.

20. *Graduated Liberty:* Link increased liberty from urine surveillance and parole officer contacts to the fulfillment of offender contract contingencies, especially that of time without violation. Conversely, make positive urinalysis result in loss of liberty and increased surveillance.

21. *Self-Help Groups:* Incorporate self-help programming (either linked with an existing self-help network, such as NA or AA, or with graduate groups developed by the program).

Individual-Level Principles

1. *Self-Identification:* Assist addict offenders to identify personal impediments to recovery.

2. *Motivation:* Provide addict offenders with incentives, positive or otherwise, to participate in recovery programs.

3. *Involvement:* Involve offenders in program planning, rather than externally imposing treatment on them. Help prisoners help themselves.

4. *Reflection:* Allow offenders some minimal contact with general population (for example, in the mess hall and recreation areas) so they have an opportunity to test their progress in higher risk environments and to see how much they have changed since inception of treatment.

5. *Reinforcement:* Reinforce prosocial behaviors rather than attempting to directly reduce the frequency of negative behavior. Successful programs discourage antisocial behavior by not giving it undue attention.

6. *Reward:* Reward positive inmate behavior change with greater privileges, early release, better housing, better clothes, better jobs, and more pay. Mete out sanctions for negative behavior (e.g., loss of good time, loss of pay, lesser housing, less desirable job assignments) for failing to meet contracted expectations. For most inmates, the most motivating incentives are reductions of time to be served, eligibility for less secure placement, safety, comfort, and status rewards.

7. *Transition:* On release, insure that there is a transition to a community-based treatment program if necessary and make provision for the releasee's basic survival and security needs to be attended to, particularly his or her housing and employment needs.

The guidelines above proved very useful for states developing comprehensive drug treatment strategies for their correctional systems during the REFORM project. They were designed to (1) engender more explicit drug treatment policies and a broader sharing of information about the extent and severity of the drug abuse problem within each state's criminal justice system, including the social, psychological, and drug-using characteristics of offenders; (2) enhance cooperation among criminal justice agencies and drug abuse treatment programs; and (3) align the custody system, the treatment system, and participating inmates toward a common objective: reducing recidivism.

NEW DIRECTIONS IN PRISON DRUG TREATMENT

A national town meeting was convened by Project RECOVERY on correctional substance abuse treatment. The meeting, which was held in July 1992 in San Diego, included a panel of national leaders, policymakers, and practitioners representing the fields of corrections, social services, and substance abuse who explored the theme "The Promise of Correctional Substance Abuse Treatment: Moving the Agenda Forward." They were asked to generate a "shared vision" of the current status of correctional substance abuse treatment and suggest recommendations for the next steps that would "move the agenda forward." A summary of the major statements, arguments, and recommendations that comprised the "shared vision" discussed at the town meeting is presented below:

In order to generate a national consensus to action to help end the human suffering of chemical abuse, and to reduce the numbers of wasted lives of incarcerated men and women, it is necessary to impress on policymakers the nature of the human and economic relationships between crime and drugs.

A successful strategy to reduce crime on our streets and improve the quality of life in our country necessitates impressing on policymakers the futility of continuing to warehouse people in prisons and the social and economic costs that policy engenders. We need to focus their attention on how successful and cost-effective we are likely to be in reducing crime and changing the quality of life by employing tested technologies of human change with persons already incarcerated.

Continuing current incarceration policies wastes dollars. In austere fiscal times like these, wasting money in one sphere causes public schools to languish, roads not to be repaired, hospitals not to be built, and other worthwhile programs to be sacrificed in order to support an already massive, and rapidly expanding, corrections system. Despite a doubling of the state and federal prison populations in the past 10 years, a fourfold increase in the national prison population in the past 20 years, and enormous resources spent on interdicting drug trafficking, there are no real drug shortages on the street and our streets are no safer, our homes no more secure.

There is convincing evidence that intensive treatment of substance-abusing offenders does work. Treatment begun in prison and continued in the community after release reduces substance abuse and criminality and returns people to tax-paying useful roles in the community. Moreover, the costs of such treatment are offset by the savings produced within 2 years. Further, prison administrators need to know that the "safe space" created by having such programs considerably reduces problematic behavior in prison. Policymakers also need to understand that most drug-using offenders do not voluntarily enter or stay in treatment in the community unless compelled to, and that prison programs represent a special opportunity to bring to bear effective treatment technologies.

It must be conveyed to policymakers that now is the time to shift resources from building and operating prisons, which we know does not work, to investing in effective substance abuse intervention and treatment programming. Such programming needs to be devised that responds to the special, and differential, needs of men and women, offenders of different races and cultures, as well as for youth who are incarcerated. Without such programming, these offenders will reemerge from their institutions more damaged than when they entered, and therefore more dangerous to society, or at best essentially unchanged and prepared to resume their predatory ways.

The goal of effective substance abuse-treatment operating in concert with the criminal justice system is not some elusive, far off dream. It has already begun in some states and in the Federal Bureau of Prisons.

The panel agreed on a shared vision of new programs, policies, and practices that policymakers could adopt today to move the public safety agenda forward and to make substantial progress in the war against crime and substance abuse. Panel recommendations included the following:

1. Creating a new mission for corrections—where correctional practitioners at all levels, from the security officers and program staff to top management—accept the responsibility for and direct their efforts to reducing crime and substance abuse.

2. Building accountability into treatment and corrections, so that all agents of treatment and the criminal justice system at all levels and functions are rewarded for achieving success in reducing recidivism—and held accountable for it.

3. Making adequate resources available for the comprehensive and effective training of all agents of treatment and habilitation services, to insure that they all understand their roles in promoting recovery and have the skills and support to insure success.

4. Fostering an array of rehabilitative programming apart from but in concert with drug abuse treatment to meet the diverse needs of multiproblem offenders: in literacy, numeracy, vocational preparation, problem-solving skills, life skills, mental health, and the like.

5. Engendering a broad national consensus that treatment works and is cost-effective.

6. Orchestrating a diversity of people (judges and prosecutors; wardens, psychologists, and psychiatrists; teachers, counselors, and correctional officers) and organizations to work in this common cause.

7. Enacting comprehensive sentencing reform that is nonracist in intent and effect and supports recovery and habilitation.

8. Acknowledging and supporting substance abuse treatment as a right for all those who need it, and making adequate resources available to enable this right.

9. Empowering recovering people to improve their home communities ("giving back")—helping the homeless, the aged, and the infirm and rebuilding the community. Persons in recovery can assume a central role in reaching out to and treating those not yet in recovery and, by their actions and example, serve as positive role models—a "Domestic Peace Corps" of recovered persons.

10. Acknowledging substance abuse treatment and recovery as an effective means of addressing child abuse, violence against women, child abandonment, incest, sexual molestation, and other social pathologies—truly supporting "family values."

11. Educating media representatives and orchestrating media releases so that stories of successful recovery get more press attention and public acknowledgment than stories of crime, violence, and failure.

12. Developing treatment models and practice that are age-, race-, class-, and gender-appropriate.

13. Implementing an effective, intensive substance abuse therapeutic community in every federal prison and every state prison system.

The considerations and recommendations generated by the panel were similar to those produced by other groups (American Bar Association, 1992; American College of Physicians, 1992; and the National Institute on Drug Abuse [Leukefeld and Tims], 1992), which indicates a growing impetus for action.

The future of prison drug treatment appears optimistic. Currently, there is growing public support for implementing correctional substance abuse treatment programs. Many states have been influenced by the hard work of the people who participated in Projects REFORM and RECOVERY. They have been instrumental in creating a sense of optimism and increasing the acceptance of habilitation and treatment as a central goal of corrections in America. An example of this profound shift in correctional policy is a billion-dollar bond package that was recently supported by voters in Texas for the construction of new correctional treatment facilities that will serve 14,000 inmates with significant substance abuse problems. However, a note of caution has been sounded by many experienced practitioners, who warn that the quality of treatment efforts may suffer during periods of rapid expansion. We believe that the development of effective correctional substance abuse treatment will be well served by the implementation of the treatment components and the recommendations discussed in this chapter.

REFERENCES

American Bar Association (1992). *Responding to the problem of drug abuse: Strategies for the criminal justice system.* The Report of an Ad Hoc Committee of the Criminal Justice Section of the American Bar Association.

American College of Physicians, National Commission on Health Care, and American Correctional Health Services Association (1992). The crisis in correctional health care: The impact of the national drug control strategy on correctional health services. *Annals of Internal Medicine, 117*(1), 71-77.

Ball, J. C. (1986). The hyper-criminal opiate addict. In B. D. Johnson & E. Wish (Eds.), *Crime rates among drug abusing offenders* (pp. 81-104). Final Report to the National Institute of Justice. New York: Narcotic and Drug Research, Inc.

Ball, J. C., Rosen, L., Flueck, S. A., & Nurco, D. N. (1981). The criminology of heroin addicts when addicted and when off opiates. In J. A. Inciardi (Ed.), *The drug-crime connection* (pp. 39-65). Beverly Hills, CA: Sage.

Ball, J. C., Shaffer, J. W., & Nurco, D. N. (1983). Day to day criminality of heroin addicts in Baltimore: A study in the continuity of offense rates. *Drug and Alcohol Dependence, 12*, 119-142.

Barr, H., & Antes, D. (1981). Factors related to recovery and relapse in follow-up. Final Report of Project Activities, Grant No. 1-H81-DA-01864. Rockville, MD: National Institute on Drug Abuse.

Brook, R., & Whitehead, P. (1980). *Drug-free therapeutic community.* New York: Human Sciences Press.

Brownstein, H. H., & Goldstein, P. J. (1990). A typology of drug related homicides. In R. Weisheit (Ed.), *Drugs, crime and the criminal justice system* (pp. 171-192). Cincinnati, OH: Anderson.

Chaiken, M. (1986). Crime rates and substance abuse among types of offenders. In B. Johnson & E. Wish (Eds.), *Crime rates among drug-abusing offenders* (pp. 12-54). Final Report to National Institute of Justice. New York: Narcotic and Drug Research, Inc.

Chaiken, J. M., & Chaiken, M. R. (1982). *Varieties of criminal behavior.* Santa Monica, CA: The Rand Corporation.

Chaiken, J. M., & Chaiken, M. R. (1983). Crime rates and the active offender. In J. Q. Wilson (Ed.), *Crime and public policy* (pp. 11-29). New Brunswick, NJ: Transaction Books.

Collins, J. J., Hubbard, R. L., & Rachal, J. V. (1985). Expensive drug use in illegal income: A test of explanatory hypotheses. *Criminology, 23*(4), 743-764.

DeLeon, G. (1984). Program based evaluation research in therapeutic communities. In F. Tims & J. Ludford (Eds.), *Drug abuse treatment evaluation: Strategies, progress, and prospects* (pp. 69-87). Rockville, MD: National Institute on Drug Abuse.

DeLeon, G. (1985). The therapeutic community: Status and evolution. *International Journal of the Addictions, 20*, 823-844.

DeLeon, G., Wexler, H., & Jainchill, N. (1982). The therapeutic community: Success and improvement rates 5 years after treatment. *The International Journal of the Addictions, 17*, 703-747.

Falkin, G. P., Wexler, H. K., & Lipton, D. S. (1992). Drug treatment in state prisons. In D. R. Gerstein & H. J. Harwood (Eds.), *Treating drug problems* (Vol. II, pp. 89-132). Washington, DC: National Academy Press.

Field, G. (1989). *A study of the effects of intensive treatment on reducing the criminal recidivism of addicted offenders.* Oregon Correctional Treatment Program.

Goldstein, P. J. (1981). Getting over: Economic alternatives to predatory crime among street drug users. In J. A. Inciardi (Ed.), *The drug/crime connection* (pp. 67-84). Beverly Hills, CA: Sage.

Goldstein, P. J. (1985, Fall). Drugs and violent behavior. *Journal of Drug Issues,* 493-506.

Gropper, B. A. (1985). *Probing the links between drugs and crime.* Washington, DC: U.S. Department of Justice.

Holland, S. (1982). *Residential drug-free programs for substance abusers: The effect of planned duration on treatment.* Chicago: Gateway Houses.

Hubbard, R., Marsden, M. E., Rachal, J. V. et al. (1989). *Drug abuse treatment: A national study of effectiveness.* Chapel Hill, NC: The University of North Carolina Press.

Inciardi, J. A. (1979, July). Heroin use and street crime. *Crime and Delinquency,* 33-346.

Innes, C. A. (1988). *Profile of state prison inmates: 1986.* Bureau of Justice Statistics Special Report. Washington, DC: Department of Justice.

Johnson, B. D., Goldstein, P., Preble, E., Schmeidler, J., Lipton, D. S., Spunt, B., & Miller, T. (1985). *Taking care of business: The economics of crime by heroin abusers.* Lexington, MA: Lexington Books.

Johnson, B. D., Williams, T., Dei, K. A., & Sanabria, H. (1990). Drug abuse in the inner city: Impact of hard-drug users and the community. In M. Tonry & J. Q. Wilson (Eds.), *Drugs and crime* (Vol. 13, pp. 9-67). Chicago: The University of Chicago Press.

Leukefeld, C. G., & Tims, F. M. (1992). Directions for practice and research. In C. G. Leukefeld & F. M. Tims (Eds.), *Drug abuse treatment in prisons and jails* (pp. 279-293). National Institute on Drug Abuse, Monograph Series No. 118. Washington DC: NIDA.

Lipton, D. S. (1983). *Important conditions for successful rehabilitation.* Paper presented at the 1983 Bellevue Forensic Psychiatry Conference, New York City.

Lipton, D. S. (1991, June 6). Testimony before the Subcommittee on Crime and Criminal Justice, Judiciary Committee, U.S. House of Representatives.

Lipton, D., Martinson, R., & Wilks, J. (1975). *The effectiveness of correctional treatment.* New York: Praeger.

Lipton, D. S., & Wexler, H. K. (1988). The drug-crime connection: Rehabilitation shows promise. *Corrections Today, 50*(5), 144-147.

McGlothin, W. H., Anglin, D. M., & Wilson, B. D. (1977). *An evaluation of the California Civil Addict Program.* Rockville, MD: National Institute on Drug Abuse.

National Criminal Justice Association. (1990). States' policy and practices in developing and providing treatment for drug dependent offenders. *A final report of the joint National Criminal Justice Association/National Governors' Association project on treatment options for drug dependent offenders.* Washington, DC: U.S. Department of Justice, Bureau of Justice Assistance.

Speckart, G., & Anglin, D. M. (1986). Narcotics use and crime: A causal modeling approach. *Journal of Quantitative Criminology, 2,* 3-28.

Tims, F. M. (1981). *Effectiveness of drug abuse treatment programs.* National Institute on Drug Abuse Treatment Research Report. DHHS Publication No. ADM 84-1143. Washington, DC: U.S. Government Printing Office.

Wexler, H. K. (1986). Therapeutic communities within prisons. In G. DeLeon & J. T. Ziegenfuss (Eds.), *Therapeutic communities for addictions: Readings in theory, research and practice* (pp. 227-237). Springfield IL: Charles C Thomas.

Wexler, H. K., Blackmore, J., Lipton, D. S. (1991). Project REFORM: Developing a drug abuse treatment strategy for corrections. *Journal of Drug Issues, 21*(2), 473-495.

Wexler, H. K., Falkin, G., & Lipton, D. (1988). *A model prison rehabilitation program: An evaluation of the Stay'n Out therapeutic community.* Final Report to the National Institute on Drug Abuse. New York: Narcotic and Drug Research, Inc.

Wexler, H. K., Falkin, G. P., & Lipton, D. S. (1990). Outcome evaluation of a prison therapeutic community for substance abuse treatment. *Criminal Justice and Behavior, 17*(1), 71-92.

Wexler, H. K., & Lipton, D. S. (1987). Interventions that "work" with drug involved offenders. *National Institute of Justice Briefing Paper,* 1-23.

Wexler, H. K., Lipton, D. S., Blackmore, J., Ryder, J., Cumo, J., & Wilson, T. (1992). *Establishing substance abuse treatment programs in prisons: A practitioner's handbook.* Washington, DC: Center for Substance Abuse Treatment.

Wexler, H. K., Lipton, D. S., & Johnson, B. D. (1988). *A criminal justice system strategy for treating drug offenders in custody.* Washington, DC: National Institute of Justice, Issues and Practices.

Wexler, H. K., & Williams, R. (1986). The Stay'n Out therapeutic community: Prison treatment for substance abusers. *Journal of Psychoactive Drugs, 18,* 221-230.

Wish, E. D., Brady, E., & Cuadrado, M. (1986). *Urine testing of arrestees: Findings from Manhattan.* New York: Narcotic and Drug Research, Inc.

Chapter 11

SUBSTANCE ABUSE AND HIV AMONG CRIMINAL JUSTICE POPULATIONS
Overview From a Program Evaluation Perspective

JAMES E. RIVERS

INTRODUCTION

A wide variety of "malfunctions"—usually defined at organizational, community, and social institutional levels—are recognized as current social problems in American society. Public and private sectors expend major personnel and fiscal resources both to establish new human service programs to ameliorate these problems and to improve program processes and outcomes. This chapter highlights the need to better conceive, design, deliver, and evaluate specified human services programming for certain institutionally and behaviorally defined populations. It begins with Rossi and Freeman's (1989) conclusions that (a) crucial human service program development and change decisions are far too often based on "speculation, impressionistic observations, and even biased information" and (b) an adequate understanding of the nature and scope of the problem it is meant to address as well as precise information about the corresponding program targets and the context in which the intervention will operate is essential prior to detailed program design and implementation (p. 71).

This chapter examines two major social problems—substance abuse and the human immunodeficiency virus (HIV)/acquired immune deficiency syndrome (AIDS)—as they intersect with a third—crime—in the criminal justice system. The limited, yet significant, objective of this discussion is to present information needed to construct informed, pragmatic, and implementable answers to a single focused question: *How can risk of HIV infection/transmission best be minimized among drug users within the boundaries of the criminal justice system?* Toward this end, an overview is provided from the relevant literature of multiple disciplines and fields of study; Akers (1992) notes that a field is problem-defined whereas a discipline is perspective-defined and the whole range of knowledge and research on the problems of the field of criminal justice cannot be contained within one discipline. The objective of this presentation is to stimulate and contribute to a program planning process by helping to define and diagnose problems in ways that will lead to the selection of the most appropriate targets and interventions and that will allow the application of systematic and reproducible evaluation procedures. Framed as a nascent (pre-planning) phase in a program evaluation, this discussion can be characterized as an attempt to define and specify the problems and their location and scope, to review proposed interventions, and to discuss the issues in selecting target populations.

PROBLEM IDENTIFICATION/SPECIFICATION AND SCOPE BY LOCATION

Substance Abuse in the General Population

Although there is broad agreement across all segments of American society that substance abuse is a major social problem, there is significant disagreement in how best to characterize the problem, that is, as primarily moral, health (physiological and/or mental), social welfare, or legal in nature. Consequently, how resources should be allocated among responding agencies, programs, and target populations often is disputed. This disagreement further confounds the already methodologically difficult task of estimating (with confidence in its accuracy) the extent of substance abuse per se or defining and measuring the numerous problems correlated with or caused by substance abuse.

Among the more sophisticated attempts in this regard is the recent analysis produced by the National Academy of Sciences Institute of Medicine (IOM), which, in estimating the extent of need for substance abuse treatment services, also made a number of specific prevalence estimates. The editors of this report state: "During any given month in the past 20 years, at least 14 million (in the peak months, more than 25 million) individuals consumed some kind of illicit drug" (Gerstein & Harwood, 1990, p. 59). (Note that this estimate does not include alcoholism/alcohol abuse or misuse of prescription drugs.) Their estimate of those who are "dependent" or "abusers" ("clearly" or "probably" needing treatment) was 4.6 million with another 2.9 million "users" estimated as "possibly" needing treatment (Gerstein & Harwood, 1990, pp. 77-80, 92-99).

More specifically, the Centers for Disease Control (CDC) fairly recently estimated the number of injection drug users (IDUs) in the United States to be from 1.1 to 1.3 million (Centers for Disease Control, 1987). Injection drug use is of major concern primarily because of its role in HIV transmission via the practice of "needle sharing." Although the CDC estimate is more specific, its accuracy has been challenged; Spencer (1989) argues that it could well be off by a factor of 2.

In addition, crack cocaine increasingly is being implicated in the spread of HIV and other sexually transmitted diseases. The crack-HIV association is principally via elevated risks resulting from drug-driven (psychological, physiological, and economic) sexual behaviors, increasing the probabilities that the crack user will have unprotected sexual relations with HIV-infected persons, especially other drug users.

Substance Abuse Among Criminal Populations

Substance Abuse Among Arrestees. Drug users per se, and particularly the more frequent users, are very likely to be arrested and incarcerated at some point (Inciardi, 1981, 1986; McBride, 1978; McBride & McCoy, 1982). As a subgroup of drug users, injection drug users have high rates of arrest and incarceration according to self-reports in survey studies (Inciardi, 1979; Nurco, Ball, Shaffer, & Hanlon, 1985). For example, from among 26,000+ "street" IDUs recruited into multisite projects designed to reduce HIV infection risks, virtually all reported at least one lifetime arrest (most many times) and 12% reported very recent arrests, that is, they were facing criminal charges at the time of the interview (Inciardi, McBride, Platt, & Baxter, 1992).

Information about drug use among samples of arrestees (males and females, those accused of drug-law violations and for other crimes) began to be routinely collected by the National Institute of Justice's Drug Use Forecasting (DUF) system in 1987 from a panel of U.S. cities, using analysis of urine specimen and confidential interviews (National Institute of Justice, 1990). Although there is variation in the data between and within cities, by race/ethnicity, gender, and so on, the central tendency since the program's inception is for about two-thirds of all DUF participants to test positive at time of arrest for at least one illicit drug. Wish (1990)—extrapolating from DUF sample data from 20 cities to official arrest statistics for 41 non-DUF cities with populations of 250,000 or more—estimated that there were 1.3 -1.7 million of the total 1988 arrestees in the 61 U.S. cities who would have tested positive for cocaine alone, had DUF programs been in place in each city.

By combining DUF interview and urine test results, the Institute of Medicine analysts cited above also made estimates and projections regarding the number of arrestees needing substance abuse treatment. Based on spring 1988 DUF data, it was projected that 700,000 arrestees (29%) "probably" needed treatment and that another 1.2 million cases could be considered as "possibly" needing treatment, that is, if the ambiguous cases were added (Gerstein & Harwood, 1990, p. 101).

Anglin and Hser (1992) used DUF arrestee and publicly funded treatment programs admission data to estimate the number of 1989 injection drug users (any drug) and cocaine users in Los Angles County. They estimated that "there could be as many as 190,000 criminals who were IDUs and 371,000 who were using cocaine." They contrasted these estimates to counts of total county treatment admissions for 1989 of 20,000 IDUs and 7,400 cocaine users (p. 47).

Substance Abuse Among Probationers. Further, the IOM analysts used a 1986 survey of state prisoners (Innes, 1988), and other reported censuses to estimate that 580,000 of 2,231,000 ($\approx$ 26%) of those being supervised by probation authorities needed substance abuse treatment services (Gerstein & Harwood, 1990, p. 84).

Substance Abuse Among Jail Inmates. Some arrestees are convicted or plead guilty to crimes that result in their incarceration in local jails for more extended periods—typically, for 1-year maximums. The data regarding the proportion or numbers of jail inmates who are substance abusers is sparse, although the DUF data cited above is suggestive. Also indicative is the national data from among the "street" IDUs recruited into HIV risk reduction projects; an overwhelming majority (83%) reported at least one lifetime instance of incarceration, and 30% of those who had been incarcerated during the 5 years prior to interview had spent a year or more in jail or prison (Inciardi et al., 1992).

The IOM study cited above reported an estimate of 60,000 inmates serving time in county jails who need treatment, that is, who were "daily drug users at the time of their offense" and "all of them probably met the diagnostic criteria for drug dependence" (Gerstein & Harwood, 1990, p. 83).

Substance Abuse Among Federal and State Prisoners. Based on 1987 state and federal prison census data (Greenfield, 1989) and using Innes's (1988) and Flannigan and Jamison's (1988) research as the basis for estimation, IOM investigators projected that 250,000 of 584,000 ($\approx$ 43%) prison inmates were daily users at the point of their offense and needed substance abuse treatment (Gerstein & Harwood, 1990, p. 83).

Substance Abuse Among Parolees. Finally, the IOM study cited above estimated that 150,000 of 350,000 ($\approx$ 45%) being supervised by parole authorities needed substance abuse treatment services (Gerstein & Harwood, 1990, p. 84).

HIV in the General Population

The first cases of acquired immune deficiency syndrome (AIDS) in the United States probably occurred around 1977. It was first identified and described as a singular disease entity in 1981 (Centers for Disease Control [CDC], 1981) and was early associated with homosexual men; in early 1982, more than 90% of the 159 cases that had been reported were bisexual or homosexual males and only 1 reported case was a female. Soon, however, the disease was being reported among intravenous and other injecting drug users, hemophiliacs, and other blood transfusion patients (CDC, 1982).

The most common means by which the human immunodeficiency virus (HIV)—which causes AIDS—is transmitted between humans include sexual intercourse of any form with an infected person, contaminated hypodermic syringes or needles, transfusion of infected blood or blood products, and perinatal transmission from infected mother to fetus. Basically, HIV results in a spectrum of conditions associated with immune dysfunction, and AIDS is best described as a severe manifestation of HIV infection (Inciardi, 1992. p. 178).

The overall dimensions of the current HIV/AIDS epidemic are hard to determine, particularly because those who represent the largest component of the epidemic—those who are HIV infected—tend to remain asymptomatic for several years after their infection. Turner, Miller, and Moses (1989) state that "at present, there are no reliable data on the current prevalence of HIV in the United States, although . . . the most plausible estimates of prevalence lie in the vicinity of 1 million infected persons, with a range of 0.5-2 million" (pp. 4-5). The CDC recently reported that injection drug use was a risk factor for 24.5% of the HIV-positive results among almost 2 million persons receiving HIV-antibody tests by public health departments in 1991 (CDC, 1992).

Currently, about 30% of all reported AIDS cases have IDU as the attributed means of infection. Somewhat over one-half of the reported AIDS cases among heterosexuals infected through sexual contact (a majority of whom are women) implicate IDU sexual partners. Further, 71% of pediatric HIV cases are children infected perinatally by HIV-infected mothers who were IDUs or the sexual partners of IDUs (CDC, 1989).

HIV Among Criminal Justice Populations

Incarceration undeniably represents a high-risk environment for HIV infection (Walker & Gordon, 1980), first by virtue of the elevated prevalence of AIDS cases among prisoners compared to the general population (cf. Moini & Hammett, 1990; data cited below). A second set of HIV infection risk factors that remain at high levels within the jail and prison setting is drug use and needle sharing. Third, homosexual behavior, even among men who are heterosexual in their "outside world" lives, is commonplace within correctional facilities. The extent of such behavior obviously will vary by time and place, but estimates across many studies place the range at 30%-45% of all inmates who will engage in such activities (voluntarily or by force) during their incarcerations (Clemmer, 1958, pp. 249-273; see also Buffum, 1972; Gagnon & Simon, 1968; Irwin, 1985; Kassebaum, 1972; Sykes, 1965).

HIV Among Arrestees. Although there are no known programs or projects that target arrestees for HIV testing, Wish, O'Neil, and Baldau (1990) make some inferences from a sample of 1,507 DUF respondents from five cities during the September-December 1987 reporting period. Self-reports of any injection drug use ever ranged from 19% to 51% among these DUF cities. Wish and his colleagues suggest that projections of HIV seroprevalence among arrestees could be made by using estimates available from other sources of seropositivity rates among IDUs in the respective cities.

Indeed, there is some evidence to support the notion that IDUs among arrestees and IDUs in the "general population" may be comparable. Leukefeld, Battjes, and Pickens (1989) report HIV infection risk behaviors (and by inference, infection rates) to be not significantly different in a cohort of IDUs entering community-based methadone maintenance treatment between those who were criminal-justice involved and those who were not. Similarly, McBride and Inciardi (1990) report that there were only minor and statistically insignificant differences in risk behaviors by weeks in jail during the past 5 years among IDUs recruited into a Miami HIV risk reduction program.

HIV Among Jail Inmates. Moini and Hammett (1990), analyzing National Institute of Justice survey data on diagnosed AIDS current (as of October 1989) cases, reported 1,750 cases in city and county jails. This translates to an annual incidence (new AIDS cases, rate per 100,000) of 202 (compared to the 1989 incidence rate of 14.65 for the general population).

Homosexual behavior is thought to occur regularly in jails as well as prisons; Van Hoeven, Rooney, and Joseph (1990) found inferential evidence to support this assumption in their study of New York City correctional facilities in which 27 inmates acquired gonorrhea from in-jail sexual activity in a 3-month period. Indeed, others have found that homosexually transmitted diseases are not rare (Alcabes & Brawlow, 1988; Flucker, 1976).

McCusker, Koblin, Lewis, and Sullivan (1990) also found that high-risk sexual practices are not the sole province of federal and state prisoners. In a study involving IDU county jail inmates, the participants were reported to be more likely to have engaged in risky sexual practices (e.g., sexual contact with two or more partners, failure to use condoms—usually considered contraband in correctional facilities) than men in drug treatment centers and other treatment sites (an HIV clinic, an STD clinic, and two community health centers).

HIV Among Federal and State Prisoners. Incarcerates, particularly those who have been convicted of crimes sufficiently serious to result in state prison sentences, are more likely (than the general population in their area) to be HIV-infected *when they enter* correctional facilities because of a general propensity to be risk-takers (not observe norms or taboos, codified as laws), including sexual and drug use risk behavior. Among the scant research literature in this area are the findings of Vlahov et al. (1989), who reported that the HIV seropositive rate among new 1988 inmates in Maryland was 8.4%, and Truman et al. (1989), who found 17% of a sample of inmates entering a NY state corrections facility to be seropositive.

In the same analysis by Moini and Hammett (1990) cited above, they reported 3,661 diagnosed current (as of October 1989) AIDS cases in state and federal prisons. To provide a better perspective, these numbers translate to an annual incidence (new AIDS cases, rate per 100,000) of 202 for state and federal prisons in 1989. In contrast, the 1988 incidence rate for state and federal prisons was less than 100.

Numerous studies suggest the widespread use of drugs and needle-sharing in U.S. correctional facilities (Gross, 1986; Inciardi & Page, 1991; Thomas & Cage, 1977; Vigdal & Stadler, 1989). British evidence is consistent with this conclusion; of 50 IDUs who all had experienced incarceration, 47 reported having used at least one illicit drug and 33 had injected drugs—of whom 26 shared injection equipment—while in jail or prison (Carvell & Hart, 1990).

The presentation above supports the conclusion of McBride and Inciardi (1990), who state that the evidence regarding the extent of substance abuse and HIV among criminal justice populations should bring to the forefront, once again, the issue of coerced treatment and increased linkages between the criminal justice system and treatment and should focus immediate attention on measures to reduce the spread of HIV in criminal justice populations through AIDS education/prevention and substance abuse treatment programs. They state that criminal justice settings deserve significantly more attention as intervention points for those with IDU histories. The importance of substance abuse and HIV prevention and intervention strategies is highlighted by the high-risk profiles of the inmates who pass through criminal justice systems, a majority of whom have never been in substance abuse treatment (National Institute on Drug Abuse [NIDA]/NOVA, 1990).

REVIEWING PROPOSED INTERVENTIONS

Our society in general has not reached a consensus on a multitude of issues regarding HIV/AIDS and most of our social institutions and systems—education, business, the military, and the correctional system—have not yet developed consistent policies with respect to the identification, management, and treatment of HIV-antibody-positive individuals. Courts in different jurisdictions have added to this inconsistency in policy with divergent interpretations and rulings with respect to the issues of inmate HIV screening programs and segregation policies for infected prisoners. It is likely that AIDS-related legal cases—which already claim the record as the largest body of cases attributable to a single disease entity (Gostin, 1990)—will continue to grow.

Issues yet to be resolved include the following:

1. The degree to which a real risk of communicability of the virus exists
2. The degree to which an incarcerated individual can give truly voluntary informed consent regarding HIV testing
3. The extent to which management strategies such as HIV antibody screening and segregation or isolation may constitute a violation of prisoners' civil rights
4. The right of an inmate, once diagnosed, to refuse medical care
5. The availability of correctional system resources to deal effectively with HIV/AIDS issues, for example, to provide adequate medical care to the HIV/AIDS-infected or to provide adequate protection for the noninfected

Many of the following recommendations, unless otherwise attributed, are abridged from those developed by participants at the NIDA's AIDS Community Prevention meeting and reported by Leukefeld, Battjes, and Amsel (1990). They are particularly relevant for interventions that target non-incarcerated criminal justice subpopulations, namely, arrestees, probationers, and parolees. Other noted recommendations are more appropriate for jailed and imprisoned at-risk populations.

- Recommendations or guiding principles for community intervention programs are that interventions should (a) incorporate multiple and repeated components to increase the likelihood of durable effects on the target group; (b) be designed and implemented as components of a variety of community resources and in the context of other major social problems, not as isolated activities or detached programs; (c) incorporate outreach and case management staff to aggressively seek out the target groups (IDUs, their spouses, and other sexual partners) and to link them with relevant community resources; and (d) be flexible and accepting of targeted individuals' reluctance and designed to build on their own motivation, rather than imposing behavioral standards as eligibility criteria that are unlikely to be met.
- The public health goals of reducing the spread of HIV and drug abstinence, as practical matters, should be considered as separate issues. Interventions with IDUs who are not in substance abuse treatment should have a dual focus—encouraging risk-reduction efforts and entry into treatment. Further, prevention efforts must include the sexual partners of IDUs, primarily to provide knowledge, coping skills, and alternatives to unprotected, unsafe sexual relations, and the families of IDUs, enabling them to assist and support the changing of targeted risk behaviors by the IDUs.

- Wish et al. (1990) note that women require special attention because of the special risk of HIV infection resulting from more serious drug problems and the likelihood of their having had multiple sexual partners through prostitution. They suggest that female arrestees, given their smaller number, could be provided with HIV/AIDS education—designed specifically for women at high risk—by local health department personnel stationed in central booking or, preferably, within the detention facilities themselves.

- It is acknowledged that abstinence is the most effective means of HIV prevention and that helping drug users (especially IDUs) cease their drug use is desirable, although many drug users will be unwilling or unable to quickly stop, even with help. Nevertheless, drug abuse treatment is conceptually an important element in community AIDS prevention. To fully realize the potential of substance abuse treatment programming as a major component of an AIDS prevention strategy, (a) treatment capacity must be expanded, (b) treatment seekers should receive same-day intake services from an always open treatment system, (c) once capacity permits, community outreach should be conducted, (d) services should be culturally specific and linguistically appropriate, and, (e) additional treatment personnel must be trained specifically to provide these services.

- Outreach and intervention efforts should employ both indigenous workers—who have ready credibility and can penetrate drug-using subcultures and neighborhoods—and others with a range of expertise and background experiences. Outreach should include both the street and various community agencies/locations, for example, public housing programs, single-room-occupancy hotels, homeless shelters, sexually transmitted disease clinics, public health centers, hospital emergency rooms, and the criminal justice system.

- Given the large number of IDUs who are involved with the criminal justice system, lockups, jails, prisons, and probation and parole offices can provide important access points for AIDS education to encourage behavior change and to facilitate referral to drug abuse treatment. Linkages between the criminal justice system and drug abuse treatment should facilitate initiation of treatment prior to institutional discharge and provide for the ongoing involvement of probation and parole officials in support of the treatment process.

  Wish and his colleagues (Wish et al., 1990) specifically advocate approaching drug users among arrestees and persons supervised by the criminal justice system who "should be considered to be at much greater risk of illicit drug use and AIDS than the general population" (p. 12). They argue that street criminals—who take lots of risks, are very active, yet are often rapidly released to the street after arrest—may be better targets for HIV-risk intervention programming than populations incarcerated in state prisons. Inciardi et al. (1992) suggest that these interventions include face-to-face education sessions, videotapes, and written materials (appropriate to the literacy level of the target group in reading difficulty) explaining HIV risk behaviors and countermeasures, HIV antibody counseling and substance abuse treatment, and the location of local service providers.

- Inciardi et al. (1992) feel that it is clearly unlikely that the high-risk behaviors of criminal justice system involved drug users—particularly IDUs and their sexual partners—will change significantly without major increases in prevention and intervention efforts. These should include:

  1. The provision of voluntary—with a reasonable expectation of service utilization (Andrus et al., 1989)—HIV antibody testing and counseling services for all arrestees and newly incarcerated inmates.

  2. The provision of HIV/AIDS education, minimally to targeted high-risk individuals. Although such programs are becoming increasingly available in the criminal justice system, they are not yet universally available, nor are they always adequate (Moini & Hammett, 1990).

  3. Opportunities to voluntarily participate in appropriately safeguarded clinical trials in the search for effective AIDS medications. The usual reasons for not conducting clinical research with inmate populations may not be sufficient or applicable, given the potential benefits for HIV-positive individuals.

- Special target communities, for example, African Americans, Hispanics, women, adolescents, prostitutes, the homeless, lesbians, and gay men, need specific outreach and intervention programs. Community-based, multi-service centers are necessary to provide adequate health care to complement the services of substance abuse treatment programs and to relieve the drain on their budgets.

- Community AIDS prevention efforts must include those who are already infected in order to reduce their likelihood of transmitting HIV to others. Messages for those infected need to communicate "living with HIV infection" not "dying from AIDS" and to stress respectful protection for those with whom the HIV/AIDS-infected have intimate contact.

- Day (1991), although among a minority, should be given serious attention when she advocates testing all new prison inmates for HIV and segregating HIV-positive prisoners if they engage in behavior that increases the risk of transmitting the virus, such as battery, sexual intercourse, or IV drug use.

SELECTING SPECIFIC TARGET POPULATIONS

Obviously, in practice, the processes of defining and specifying problems, their location and scope, and in reviewing possible interventions require either a priori or emergent assumptions regarding potential target populations. It should be apparent at this point, however, that target definitions are easier to write than to employ in the more exacting processes of needs assessment and program design.

Target specification attempts to establish boundaries or rules determining who or what is included and excluded when the specification is applied. Twin risks in specifying target populations are to make the definition either too broad (overinclusive) or too restrictive (underinclusive). The former may result in an overestimation of need, an uneconomical investment in a policy or intervention whose targets have little to gain from it, or a dilution of the program to serve an excessively large target group. The latter may result in eliminating key groups or large numbers of individuals who in fact should be included (Rossi & Freeman, 1989, p. 103).

For target definitions to be useful, they must be feasible to apply, employing characteristics of targets that are not too difficult to easily observe or for which existing data contain appropriate measures. Overly complex definitions requiring much detailed information are similarly difficult to apply; there is an inverse relationship between the number of definitional criteria and the numbers who can qualify for inclusion in the target population. Complex definitions are therefore akin to narrow ones and they carry with them the same risks (Rossi & Freeman, 1989, p. 103).

As program planning continues, procedures must be devised whereby targets can be efficiently and economically distinguished from nontargets during the project's implementation. These target-definition procedures can involve a number of important concepts that are borrowed from medical epidemiology:

Incidence refers to the number of new cases of a particular problem that is identified or arise in a defined geographical area during a specified period of time. *Prevalence* is the number of existing cases in a particular geographic area at a specified time. (Incidence is of interest when dealing with disorders of short duration, prevalence is the operative concept when dealing with chronic problems that require long-term management and treatment efforts.) A *population at risk* (a concept particularly useful for prevention projects) is that segment of a population that is exclusively or largely subject, with significant probabilities, to developing a given condition. *Need*, in contrast to *at-risk*, signifies a population that currently manifests a given condition and can usually be defined by a precise criterion for inclusion, for example, a screening technique. *Demand*, in the human services arena, often is incorrectly measured by level of *utilization*, with results interpreted as signifying level of desire for the services being offered. (Such use ignores potential influences of affordability, accessibility, acceptability, real and/or perceived barriers [psychological, fiscal, geographical, cultural, etc.] to utilization.) *Sensitivity* denotes the likelihood of correctly identifying targets who should be included in a program because they have a specified disease or condition, that is, the ability to detect "true positives." *Specificity*, however, is defined as the likelihood of correctly excluding from the target population those persons or units who do not have the relevant condition, that is, "false positives." *Rates* are proportions (percentages) or ratios (cases per given population aggregation), information that is particularly useful in the analysis of potential target population to maximize opportunities to include the most appropriate participants and tailor the program to the particular characteristics of sizable groups. For example, estimates of target populations may be made at several levels of disaggregation by age, gender, race, ethnicity, or religious background; statistical techniques may be used to take multiple sociodemographic characteristics into account simultaneously (Rossi & Freeman, 1989, p. 197).

Successful evaluation depends on both explicit, agreed-on objectives and a detailed description of how they are to be achieved. An *intervention or impact model* is an attempt to translate conceptual ideas regarding the regulation, modification, and control of behavior or conditions among targeted populations into hypotheses on which action can be based. It takes the form of a statement about the expected relationships between a program and its goal, setting forth the strategy for closing the gap between the objectives set during the planning process and the existing behavior or condition. It must contain a causal hypothesis, an intervention hypothesis, and an action hypothesis.

The *causal hypothesis* is a set of hypotheses about the influence of one or more processes/determinants on the behavior/condition that the program seeks to modify; these refer to how the problem at issue is brought about in vivo, without the intervention of the program to be designed. Causal hypotheses can be found in the relevant substantive scientific literature concerning the problem. Especially critical for the purposes of program design are causal hypotheses that relate the problem to processes that programs can affect, that is, that contains "operational" terms capable of measurement in an evaluation.

The *intervention hypothesis* is a statement that specifies the relationship between what is going to be done in the program and the processes or determinants specified in the causal hypothesis of the behavior or condition to be ameliorated or changed. The *action hypothesis* is needed to assess whether the intervention—even if it results in a desired change in the causal variable—is necessarily linked to the outcome, that is, to changes in the behavior or condition to be modified. (An action that is planned and carried out as an intervention takes place under conditions that may differ in important ways from those that obtain when such actions "ordinarily" occur.)

The interplay between defining the target population and developing an impact model is so strong that in some ways the distinction between the two tasks is artificial. The impact model must include a set of hypotheses about the plausibility of one event leading to another. Such hypotheses rest on predictions about the characteristics of the target population in relation to the intervention. Hence, although we need to know a great deal about a target population at the outset of planning, the development of plans may lead to the redefinition of specific program targets. Similarly, a consideration of target specification for a particular program may lead to a reconsideration of the program's design.

The discussion above includes a set of rational "ideal" techniques that can be used to aid in the target selection process. However, the present discussion recognizes that, in practice, target selection and other programming decisions must take myriad factors into account, including the complex relationships among need, demand, utilization, and resource structures. These factors include measured or estimated service needs; willingness of populations to demand and use services; social, economic, and psychological barriers to services that exist or are believed to exist for population at-risk/in-need; and, the social and economic costs of providing different types of service. If such barriers exist or are perceived to exist, interventions that will change a population's ability and/or willingness to use services are necessary. Further, policy and program decisions are contingent on policy goals regarding the populations to be targeted, for example, all or the largest number possible per se or in specified need categories (for example, high risk adolescents; racial or ethnic minorities; pregnant and postpartum women; inner-city residents; intravenous drug users; sexual partners of IDUs; arrestees versus incarcerates); at the lowest possible cost per unit; such that each person in the service area has equal access.

Also understood is the fact that final programming decisions emerge out of a political process involving interested groups and organizations as well as the persons with specific policy and administrative decision-making responsibilities (Goldsmith et al., 1989, p. 80). There is certainly agreement with those who have pointed out that political action, as well as cultural values, are legitimate influences on programming decisions in a democratic society (Cook, 1983). And, finally, it must be conceded that "decision makers" often have very little true discretion in making choices from among apparent options because of prior choices (Weiss, 1980).

CONCLUSION

Correctly defining and identifying problem targets is crucial to the success of interventions from the earliest stage, when stakeholders begin to converge in their definition of problems, throughout the extended period during which policy becomes authorized, funded, and implemented programming. The definitions and estimates of intervention targets are always in flux to some degree, but they are critically important at two junctures: in the pre-design phase of laying out policy alternatives and during the course of designing specific programs (Rossi & Freeman, 1989, p. 97).

A crucial issue in the definition of target problems and populations arises from the differing perspectives of professionals, politicians, and the range of other stakeholders involved—including, of course, the potential recipients of services. Discrepancies may exist, for example, between the views of legislators at different levels of government, community action groups, and the stakeholders affected by the problem and the programs that are put into place. Information collected about varying perspectives on needs may lead to a reconceptualization of the problem or the prospective intervention or even indicate the advisability of abandoning the program (especially if the different perspectives turn out to be both highly contradictory and intensely held by the various stakeholders [Rossi & Freeman, 1989, pp. 104-105]). The same situation exists regarding program design. In aid of this universal problem we should remember that although science and evaluation research cannot establish which viewpoint is "correct," they can provide definitions and diagnoses of problems in ways leading to the selection of the most appropriate targets and interventions and that will allow the application of systematic and reproducible evaluation procedures. In so doing, they can also eliminate some conflicts that might arise from groups talking past each other.

In conclusion, there would seem to be a critical need to initiate a dialogue and provide common analytic framework/consensus process for discussing the issues and beginning to devise a workable policy that can be translated into complementary programs, demonstration projects, measurable objectives, and evaluation studies. This dialogue should include all of the key stakeholders from within the public health and criminal justice arenas and at each potential level (federal, state, and local) of program or project implementation.

Demonstration projects are probably better alternatives than large-scale systemwide programs at this point. Such demonstrations are useful to test bolder innovations that can be later introduced as part of a new policy. The settings are circumscribed, allowing explorations without taking major resources from current policy. They are often fundable when existing programs are widely held to be ineffective and/or difficult to improve or when the political climate favors exploration of bold (or desperate) alternatives.

Care should be taken, however, to avoid some of the limitations of demonstrations, namely, too short allocated times to permit clear or persuasive measurement of improved outcomes; excessive reliance on the enthusiasm and motivation of those who conceptualize, sponsor (at higher government levels—and who may be gone with a change in administration), create, implement, and/or operate the demonstration; use of conditions that are atypical and/or difficult to replicate as components of organizational routines; lack of synchronization with policy windows of opportunity; and naive assumptions that demonstrated superiority will perforce result in continued funding, widespread knowledge of the project and evaluation results, or new policy.

This discussion concludes by mirroring the sentiments of Inciardi and his colleagues (Inciardi et al., 1992), who conclude that:

> The development and implementation of programs to provide HIV/AIDS education to criminal justice populations would require an enormous and concerted effort on the part of many government agencies. Yet, such an effort would not be impossible to mount, and the resulting impact on public health could be both meaningful and measurable. Additionally, because

such interventions would reach members of several overlapping high-risk groups, it likely would be very cost-efficient and—especially with reference to the medical costs attendant to a course of treatment for full-blown AIDS—cost-effective, as well.

REFERENCES

Akers, R. L. (1992). Linking sociology and its specialties: The case of criminology. *Social Forces, 71*(1), 1-16.

Alcabes, P., & Brawlow, C. (1988). A cluster of cases of penicillinase-producing Neisseria Gonorrhoea in an adolescent detention center. *New York State Journal of Medicine, 88*, 495-496.

Andrus, J. K., Fleming, D. W., Knox, C., McAlister, R. O., Skells, M. R., Conrad, R. E., Horan, J. K., & Foster, L. R. (1989). HIV testing in prisoners: Is mandatory testing mandatory? *American Public Health Journal, 79*, 840-842.

Anglin, D., & Hser, Y. (1992). *Multimethod approaches for estimating numbers of illicit drug users.* Resource Materials for State Needs Assessment Studies. Washington, DC: Center for Substance Abuse Treatment.

Buffum, P. C. (1972). *Homosexuality in prisons.* Washington, DC: Government Printing Office.

Carvell, A.L.M., & Hart, G. J. (1990). Risk behaviors for HIV infection among drug users in prison. *British Medical Journal, 300*, 1383-1384.

Centers for Disease Control (CDC). (1981, June 5). Pneumocystis pneumonia—Los Angeles. *Morbidity and Mortality Weekly Report, 30, 52.*

Centers for Disease Control (CDC). (1982, January 28). Epidemiologic aspects of the current outbreak of Kaposi's sarcoma and opportunistic infections. *New England Journal of Medicine, 306,* 248-252.

Centers for Disease Control (CDC). (1987). Human immunodeficiency virus infection in the United States: A review of current knowledge. *Morbidity and Mortality Weekly Report, 36*(Suppl. S-6), 1-48.

Centers for Disease Control (CDC). (1989, December). *HIV/AIDS Surveillance Report.*

Centers for Disease Control (CDC). (1992, August 28). Publicly funded HIV counseling and testing—United States, 1991. *Morbidity and Mortality Weekly Report, 34,* 613-617.

Clemmer, D. (1958). *The prison community.* New York: Reinhart.

Cook, T. D. (1983). Evaluation: Whose questions should be answered? In G. R. Gilbert (Ed.), *Making and managing policy: Formulation, analysis, evaluation* (pp. 193-217). New York: Dekker.

Day, L. (1991). *AIDS: What the government isn't telling you.* Palm Desert, CA: Rockford Press.

Flannigan, T. J., & Jamison, K. M. (Eds.). (1988). *Sourcebook of criminal justice statistics— 1987.* Bureau of Justice Statistics, NCJ-111612. Washington, DC: U.S. Department of Justice.

Flucker, J. L. (1976). A 10-year study of homosexually transmitted infection. *British Journal of Venereal Diseases, 52,* 155-160.

Gagnon, J. H., & Simon, W. (1968). The social meaning of prison homosexuality. *Federal Probation, 32,* 23-29.

Gerstein, D. R., & Harwood, H. J. (Eds.). (1990). *Treating drug problems: A study of the evolution, effectiveness, and financing of public and private drug treatment systems.* Washington, DC: National Academy Press.

Goldsmith, H., Lin, E., Jackson, D., Manderscheid, R. W., & Bell, R. A. (1989). The future of mental health needs assessment. In C. A. Taube, D. Mechanic, & A. A. Hohmann (Eds.), *The future of mental health services research* (pp. 79-93). ADM 89-1600. Washington, DC: Government Printing Office.

Gostin, J. D. (1990). The AIDS litigation project: A national review of court and Human Rights Commission decisions, Part I: The social impact of AIDS. *Journal of the American Medical Association, 263,* 1961-1970.

Greenfield, L. A. (1989). *Prisoners in 1988.* Bureau of Justice Statistics, NCJ-116315. Washington, DC: U.S. Department of Justice.

Gross, J. (1986, February 15). 2 prisoners charged in heroin sales by phone. *New York Times* pp. 29, 33.

Inciardi, J. A. (1979). Heroin use and street crime. *Crime & Delinquency, 25,* 335- 346.

Inciardi, J. A. (Ed.). (1981). *The drugs/crime connection.* Beverly Hills: Sage.

Inciardi, J. A. (1986). *The war on drugs: Heroin, cocaine, crime, and public policy.* Palo Alto, CA: Mayfield.

Inciardi, J. A. (1992). *The war on drugs II: The continuing epic of heroin, cocaine, crack, crime, AIDS, and public policy.* Palo Alto, CA: Mayfield.

Inciardi, J. A., McBride, D. C., Platt, J. J., & Baxter, S. (1992). Injection drug users, incarceration, and HIV: Some legal and social service delivery issues. In B. S. Brown (Ed.), *The national AIDS demonstration research program.* Westport, CT: Greenwood Press.

Inciardi, J. A., & Page, J. B. (1991). Drug sharing among intravenous drug users. *AIDS, 5,* 772-774.

Innes, C. A. (1988). *State prison inmate survey, 1986: Drug use and crime.* Bureau of Justice Statistics Special Report, NCJ-111940. Washington, DC: U.S. Department of Justice.

Irwin, J. (1985). *The jail: Managing the underclass in American society.* Berkeley, CA: University of California Press.

Kassebaum, G. (1972, January). Sex in prison. *Psychology Today,* p. 39.

Leukefeld, C. G., Battjes, R. J., & Amsel, Z. (1990). Community prevention efforts to reduce the spread of AIDS associated with intravenous drug abuse. *AIDS Education and Prevention, 2*(3), 235-243.

Leukefeld, C. G., Battjes, R. J., & Pickens, R. W. (1989). Aids prevention: Criminal justice involvement of intravenous drug abusers entering methadone treatment. *The Journal of Drug Issues, 21,* 673-683.

McBride, D. C. (1978). Criminal justice diversion. In J. A. Inciardi & K. C. Haas (Eds.), *Crime and the criminal justice process.* Dubuque, IA: Kendall-Hunt.

McBride, D. C., & Inciardi, J. A. (1990). AIDS and the IV drug user in the criminal justice system. *The Journal of Drug Issues, 20,* 267-280.

McBride, D. C., & McCoy, C. B. (1982). Crime and drugs: The issues and the literature. *The Journal of Drug Issues, 12,* 137-152.

McCusker, J. B., Koblin, B., Lewis, B. F., & Sullivan, J. (1990). Demographic characteristics, risk behaviors, and HIV seroprevalence among intravenous drug users by site of contact: Results from a community-wide HIV surveillance project. *American Journal of Public Health, 80,* 1062-1067.

Moini, S., & Hammett, T. M. (1990). *1989 update: AIDS in correctional facilities.* Washington, DC: Office of Justice Programs, National Institute of Justice.

National Institute of Justice (NIJ). (1990, March). *DUF: 1988 drug use forecasting annual report.* NIJ Research in Action. Washington, DC: National Institute of Justice.

National Institute on Drug Abuse (NIDA)/NOVA (1990). NADR finds differences in IVDUs with and without drug treatment histories. *Network, 2,* 1-7.

Nurco, D. N., Ball, J. C., Shaffer, J. W., & Hanlon, T. F. (1985). The criminality of narcotic addicts. *Journal of Nervous and Mental Disease, 173,* 94-102.

Rossi, P. H., & Freeman, H. E. (1989). *Evaluation: A systematic approach* (4th ed.). Newbury Park, CA: Sage.

Spencer, B. D. (1989). On the accuracy of current estimates of the numbers of intravenous drug users. In C. F. Turner, H. G. Miller, & L. E. Moses (Eds.), *AIDS, sexual behavior, and intravenous drug use.* Washington, DC: National Academy Press.

Sykes, G. M. (1965). *The society of captives: A study of a maximum security prison.* New York: Atheneum.

Thomas, C. W., & Cage, R. J. (1977). Correlates of prison drug use: An evaluation of two conceptual models. *Criminology, 18,* 193-209.

Truman, B. I., Morse, D., Mikl, J., Lehman, S., Forte, A., Broaddus, R., & Stevens, R. (1989, June). *HIV prevalence and risk factors among prison inmates entering New York State prisons.* Stockholm: IV International Conference on AIDS.

Turner, C. F., Miller, H. G., & Moses, L. E. (Eds.). (1989). *AIDS, sexual behavior, and intravenous drug use.* Washington, DC: National Academy Press.

Van Hoeven, K. H., Rooney, W. C., & Joseph, S. C. (1990). Evidence for gonococcal transmission within a correctional system. *American Journal of Public Health, 80,* 1505-1506.

Vigdal, G. L., & Stadler, D. W. (1989, June). Controlling inmate drug use. *Corrections Today,* pp. 96-97.

Vlahov, D., Brewer, F., Castro, K. G., Narkunas, J. P., Salive, M. E., Ullrich, J. , & Munoz, A. (1989). Prevalence of antibody to HIV-1 among entrants to US correctional facilities. *Journal of the American Medical Association, 265,* 1129-1132.

Walker, B., & Gordon, T. (1980). Health and high density confinement in jails and prisons. *Federal Probation, 44,* 53-58.

Weiss, C. H. (1980). Knowledge creep and decision accretion. *Knowledge: Creation, Diffusion, Utilization, 1,* 381-404.

Wish, E. D. (1990). U.S. drug policy in the 1990's: Insights from new data from arrestees. *The International Journal of the Addictions, 25*(3a), 377-409.

Wish, E. D., O'Neil, J., & Baldau, V. (1990). Lost opportunity to combat AIDS: Drug abusers in the criminal justice system. In C. G. Leukefeld, R. J. Battjes, & Z. Amsel (Eds.), *AIDS and intravenous drug use: Future directions for community-based prevention research.* Rockville, MD: National Institute on Drug Abuse.

NAME INDEX

SUBJECT INDEX

Accreditation, 46
Action hypothesis, 241
Addiction:
    as symptom, 35
    criminal aspects of, 128, 130
Addiction Severity Index, 60
Addictive disease, 50
Addictive Disease Treatment Program, Philadelphia, 57
Administration:
    commitment from, 66
    evaluation goals and, 70
    roles of, 204
    supportive relationships with, 214
Admission, diagnosing clients at, 21
Adolescent(s), *see* Youth offenders
Adolescent agency coordinating work group, 107-108
Adolescent Assessment/Referral System, 106
Adult education funds, 75
Advisory boards, 218
Advocacy functions, case management and, 88, 90
Aftercare, 51, 53, 54
    costs of, 82
    court order and, 69
    cycles of, 22
    federal Bureau of Prisons and, 200
    TASC and, 134
    youth offenders and, 119-120

Aftercare meetings, 58
Aftercare plan, 65-66
Age, relapse and, 117
Agency for Community Treatment Services, Inc., 107
Aggression replacement training, 13
Aggressive behavior, 70
AIDS medications, 238
AIDS risk, *see* HIV/AIDS risk
Alcoholics, 45
Alcoholics Anonymous (AA), 32, 48
Alcohol Use Inventory, 11
Alternatives to incarceration, 90
American Association of Correctional Psychologists, 46
American Jail Association, 46, 48
Amity, Inc., 57
Anger management, 62
Anonymous Fellowships, 9, 50, 65
    women offenders and, 9, 13, 18
Anti-Drug Abuse Act of 1986, 34, 149, 215
Anti-Drug Abuse Act of 1988, 74
Antisocial behaviors, 62, 212
    educational problems and, 101
Antisocial personality disorder, 45
Antisocial thinking, 34
Anxiety, 62, 63
Applied Evaluation Demonstration Projects, 88
Area networks, 10

Arrests:
  follow-up and, 72-73
  history of, 136, 142-143, 173-174
Arrestees:
  HIV among, 233-234
  substance abuse among, 230-231
Assertive case management, 85
Assertive community treatment model, 90-91
Assertiveness, 8, 19, 62
Assessment, 59-60, 67
  family members and, 109
  federal Bureau of Prisons and, 197-198
  Focused Offender Disposition Program
    and, 149-162
  HIV/AIDS risk, 154
  Project REFORM and, 216
  selection for treatment and, 68-70
  TASC and, 128
  youth and, 104-110, 112
Asset forfeiture, 2
At risk population, 240

Behavior:
  clear consequences for, 67
  prosocial, 7
Behavioral contingencies, Project REFORM
  and, 219
Behavioral skills training, 64
Behavior change, therapeutic communities
  and, 35, 55
Biopsychosocial model of treatment, 8
Block grants, 73-74
Bond, 69, 136
Breathalyzer tests, 108
Bureau of Justice Assistance, 149-162, 215
Bureaucratic constraints, 20, 38

California Civil Addict Program, 138
California Institute for Women (CIW), 13-14
Career opportunities, for women, 23
Case management approach, 14, 48, 65-66,
    81-93
  assertive, 85
  origins of, 84-86
  Project REFORM and, 219
  TASC and, 135

youth offenders and, 111, 113
Causal hypothesis, 240-241
Center for Substance Abuse Treatment, 217
Chemical dependency programs, 50-51
Child care, 82, 83
Children, 82, 83
  crack cocaine and, 1-2
  women prisoners and, 23
Child welfare system, 23
Civil commitment, women drug offenders
  and, 6
Classification, Focused Offender Disposi-
  tion Program and, 151
Client data bases, 139
Clinical Research Centers, 194
Clonidine, 59
Cocaine Anonymous, 9
Cocaine use, 1
  crime and, 130-131
  youth offenders and, 100, 108
  See also Crack cocaine
Cognitive behavioral program, 14, 64, 68, 111
Combined Addicts and Professional Serv-
  ices, Inc., 16
Commitment:
  to conforming behavior, 153
  to receive treatment, 53, 70
Communication skills, 53, 62, 199
Communications channels, 20-21
Community:
  reentry into, 17
  safety and, 140
  supervision in, 22
Community AIDS prevention efforts, 238
Community services:
  case management and, 84
  psychoeducational programs and, 54
  women offenders and, 6-7
Community support systems, youth and, 120
Comparison group, 72, 141
Comprehensive Assessment Battery, 106
Confidentiality, 22, 198
Conflict, history of, 61
Conforming behavior, commitment to, 153
Confrontation, 33, 56, 62
Construction funding, 74
Construction trades, 23
Continuing Criminal Enterprise (CCE), 2

ABOUT THE AUTHORS

M. DOUGLAS ANGLIN, Ph.D., is Adjunct Professor in UCLA's Department of Psychiatry (Neuropsychiatric Institute) and Director of the UCLA Drug Abuse Research Center (DARC). For 20 years, he has been involved in numerous federally and state funded research projects on drug abuse, most of which deal with the evaluation of community treatment, criminal justice, and other interventions for heroin and cocaine users. His work has brought nationwide recognition and invitations to serve as an advisor to various organizations·on drug abuse issues. Anglin is author or coauthor of over 70 articles for scientific books and journals.

RICHARD DEMBO, Ph.D., is Professor in the Department of Criminology at the University of South Florida in Tampa, Florida. He received his Ph.D. in sociology from New York University in 1970. He has conducted research on the relationship between drug use and delinquency; has published numerous articles and chapters for books in the fields of criminology, substance use, mental health, and program evaluation; and has guest-edited four special issues of journals addressing the problem of drug abuse. He has a long-term interest in applying research technology to social problems with a view to improving understanding of these problems and in developing innovative programs and service delivery systems. Since 1986, he and his associates have been pursuing a longitudinal study of a group of juvenile detainees.

JAMES A. INCIARDI is Director of the Center for Drug and Alcohol Studies and Professor in the Department of Sociology and Criminal Justice at the University of Delaware. He received his Ph.D. in Sociology from New York University in 1973. Prior to the establishment of the Center, from 1976 through mid-1991, he was director of the University's Division of Criminal Justice. Inciardi has an appointment in the Comprehensive Drug Research Center at the University of Miami School of Medicine, and he is a member of the South Florida AIDS Research Consortium. Before coming to Delaware, he was director of the National Center for the Study of Acute Drug Reactions at the University of Miami, vice president of the Washington, D.C.-based Resource Planning Corporation, and associate director of research of the New York State Narcotic Addiction Control Commission. With almost 30 years' experience in the drug field, he has done extensive consulting work both nationally and internationally and has published more than 150 articles, chapters, books, and monographs in the areas of substance abuse, criminology, criminal justice, history, folklore, social policy, AIDS, medicine, and law.

DOUGLAS S. LIPTON, Ph.D., is Senior Research Fellow at the National Development and Research Institutes (NDRI), where from 1988 to 1992 he was Director of Research. Since 1972, he has served as Director of Research and as Deputy Director of the New York Division of Substance Abuse Services (DSAS) in charge of state drug abuse research. He has evaluated drug abuse control and treatment programs around the world for the United Nations; has been the recipient of many research grants; and has authored and coauthored numerous publications and presentations. After completing his doctoral work at Vanderbilt University, he became Director of Research and Planning for the New York City Department of Corrections in 1964; conducted research and served as director of the Social Restoration Research Center in 1965; and in 1967 joined Governor Rockefeller's Special Committee on Criminal Offenders as assistant director. In the early 1970s, as Assistant Director of the New York State Crime Control Council, the state Office of Crime Control Planning, and the state Division of Criminal Justice, Lipton made major contributions to state crime control efforts.

DOROTHY LOCKWOOD is Associate Scientist with the Center for Drug and Alcohol Studies at the University of Delaware. She received her M.A. in Sociology from the University of Delaware in 1987. She is the Co-Principal Investigator and Project Director of a 5-year therapeutic community/work release treatment demonstration grant funded by the National Institute on Drug Abuse. Prior to joining the Center, she was research specialist at the Delaware Council on Crime and Justice where she conducted policy-oriented research on both the adult and juvenile justice systems and evaluations of state-operated offender programs. She has authored numerous publications and presentations on drug abuse treatment for offenders, therapeutic communities, women and drug use, and substance abuse.

STEVEN S. MARTIN is Associate Scientist with the Center for Drug and Alcohol Studies at the University of Delaware. He received an M.Sc. in Economics from the London School of Economics in 1973 and an M.A. in Sociology from the University of Michigan in 1978. He is the Co-Principal Investigator and Project Director of a 5-year assertive case management treatment demonstration grant funded by the National Institute on Drug Abuse. He previously worked as a research associate on an NIDA grant at Baylor College of Medicine, then as a scientific analyst at the Center for Prevention Research at the University of Kentucky. He taught in the Sociology and Criminal Justice Department at Delaware before joining the Center. Beside his work with the Center, he continues as a consultant with the Kentucky Prevention Center. He has coauthored a number of articles in the areas of survey research, attitudes and behavior, delinquency, and substance abuse.

DUANE C. MCBRIDE received a master's degree in sociology from the University of Maryland and a Ph.D. in sociology from the University of Kentucky. Since receiving his degree, he has been actively involved in a variety of drug abuse and crime and drugs research projects funded by the National Institute on Drug Abuse and the U.S. Department of Justice. He has also authored or coauthored two books and more than 40 monographs, articles, and chapters in the substance abuse field. His research and teaching career has spanned two decades. Most of those years were spent on the faculty of the Department of Psychiatry at the University of Miami School of Medicine where he served as a research professor. Currently he serves as Professor and Chair of the Behavioral Sciences Department at Andrews University. He also chairs the Research Center of the Institute of Alcoholism and Drug Dependency at Andrews University.

HAO PAN is a graduate student in the Department of Sociology and Criminal Justice at the University of Delaware. He received his B.A. degree at the Chongging Institute of Architecture and Engineering and his

M.A. degree in sociology at the University of Delaware. His doctoral dissertation deals with social reorganization and law in contemporary China.

ROGER H. PETERS, Ph.D., is Assistant Professor in the Department of Law and Mental Health at the Florida Mental Health Institute (FMHI), University of South Florida in Tampa. He has been a faculty member at the University since 1986, after receiving his doctorate in clinical psychology from the Florida State University and completing a predoctoral internship at the University of North Carolina School of Medicine, Department of Psychiatry. He has worked for the past several years to design and evaluate the Hillsborough County Sheriff's Office Substance Abuse Treatment Program, one of three in-jail model demonstration projects funded by the Bureau of Justice Assistance. He has also helped to evaluate results of a nationwide survey of in-jail substance abuse treatment services, sponsored by the Bureau of Justice Assistance. He has served as a consultant to the Center for Substance Abuse Treatment and the American Jail Association in developing substance abuse treatment programs and evaluation initiatives within criminal justice settings.

MICHAEL L. PRENDERGAST, Ph.D., Assistant Research Historian, UCLA Drug Abuse Research Center (DARC), has been involved in drug abuse research for 12 years. He is currently involved in two projects funded by the National Institute of Justice on treatment for drug-abusing offenders generally and for drug-abusing women offenders; he is also working on drug policy issues within California. His interests include treatment improvement, criminal justice treatment, drug control policy, and the history of drug issues.

JAMES E. RIVERS is Associate Professor in the Department of Epidemiology and Public Health at the University of Miami and Deputy Director of the University's Comprehensive Drug Research Center, where he coordinates over 30 laboratory, clinical, and survey research projects. He received his Ph.D. from the University of Kentucky. His 17 years in the substance abuse field include experience in information systems development, as a founding member of NIDA's Community Epidemiology Work Group, and as "Drug Czar" for Metro-Dade County (Greater Miami), Florida. He was also a founding member of The Miami Coalition for a Drug Free Community, served on both its law enforcement/courts/corrections and treatment task forces, and is the evaluator for this 5-year federally funded anti-drug abuse community organizing project. His research emphasizes substance abuse indicator data bases, geographic information systems, services needs assessments, and evaluations of substance abuse treatment programs and HIV risk reduction projects.

FRANK R. SCARPITTI is Professor of Sociology and the Chairperson of the Department of Sociology and Criminal Justice at the University of Delaware. He received his Ph.D. in Sociology from Ohio State University in 1962. He previously held teaching and research positions at Rutgers University and Ohio State University. In 1981, he served as president of the American Society of Criminology. His research on community mental health won the American Psychiatric Association's Hofheimer Prize in 1967. He is the author, coauthor, or editor of numerous books and monographs, including *Schizophrenics in the Community* (1967), *Combatting Social Problems* (1967), *Youth and Drugs* (1969), *Group Interaction as Therapy* (1974), *Deviance* (1975), *Social Problems* (1974, 1977, 1980), *Women, Crime, and Justice* (1980), *Drugs and the Youth Culture* (1980), *Poisoning for Profit* (1985), and *Social Problems* (1989; 1992). In addition, he has written numerous journal and magazine articles on mental health, delinquency, corrections, female crime, drug use, and organized crime.

JAMES SCHMEIDLER is Assistant Professor in the Departments of Psychiatry and Biomathematical Sciences at Mount Sinai School of Medicine, New York. He received his Ph.D. in Mathematical Statistics from Columbia University. His recent statistical research has focused on multiple comparison procedures, in addition to a variety of applied topics. He has collaborated extensively in research on psychiatry, substance abuse, and criminology.

JAMES SWARTZ is presently Director of Research at the Illinois Treatment Alternative for Special Clients (TASC) program and is an associate faculty member of the Illinois School of Professional Psychology, where he teaches research methods. He received an M.S. from Loyola University of Chicago in Behavioral Research and a Ph.D. in clinical psychology from Northwestern University. His primary research interests are in understanding the effects of drug treatment on addiction and criminal behavior, improving the efficacy and delivery of substance abuse treatment for criminal clients, and utilizing statistical models to study the multivariate relationships in both of these areas. He is currently working on a study funded by the National Institute of Justice of the implications of statewide DUF results for Illinois TASC.

BETH A. WEINMAN, M.A., is the National Drug Abuse Coordinator with the Federal Bureau of Prisons. She has over 15 years' experience working in criminal justice system programming, including programs for juveniles, victims, judges and other court personnel, probation and parole, corrections, offender case management, treatment/client matching, and drug treatment for the drug-dependent offender. Before joining the Federal Bureau of Prisons, she spent 6 years as the director of Criminal Justice Programs for the National Association of State Alcohol and Drug Abuse Directors (NASADAD). She has also worked directly with Treatment Alternatives to Street Crime (TASC) program operations in Illinois, New York, and Pennsylvania. She has written extensively on offender treatment and case management theories.

JEAN WELLISCH, Ph.D., is Research Associate with the UCLA Drug Abuse Research Center (DARC). Currently, she is working on DARC's Comprehensive Review of Drug Abuse Treatment in the Criminal Justice System, which is being conducted for the National Institute of Justice (NIJ), and she is Co-Principal Investigator on a review of Criminal Justice Drug Treatment Programs for Women Offenders, also for NIJ. She is the principal author of several articles (in press) on the characteristics and treatment of drug-abusing women and on federal promotion of linkages between the drug treatment and criminal justice systems.

HARRY K. WEXLER, Ph.D., is Senior Principal Investigator for the Evaluation of Amity Rightturn, which is a prison-based Therapeutic Community for Substance Abusers (funded by the National Institute on Drug Abuse), and for the National Prison Treatment Technical Assistance Project (RECOVERY), a national technical assistance program designed to improve the quality and effectiveness of prison-based drug treatment in 14 states (funded by the Office of Treatment Improvement). He has worked in the drug field for the past 25 years and currently serves on the editorial boards of substance abuse and psychology journals. He has published numerous articles in scholarly and policy journals. He also serves or has held appointments at several universities, including Columbia University, New York University, City University of New York, and UCLA; is active in many professional organizations; and often makes presentations at national conferences.

LINDA WILLIAMS received her B.A. in Criminology from the University of South Florida in Tampa and is currently Senior Statistician on a research study on foster care. She has been involved in research and service projects involving detained youths since 1984 and has had a major role in an ongoing longitudinal study of juvenile detainees, with Richard Dembo, that began in 1986. She has coauthored numerous publications in professional journals on criminology, substance use, mental health, and program evaluation. She has a long-term interest in the welfare of troubled youths, substance use, drug abuse prevention, and mental health.